Human Resource Management for Events

Books in the series

Event Feasibility
William O'Toole

Events Design and Experience
Graham Berridge

Events Management (second edition)
Glenn A. J. Bowdin, Johnny Allen, William O'Toole, Rob Harris and Ian McDonnell

Innovative Marketing Communications: Strategies for the Events Industry
Guy Masterman and Emma Wood

Management of Event Operations
Julia Tum, Philippa Norton and J. Nevan Wright

Marketing Destinations and Venues for Conferences, Conventions and Business Events
Rob Davidson and Tony Rogers

Human Resource Management for Events
Lynn Van der Wagen

Human Resource Management for Events

Managing the event workforce

Lynn Van der Wagen

AMSTERDAM • BOSTON • HEIDELBERG • LONDON • NEW YORK • OXFORD
PARIS • SAN DIEGO • SAN FRANCISCO • SINGAPORE • SYDNEY • TOKYO
Butterworth-Heinemann is an imprint of Elsevier

Butterworth-Heinemann is an imprint of Elsevier
Linacre House, Jordan Hill, Oxford OX2 8DP, UK
30 Corporate Drive, Suite 400, Burlington, MA 01803, USA

First edition 2007

British Library Cataloguing in Publication Data
A catalogue record for this book is available from the British Library

Library of Congress Cataloging-in-Publication Data
A catalog record for this book is available from the Library of Congress

ISBN–13: 978-0-7506-6998-6
ISBN–10: 0-7506-6998-5

For information on all Butterworth-Heinemann publications
visit our web site at http://books.elsevier.com

Cover image by Craig Golding, Fairfaxphotos.com. Reproduced with permission

Typeset by Charon Tec Ltd, Chennai, India
www.charontec.com
Printed and bound in Great Britain

06 07 08 09 10   10 9 8 7 6 5 4 3 2 1

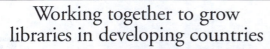

Contents

Series editors

Glenn A. J. Bowdin is Principal Lecturer in Events Planning at the UK Centre for Events Management, Leeds Metropolitan University where he has responsibility for managing events-related research. He is co-author of *Events Management*. His research interests include the area of service quality management, specifically focusing on the area of quality costing and issues relating to the planning, management and evaluation of events. He is a member of the Editorial Boards for *Event Management* (an international journal) and *Journal of Convention & Event Tourism*, Chair of AEME (Association for Events Management Education), Charter Member of the International EMBOK (Event Management Body of Knowledge) Executive and a member of Meeting Professionals International (MPI).

Don Getz is a Professor in the Tourism and Hospitality Management Program, Haskayne School of Business, University of Calgary. His ongoing research involves event-related issues (e.g. management, event tourism, events and culture) and special-interest tourism (e.g. wine). Recent books include *Event Management and Event Tourism* and *Explore Wine Tourism: Management, Development, Destinations*. He co-founded and is a member of the Editorial Board for *Event Management* (an international journal).

Professor Conrad Lashley is Professor in Leisure Retailing and Director of the Centre for Leisure Retailing at Nottingham Business School, Nottingham Trent University. He is also series editor for the Elsevier Butterworth-Heinemann series on Hospitality Leisure and Tourism. His research interests have largely been concerned with service quality management, and specifically employee empowerment in service delivery. He also has research interest and publications relating to hospitality management education. Recent books include *Organization Behaviour for Leisure Services*, *12 Steps to Study Success*, *Hospitality Retail Management* and *Empowerment: HR Strategies for Service Excellence*. He has co-edited *Franchising Hospitality Services* and *In Search of Hospitality: Theoretical Perspectives and Debates*. He is the past Chair of the Council for Hospitality Management Education. He is a Chair of the British Institute of Innkeeping's panel judges for the NITA Training awards, and is advisor to England's East Midlands Tourism network.

Series preface

The events industry, including festivals, meetings, conferences, exhibitions, incentives, sports and a range of other events, is rapidly developing and makes a significant contribution to business and leisure related tourism. With increased regulation and the growth of government and corporate involvement in events, the environment has become much more complex. Event managers are now required to identify and service a wide range of stakeholders and to balance their needs and objectives. Though mainly operating at national levels, there has been significant growth of academic provision to meet the needs of events and related industries and the organizations that comprise them. The English speaking nations, together with key Northern European countries, have developed programmes of study leading to the award of diploma, undergraduate and postgraduate awards. These courses focus on providing education and training for future event professionals, and cover areas such as event planning and management, marketing, finance, human resource management and operations. Modules in events management are also included in many tourism, leisure, recreation and hospitality qualifications in universities and colleges.

The rapid growth of such courses has meant that there is a vast gap in the available literature on this topic for lecturers, students and professionals alike. To this end, the **Elsevier Butterworth-Heinemann Events Management Series** has been created to meet the need for a planned and targeted set of publications in this area.

Aimed at academic and management development in events management and related studies, the **Events Management Series**:

- provides a portfolio of titles which match management development needs through various stages;
- prioritizes publication of texts where there are current gaps in the market, or where current provision is unsatisfactory;
- develops a portfolio of both practical and stimulating texts;
- provides a basis for theoretical and research underpinning for programmes of study;
- is recognized as being of consistent high quality;
- will quickly become the series of first choice for both authors and users.

Preface

When I was asked why I wanted to write this book (rather than my novel or, more importantly, my thesis), my response was, 'because over the next few years London will host the Olympic Games; South Africa, World Cup Soccer; Shanghai, EXPO; and Australia has 800 000 Catholics visiting in 2008!' These are significant events, and they need people, they need trained people, they need motivated people, and in turn these people need visionary leadership. They need to be managed well, and this is the human resource management role. Every event supervisor is a human resource manager; his or her career depends on it.

People make events successful, and there are so many of them behind the scenes. There are ticket sellers, purchasing officers, technical assistants, media monitors, cleaners, cooks, accreditation experts, security officers, risk managers, creative designers, announcers, singers and sweepers. Mostly their skills are brought together for a very short time. There is no more challenging environment for human resource management than the event business.

Events celebrate our best moments: winning the World Cup, coming first in an Olympic 100 metre swim, Black Eyed Peas performing, receiving an award, holding a 21st birthday party, or a 90th for that matter. Small or large, events commemorate our most important moments, and they are significant in our lives and in our cultures. Because there is so much planning and organizing to be done – because the risks are high – event professionals are needed.

There are many books on event planning, on crowd management and on economic impact analysis. But to date, there has not been a book on human resource management for events. The challenge for me was irresistible. I had a background in human resource management as training manager and director of human resources in a five star hotel. This was early in my career, and I thought the hospitality industry was the most exciting there was. This was until I worked for the Sydney 2000 Olympic Games and discovered the world of events. It was not a soft entry into the business; it was conflict ridden and stressful. But, hey, it was exciting. And as every event manager will agree, all the angst is worth it when the event is a success. So with the rosy afterglow of a flawless mega event, I continued to teach in this area and became increasingly enchanted with the event business.

This book is for anyone managing people at a festival, carnival, exhibition, show, competition, race, display, match, concert or convention. The work needs to be analysed and allocated, contracts prepared and signed, people hired, procedures developed, staff trained, uniformed and fed. Things change constantly; the structure (physical and organizational) is often not in place until days or hours before the event starts. In this controlled chaos, decisions are quick, clear communication is essential and people need to be upbeat all the time. I have to confess that when working as a volunteer for the Sydney 2000 Olympic Games I became so tired of smiling, nodding and answering questions on my journey to and from work (two hours each way) that in the final days I went in mufti, carrying my volunteer uniform in my bag and saving my emotional energy for my shift. My hope is that the bonhomie of your events is such, too, that it wears you out! That's the measure of success: everyone around you is uplifted and energized, and you know that this event will be fixed in everyone's memory for a lifetime. During the 2000 Olympic Games it was said ad nauseam, 'This is a once in a lifetime opportunity'. If you are entering this profession, I hope that you have many such positive opportunities.

Acknowledgements

The help of many people and organizations has been essential in the preparation of this book. The author thanks the following organizations for their contributions: Alcatel Ottawa Children's Festival; California Traditional Music Society (CTMS) Annual Summer Solstice Folk Music, Dance and Storytelling Festival; Beijing 2008 Olympic Games; *Boat Magazine*; Canmore Folk Music Festival; Chelsea Flower Show; Edinburgh International Book Festival; Edinburgh International Festival; European Youth and Sport Forum; FIFA World Cup Soccer 2006; Food Safety, Victoria; Good Vibrations Festival; International Festival and Events Association (IFEA); Korean Film Festival; Manchester 2002 Commonwealth Games; Melbourne 2006 Commonwealth Games; National Folk Festival, Canberra; Nonprofit Risk Management Center; *North Devon Journal*; Ottawa Folk Festival; Project Management Institute; Special Olympics; Studio Festi; TAFE NSW; Trade Union Congress (TUC); Vancouver International Writers and Readers Festival; Volunteering England; Wave Aid; *Westchester County Business Journal*.

The organizations listed above gave permission for me to use their material. Every effort has been made to trace the owners of copyright material, in some cases with limited success, and I offer apologies to any copyright holders whose rights I may have unwittingly infringed.

I would also like to thank Ruth Blackwell, Glenn Bowdin, Matthew Lazarus-Hall, Roy Masters, Tony Webb, and the team who produced the book: Kathryn Lamberton, Francesca Ford, Lesley Nash and Melissa Read.

List of case studies

Part One

Human resource strategic planning: establishing the context

Part One of this book establishes a context for human resource management (HRM) in the events business. The different types of events include business events (conferences and exhibitions), sports, arts, entertainment and community events, street parades and festivals. These events may be commercial or not for profit. They may be fundraising events or simply big parties. Most events are project based, occurring once only or annually.

The functions of human resource management – recruitment, selection, induction, training, and performance management – are important parts of every event organizer's job. In the case of large events, including mega events such as the Winter Olympics or World Cup Soccer, the size of the event clearly warrants a specialist human resources team. For smaller events, these functions are undertaken by the organizer, organizing committee or area managers. In this environment, there is typically a diverse range of employment arrangements and very frequently there are volunteers involved.

The overall focus of Part One is on the development of a strategic plan for human resource management of one or more events.

Chapter 1 discusses the unique features of the event environment that differentiate it from other traditional business environments in which human resource management is practised. Chapter 2 considers planning from a macro perspective, looking at the whole workforce, which may include paid staff, volunteers and contractors who provide event services such as catering. The growth of the event team over time and the phases of organizational development are covered in Chapter 3, followed by a discussion in Chapter 4 of the issues associated with volunteer management. Chapter 5 deals with the employment of event service providers of security, cleaning, waste management and technical support (lighting and sound). Having developed an awareness of the overall responsibility that the event organizer has for the health and safety of everyone working on site, employment legislation will be discussed in more detail in Chapter 6. Finally, Chapter 7 looks at the process of job analysis, leading to the development of job descriptions, which form the basis for many other human resource functions (such as training). These are covered in Part Two when the text moves on to operational planning.

Chapter 1
The event environment

Learning objectives

After reading through this chapter you will be able to:

- Differentiate between events in terms of size, scope and type of event
- Identify a range of factors that differentiate events from more traditional ongoing business enterprises
- Discuss the management of events in terms of the creative and organizational attributes of organizers
- Describe contemporary strategic approaches to human resource management
- Differentiate between the different groups of people comprising the event workforce
- Discuss the emergence of event management as a profession.

Introduction

International sporting events such as the Olympic Games, World Cup Soccer, IAAF World Championships, America's Cup and the Commonwealth Games continue to grow in size and investment. Most importantly, this growth is matched by the almost exponential growth of the television audience that watches these world-class competitions, so much so, that the organizers of opening and closing ceremonies freely admit that these ceremonies are no longer designed for the audience seated in the stadium, even if these spectators have paid thousands of dollars for their tickets. In terms of viewer audience, 3900 million people (unduplicated) had access to the coverage of the Athens 2004 Olympic Games, compared with 3600 million for Sydney 2000. In total, 35 000 hours were dedicated to the Athens 2004 Olympic Games coverage, compared with 20 000 hours for Barcelona 1992, 25 000 for Atlanta 1996 and 29 600 for Sydney 2000, representing an increase of 27 per cent (Rogge, 2004).

The ceremonies are designed with every camera shot in mind, and CAD designs are used to visualize the on-screen effects from the various camera positions well in advance, most particularly those from high vantage points above the stadium. Major sponsors want to know beforehand how their logos will appear in the footage of the ceremony – how they will be positioned and how long they will appear on screen. There are also all sorts of political pressures brought to bear on the design of each ceremony's programme, with the host country branding itself according to the images

Snow and rain are part of any contingency planning – the stage build for the 2006 Winter Olympic Games torch relay where working conditions were less than perfect

portrayed. There are athletes, performers, players, entertainers, ushers, security staff, police and a multitude of other staff, including volunteers, working behind the scenes. Managing the interests of everyone involved, meeting deadlines on a multitude of projects that are interdependent and immutable are just a few of the challenges of this environment.

The 2005 Live 8 Concerts held in ten cities, including London, Philadelphia, Paris, Berlin, Johannesburg, Rome and Moscow, played to hundreds of thousands of people. A TV audience of several hundred million watched these gigs. In this case, the event was not a sporting event but a social justice initiative to eliminate poverty in Africa. This example further illustrates the challenges of producing an event on such a large scale, with specific political and economic aims in mind. The workforce for these events is similar in scale to sporting events such as the 2008 Olympic Games to be held in Beijing, recruiting 70 000 volunteers for the Summer Games and 30 000 for the Paralympic Games. Added to this there is the paid workforce of the organizing committee.

For most events the additional size and scope of the contractor workforce are often underestimated. Many services, such as catering and cleaning, are contracted out and there is sometimes debate about whose responsibility it is to develop the event-related knowledge and customer service skills required by contractor employees on the site. As Goldblatt (2005b, p. 118) points out, 'You are being paid for creating memorable positive experiences, and you and your staff are the critical resource that makes the guest's experience memorable. Issues such as your human resource organization, training, and employee retention are vital if you are to remain competitive.'

Events: a new context for HR management

Events are not only challenging for management in their size, scope and timeline. Human resource management remains a key success factor in smaller, locally based events involving only a limited number of people, as the range of stakeholders and participants need to be brought to one purpose. Frequently, even the organizing committee cannot agree on the primary purpose of the event! Anyone who has sat on an event committee would know this.

Essentially, the main differences between the management of an event and the management of an ongoing business enterprise is that the event is generally intangible and untested, and there is only one chance to get it right. In contrast, a retail store that doesn't sell stock in the current month can put it all on sale the following month and hope to at least recover its costs.

Events are often high-stakes ventures. At the mid-scale level, a festival can represent the labour and dreams of the whole community, while at the lower end, in terms of scale, the most obvious example is a wedding which, although small, may represent a family's life savings, thus making it a high-stakes venture which needs to run flawlessly. (One hopes it is a once in a lifetime celebration!)

Classification of events

There have been many efforts to classify events by type. The main classifications are generally business, sporting and cultural (see Table 1.1). While technically sports would come under the umbrella of culture, it is useful to differentiate this category. One way in which events can be further classified is as not-for-profit and commercial (profitable) events.

Characteristics differentiating events

Many event characteristics have already been discussed and these will be elaborated further. First, however, it is important to attempt to define 'event' and 'event product'. As Brown and James (2004) point out, there are as many definitions as there are text books. For Goldblatt (1997, p. 2) a special event is a 'unique moment in time celebrated with ceremony and ritual to satisfy specific needs'. While this definition clearly satisfies most events falling in the category of cultural events, it is not entirely satisfactory for many large-scale, commercial or corporate events such as product launches and other business events which are not necessarily celebratory. Perhaps a definition on which most writers would agree is that an event is generally a complex social endeavour characterized by sophisticated planning with a fixed deadline, often involving numerous stakeholders.

Table 1.1 Classification of events

Business	Meetings and conferences	Many associations have annual conferences around the world and the bid process for these is conducted many years in advance. For example, the 9th International Conference on Alzheimer's Disease and Related Disorders, presented by the Alzheimer's Association (USA), was the largest gathering of Alzheimer researchers in history. More than 4500 scientists from around the world attended. However, in terms of conventions, this is only mid-scale.
	Exhibitions	The world's biggest information and communication technology exhibition, CeBIT, is held annually. In 2004, a total of 6411 firms from 64 countries presented their products and systems at the Hanover show which attracted about 500 000 visitors.
		Many agricultural fairs have animal exhibitions and competitions, adding somewhat to the challenges for organizers. Bulls, horses and dogs all require careful handling!
	Incentives	Incentives are corporate events organized for high-achieving staff, often held at a resort or holiday destination, but including work-related meetings and presentations.
Sports	Competitive sports events	All grades of sporting competition from amateur to professional fall into this category, which also covers a multitude of sports ranging from baseball, cricket and football to netball and gymnastics.
	Non-competitive sports events	Fun and non-competitive activities characterize this type of sporting event, which includes runs and walks supporting charities and dragon boat races of the non-competitive variety.
Cultural	Arts	Arts festivals come in a multitude of formats, from the Adelaide Festival of Ideas to the Edinburgh Festival of classical music, opera, theatre and dance.
	Entertainment	There are many music concerts held around the world, on both a large and small scale, and featuring many different music genres.
	Television and the Internet	Many events are played out on television or the World Wide Web. The search for the 'American Idol' is an example of one such contemporary trend. In China, the equivalent is the competition for 'Super Voice Girl'.

Table 1.1 (*Continued*)

Community – historical and anniversary celebrations	Founding days, centenaries, bicentenaries and other anniversary days are often celebrated. Multicultural festivals also fall into this category.
Social action – cause-related events	Generally fundraising in nature, this type of event includes concerts such as Live 8 and relief concerts to raise money for the victims of the 2004 tsunami in South East Asia and Southern Asia and the 2005 hurricanes in the USA.
Protests	Many street protests – against globalization, for example – fall into this category. There is an annual calendar of protest events and international days of action around the world.
Life cycle/milestones	Baptisms, Bar Mitzvahs, weddings and funerals are all examples of life-cycle events. While most are small scale, 600 000 people lined the streets to watch the wedding of Charles and Diana, and one million people lined the route of Diana's funeral procession.
Religious	Ranging from small to large scale and represented, for example, by the Kumbha Mela in India, which attracted 70 million people over 44 days in 2001.

The event product is the whole package of goods and services. This is primarily the event programme but it also includes merchandise, food, service, the environment, transport, queues etc. Salem *et al.* (2004, p. 19) describe the event product as 'a unique blend of activities, which are the tools for achieving the overall event aims and satisfying customer needs'. In order to achieve its purpose, an event must meet human needs at all levels, and the management of human resources, in order to provide an optimal experience for the audience, is a critical part of product planning.

The things that make marketing of event products complex are their features of intangibility, inseparability, heterogeneity and perishability (Drummond and Anderson, 2004). In particular, the product leaves little that lasts, other than a few photos and other memorabilia. One aspect of the event product that is seldom acknowledged in discussing event marketing is its anticipatory element. Most events are something that the audience and, indeed, the participants look forward to since they are generally significant and positive social occasions. By enhancing this part of the product one can enhance service and satisfaction. Staff training usually has the event programme and related service delivery as its focus. This needs to be expanded to cover the lead-up period during which staff will be selling tickets, registering participants and providing information. Often the client works with the event management company over a long period. The service provided during this sometimes stressful time needs to be managed just as well as the actual event production.

Key characteristics of the event industry at the present time include the following:

1 *Worldwide interest.* Increasing globalization, a growing television audience and exposure to the World Wide Web have led to increased interest in events as a reflection of contemporary culture. In some extreme instances, sporting events can stop the nation and the world. This is certainly the case with some athletic events in the Summer Olympics. Two billion viewers watched Pope John Paul II's funeral. The execution of this event was doubtlessly planned in infinite detail – an extraordinary ceremony attended by the world's leaders and watched worldwide.

2 *Competitive environment.* Countries and cities involved in bid processes demonstrate the competitive nature of event procurement. Many conferences and exhibitions attract thousands of visitors and their expenditure is generally much higher than the average international visitor. All over the world – in China, in particular – there are initiatives to build bigger and better convention facilities in order to attract this lucrative segment.

3 *Economic and tourism impact.* Business, cultural and sporting events also contribute significantly to the economic and tourism impact on cities and even countries. Many cities and suburbs are branded by their hallmark events, including Edinburgh, Monaco, Rio, Calgary and Chelsea. Taken into account here is the direct expenditure of visitors and event organizers as well as the indirect (or flow on) economic effect on the wider community.

4 *Authentic or imaginative event products.* Consumers look for a point of difference and, in particular, authenticity when visiting an event as a tourist. Where leisure options are a dime a dozen, an event needs to provide the motivation to attend. In the case of annual events, the visitor needs a reason to return. WOMAD is an example of a popular and enduring event, held in several cities. WOMAD stands for World of Music, Arts and Dance, expressing the central aim of the WOMAD festival, which is to bring together and to celebrate many forms of music, arts and dance drawn from countries and cultures all over the world. The organizers say they aim to excite, to inform, and to create awareness of the worth and potential of a multicultural society.

5 *Benefits to the host community.* The community expects to be consulted when there is an anticipated impact on their local area. The community needs to know that the positive impacts will outweigh the short-term negative effects. There are many residents of Melbourne who remain opposed to the motor racing held annually in their city. On the other hand, Chinese citizens displaced by the massive construction projects of the 2008 Olympic Games demonstrated resigned acceptance to the planning priorities established by their government. Even the smallest community event must be approved by the local council, whose role it is to ensure that the event is a good fit with the community, has minimal risk and, indeed, will contribute in a positive way to the social fabric of the region.

6 *Minimizing risk.* Public liability and other insurances are significant considerations for event organizers. Safety is a primary concern, particularly as there are additional risks associated with mass gatherings. Crowd behaviour and potential fatalities at sporting and music events are worldwide issues.

7 *Political influence.* Where many large events require government support at one level or another (including local council level) there are always political considerations. In Australia, for example, a regional event is much more likely to attract funding than a city event since regional development is a political priority.

Naturally, with countries being so fiercely competitive, bidding for mega events such as the Olympic Games or World Cup Soccer requires government support at the highest level. South Africa's 2010 FIFA soccer World Cup bid win was a political success for the current government.

8 *Complex design and execution.* Most events do not carry a blueprint. They are often complex and risky artistic endeavours attracting media attention. They can involve hundreds of people as spectators, participants and workers. All of these people join together for a typically short period, ranging from a few hours to a few days. In that short time the purpose and aims of the event must be achieved. Plans must be dynamic and the whole project is often quite organic, some might say chaotic.

9 *Multiple stakeholders.* Sponsors are the most demanding of the stakeholders, which may include government, tourism bodies, emergency services, roads authorities, contractors and the local community, to name just a few, and rightly so if they have made a significant investment. In some cases, they compete against each other in terms of exposure if their expectations aren't carefully managed. Sponsors want signage, media coverage and a range of other benefits. In the simplest example, at a music festival the teenagers want to go wild, their parents want them to behave like 50 year olds, and the police would prefer that they stay at home. The bands encourage the fans to behave badly and the security staff have their hands full monitoring drug and alcohol abuse. For large events there are competing contractor organizations which have to submit tenders for event services such as security. This can become fraught with problems if the tendering is not above board and if the contracts are not awarded with sufficient time for effective implementation.

10 *Volunteer management.* Many events, large and small, are organized or staffed by volunteers. This brings further challenges as the event manager responsible for human resources needs to evaluate the specific needs of volunteers and ensure that they are met. Volunteers may be motivated by patriotism or a commitment to the cause behind the event, such as fundraising. In many cases, volunteers have high expectations of having a good time and will leave if this does not eventuate. Attrition rates will be discussed in more detail in Chapter 15. The decisions relating to the size and scope of the volunteer workforce need to be carefully considered.

Event management – art or science?

Attempts to describe the responsibilities of event managers often elaborate on the challenges of logistics and operations. For example, some writers suggest that a project management approach such as EMBOK™ (event management body of knowledge) could be used to formalize and develop the professionalism of the contemporary event manager (Goldblatt, 2005a). However, Brown and James (2004, p. 53) suggest that many practitioners 'have put aside, ignored or failed to consider the conceptual development and design of their events – the very heart and soul, the *raison d'être* of any truly great event – in favour of artificially manufacturing events that try to meet the needs of clients and stakeholders'.

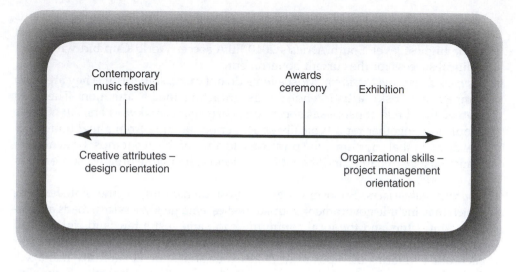

Figure 1.1 Continuum of creative and organizational input for different types of events

Brown and James' position will be taken up here as a discussion about the art and science of event management. Clearly event management is both an art and a science (see Figure 1.1). It is a science in the same way that meticulous project planning is applied to the building of a bridge. Indeed, many events involve the building of infrastructure of one sort or another. But this is only part of event management. The other part of event management is more akin to producing a movie. Here, people and resources are brought together in a creative and costly pursuit in which the audience response defines success or failure. Thus event management is in some ways like engineering, while in others it is like movie making. The question is whether one and the same person can be the artist and the scientist or whether these roles are best separated. There has to be a tension between artistic vision and operational implementation. This is illustrated in successive Olympic Games opening ceremonies where, in the short period of four years, the technology used surpasses that used in previous ceremonies. However, essentially, the opening ceremony is a production not a project. In contrast, an exhibition such as CeBIT, the largest computer show in the world, is more like a project, but one of massive proportions.

Events require vision. Chapter 13 will revisit the continuum of art and science as it applies to the design and management of events.

Contemporary human resource management

Formerly, the personnel function was associated quite narrowly with recruitment, selection and implementation of company policy. However, contemporary human resource managers see their role as being more strategic and business oriented. Where the event organization has this focus, whether in the form of a human resource department or the allocation of this function to relevant managers, there are considerable benefits.

At a strategic level, the event organization needs to decide which services should be contracted out and which kept in-house. These are critical decisions, which are driven by labour market forces. Labour cost is frequently amongst the most significant of the costs associated with running an event and is complicated by the fact that a large proportion of this cost is often hidden in agreements developed with contractors. It is important that this be acknowledged when undertaking strategic planning for human resources. A scoping exercise will determine the multitude of tasks that need to be undertaken and strategic decisions must then be made as to which of these tasks should be contracted out. A risk analysis is also necessary to ensure that the job analysis is based on sound decision making. For example, it is commonplace to contract security organizations to manage this role because their staff are adequately trained, carry the necessary licences and are expert at this type of work. (Well, of course, this is what one hopes and plans for.)

The most significant issue for strategic planners is the temporary nature of most event-related employment. Maximizing performance and achieving optimal levels of service is only possible through effective strategic human resource planning, which is undertaken by HR specialists and/or managers throughout the event organization. Human resource management is a shared responsibility.

Event human resource management

One of the most challenging tasks for the event or human resource manager is managing the people designing and staging the event, whether a festival, exhibition, street parade or competition. This is no ordinary business environment. Most organizations hold onto their employees for months or even years, giving them time to socialize and develop their skills and knowledge in the context of the particular business.

In the event environment, on the other hand, there is generally only a handful of individuals on the planning team and a mass of paid, voluntary and contractor employees working on a temporary site for anything from a few hours to a few days. Developing a vision or purpose for the event, conducting a detailed job analysis, responding to constant changes in operational planning and meeting the communication needs of all involved are just some of the tasks of the human resource manager. Indeed, most events do not have a human resource manager, and this function is undertaken by senior staff from the event manager down to the team leader. It is thus vitally important that each person in a management or supervisory role understands the human resource function and their contribution to managing the people in their temporary workforce.

This challenging and dynamic environment is one which tests people management skills to the limit. As one event manager says, 'something will always go wrong, it is how you respond to it that matters'.

Table 1.2 illustrates the different roles of those involved in staging an event. In some cases, their interests differ, commonly when the budget allocated to safety and security is not seen as sufficient. Conflict is commonplace. For example, there may

Table 1.2 Event workforce

Event committee
The role of the committee is to formally identify the primary purpose and goals of the event and to monitor progress towards those goals. The committee members generally take on responsibilities for production, marketing, staffing, operations and finance.

Event staff
The paid staff of an event organization share responsibility for designing and staging the event. Paid staff are usually experienced and qualified, if not in the events business, then in a related field. This group may be quite small until close to the event. In some cases, the paid workforce includes staff on secondment from, for example, government agencies.

Stakeholders
Multiple stakeholders from different disciplines have an impact on event planning. Stakeholders may include local government, emergency services, roads and transport, environment protection authority, police and sponsors. The owner/manager of the venue is one of the primary stakeholders.

Contractors
Few events run without the extensive use of contracting organizations to provide goods and services. These include suppliers of temporary fencing and facilities, lighting, sound, stage management, entertainment, catering and waste management.

Volunteers
Many community events involve volunteers, sometimes from the committee down. The number of volunteers varies depending on the type and scale of the event. For many sporting events, the volunteers are specialists in their areas of scoring etc. Commercial events such as exhibitions seldom require volunteers.

be a difference of opinion about the choice of entertainment – the committee members may agree but the sponsor may not approve or endorse their choice.

As Drummond and Anderson (2004, p. 88) point out, 'quality in the operational environment of events and festivals is directly related to the people delivering the service'. The customer interacts with any number of service providers, such as ticket sellers, security staff and cleaners. These people could all work for contracting organizations and are therefore not under the direct control of the event organization. Managing the quality of such interactions is imperative. The selection and training of contractor organizations and their staff will be discussed in detail in Chapters 5 and 9. In relation to the service staff whose role it is to manage customers at an event, Drummond and Anderson (2004, p. 89) stress that 'the communication and professional skills of these people influence the whole understanding of the organization in the visitor's mind'.

Event management as an emerging profession

There has been recent debate about the emergence of event management as a profession (Goldblatt, 2005a; Harris, 2004). If the level of interest by students in this area and the number of courses offered is anything to go by, one would have to accept that, indeed, this is a new profession. However, Harris (2004) analyses this issue in

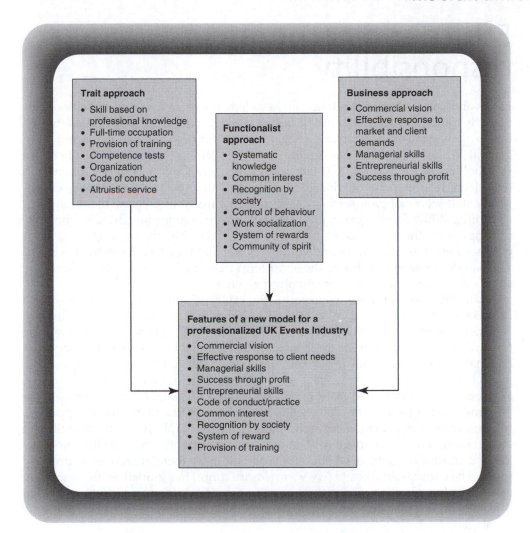

Figure 1.2 Proposed model for professionalization of events management in the United Kingdom
(Harris, V. (2004). Event management: a new profession. *Event Management* **9**, 107. Reproduced with permission.)

some detail to conclude that a lack of common purpose and unity precludes the development of the event profession in the current environment. This is largely due to the numerous industry associations representing different sectors such as conferences, exhibitions, special events, venue management and the like. While the industry is fragmented and lacks a common code, as you would find, for example, with the medical or engineering professions, there is little hope for the development of a single professional association and code of conduct. However, Harris does provide a model for the professionalization of event management, illustrated in Figure 1.2, which takes into account the trait, functionalist and business approaches. This includes the all important code of conduct.

Events carry with them a number of risks, in particular, risks associated with public safety. In South Africa, a proposal has been put forward requiring appropriate qualifications for event managers to be legislated, among other proposals for measures to ensure crowd safety.

Ethics and corporate responsibility

Ethics and corporate responsibility are key elements of an event organization, particularly human resource responsibilities such as occupational health and safety, volunteer management, contractor management and, indeed, people management in general. While Webb (2001) stresses the positive collaboration that occurred between stakeholders of the Sydney 2000 Olympic Games, particularly between unions and organizers, he does point out that goodwill played an important part in the few cases where staff were not paid for two weeks due to a range of glitches, including time recording. While for this event problems were overcome for bus drivers who were unhappy with their pay, accommodation, food and shifts, there are many smaller events where both employees and volunteers feel that they have been treated badly. This is seldom reported due to the short-term nature of the event, those involved simply deciding never to become involved again.

Of all HR responsibilities, concern for the safety of staff (and audience) is most important. Since the crowd crush at the E2 Night Club in Chicago took 21 lives in 2003, and the inferno at The Station nightclub, also 2003, claimed 100 lives in the fourth deadliest nightclub fire in US history, the National Fire Protection Association has enacted tough new code provisions for fire sprinklers and crowd management in nightclub-type venues in America. Crowd managers are required to control crowds, keep egress paths clear and assist in rapid evacuation. The Life Safety Code calls for one crowd manager for every 250 attendees and requires that they undergo approved training in crowd management techniques. This has implications for recruitment and training, HR risk management and workplace supervision, including monitoring and control of contract labour. Across the industry there are moves to improve safety. The Crowdsafe website (www.crowdsafe.com/) has guidelines for managing crowds and mosh pits and conducts ongoing research into crowd safety. Increased threats to mass gatherings are a major concern for authorities whenever large events are staged.

Case study 1.1

IFEA human resource management standard

The International Festivals and Events Association (IFEA) has a code of professional responsibility, which includes the following standard specifically related to human resource management:

Principle/Standard #4: *Members shall embrace and promote the highest standards of human resource training and management.*

Consideration #1: *In its development as an industry, festival and special event organizations and professionals must establish the highest standards of professional hiring, employment and development. As such, members should take such action as necessary to ensure that they, as individuals and organizations, establish and practice ethical hiring, termination and discipline practices for employees and associates. At a minimum, members and member organizations shall operate in compliance with all federal, local and state laws concerning the hiring, promotion and discipline of employees. Because of the industry's commitment to social and community development, members and member organizations should take every reasonable opportunity to ensure and encourage the diversity of their membership, and employee and volunteer base.*

Consideration #2: *Members and member organizations should take such action as necessary to comply with federal, state, and local Equal Opportunity Employment laws and to avoid the practice and tolerance of discrimination based on race, creed, national origin, age, handicap, political affiliation, sex, sexual orientation, religion, parental or military status, veteran status, or disability. At a minimum, members and their organizations shall comply with all laws applicable to the jurisdiction(s) in which they conduct business.*

(Reproduced by courtesy of International Festivals and Events Association (IFEA); for further information see www.ifea.com)

Reflective practice 1.1
1 Explain why you think codes of practice are necessary for event management?
2 This code looks at hiring, EEO and training. Suggest other human resource practices that could be covered by a code of practice.

While the International Festivals and Events Association (see Case study 1.1) has a voluntary code, it is likely that higher levels of legislative compliance will become necessary in many countries as more event planning elements fall under the scope of legislation. It is really a case of 'watch this space' as governments and associations work towards developing legislation, recommendations, guidelines and codes of practice which will further develop the profession of event management and raise the status of organizations which demonstrate best practice. In the United Kingdom, the *Event Safety Guide* ensures legal compliance. However, with the rapid growth of the industry in size and scale (including both mega events, such as the Olympic Games, and small community events), there will be moves to ensure much more rigorous compliance all over the world. Recognized training will become a minimum requirement for many roles in the event industry. Arcodia and Axelson (2005) show that organizations advertising for event managers rate the following five skills as most important, based on the number of times these skills were mentioned in their study of 1002 job advertisements: organizational/planning skills; general communication skills; team skills; customer service skills; and computer skills. In addition, a detailed knowledge of human resources/industrial relations legislation and codes of practice for staffing and supervision will be found on the job specification of every event manager and event human resource specialist.

Many events start from small beginnings and grow over time. The sustainability of an event is vitally important as it represents a great deal of effort and financial investment. There are many community events that fall into this category, including historical and cultural celebrations.

Case study 1.2 provides an example of a sophisticated international event that has developed since its inception in 1985 largely through a quality programme, links with schools and supportive sponsorship.

Case study 1.2

Alcatel Ottawa International Children's Festival

Attendance at the Ottawa International Children's Festival has grown in monumental numbers. The festival is fast becoming the premier family event in the Nation's Capital, and has made the Ottawa International Children's Festival a favourite destination for young people of all ages.

In a survey administered by the Ottawa Tourism & Convention Authority, 96 per cent rated their festival experience as excellent or good and said they would like to return to the festival.

Festival growth

2001–5 000
2002–9 000
2003–12 000
2004–16 000
2005–13 000

Marketing goals and objectives

Ottawa International Children's Festival exists to surround young people with excellence in the performing arts that excites their instinctive creativity and their boundless imagination, and encourages individual expression. To serve this mission we will:

- *Build local and regional public interest and awareness to ensure high festival attendance.*
- *Cultivate awareness, interest and enthusiasm for children's performance art and theatre from all over the world.*
- *Promote local and national talent to a wide audience.*
- *Promote an annual festival in the spring for school audiences, and year round programming for the general public.*
- *Strengthen local economies throughout the National Capital Region by attracting visitors, and by promoting the Children's Festival as a popular annual and local 'destination' event.*
- *Acknowledge/profile volunteers who work to make the Children's Festival a success.*
- *Identify and promote all participating sponsors.*

Festival attendance

The 2002 festival enjoyed a 400 per cent increase in attendance to 9000 audience members, with the majority of attendees being school-aged children during the weekday performances. The OTCA Visitor Impact Survey for 2003 reports that the 2003 festival was even better attended, due in part to the offering of a combination of paid and free events, resulting in just over 12 000 attendees, which included paid and free activities. This past year's festival saw another dramatic increase to 16 000 audience members.

Audience demographic: A wide cross-section of the public – from all economic and social backgrounds and ages, attendees include families, single parents, grandparents and school groups.

Ottawa International Children's Festival operating budget: $600 000.

(Reproduced with permission of Alcatel Ottawa International Children's Festival; for further information see www.ottawachildrensfestival.ca/default.asp)

Reflective practice 1.2

1 Discuss changes that are likely to impact on an event that grows from an attendance of 500 to 13 000 visitors in terms of strategic human resource planning and 'professionalization' of the workforce.

2 Given the dramatic growth of this festival over five years, discuss the formalization of human resource procedures that would be associated with the increased size and scope of the event.

3 This event targets children (and their parents) as the primary demographic. Some countries have codes of conduct and guidelines for working with children. If you were running an event for children, what consideration would you give to the increased corporate responsibility associated with running a children's event?

Chapter summary and key points

Events celebrate, inspire and commemorate. As we have seen in this chapter, to ensure their success the work must be planned and allocated according to the vision and goals for the event. Strategically, this includes management of contractor organizations and their staff as well as relationships with key stakeholders. For all but the biggest events, there is no human resource manager. This function is undertaken by the event committee and the organizer. Each manager and supervisor is responsible for his or her people, making sure that they provide optimal service in this dynamic environment. With the emerging emphasis on professionalism in the event business, human resource management has become a key focus of overall event management. Codes of practice and legislative requirements make it essential that event organizational planning is undertaken by people who are professionally qualified, in this case in human resource management as it applies to the unique environment of events management.

Revision questions

1 Using the event categories listed in this chapter, identify a real event to match each of the categories.

2 List and explain ten characteristics of the event environment most relevant to human resource management.

3 Table 1.2 shows five categories of people involved in the event workforce. Using a major or mega event, explain in detail how this event would be structured in terms of staffing, providing also, for example, the names of sponsors and/or contractor organizations.

References

Arcodia, C. and Axelson, M. (2005). A review of event management job advertisements in Australian newspapers. In *The Impacts of Events*. University of Technology, Sydney.

Brown, S. and James, J. (2004). Event design and management: ritual sacrifice?. In I. Yeoman *et al.* (eds), *Festival and Events Management: An International Arts and Culture Perspective*. Elsevier Butterworth-Heinemann.

Drummond, S. and Anderson, H. (2004). Service quality and managing your people. In I. Yeoman *et al.* (eds), *Festival and Events Management*. Elsevier Butterworth-Heinemann.

Goldblatt, J. (1997). *Special Events*, 2nd edn. John Wiley and Sons Inc.

Goldblatt, J. (2005a). An exploratory study of demand levels for EMBOK™. In *The Impacts of Events*. University of Technology, Sydney.

Goldblatt, J. J. (2005b). *Special Events: Event Leadership for a New World*, 4th edn. Wiley.

Harris, V. (2004). Event management: a new profession. *Event Management*, **9**, 103–9.

National Fire Protection Association. Life Safety Code. Viewed 15 May 2006, www.nfpa.org/aboutthecodes/AboutTheCodes.asp?DocNum=101.

Rogge, J. (2004). Global viewing of Athens 2004 Olympic Games breaks records. International Sports Television Convention (Sportel), Monaco.

Salem, G., Jones, E. and Morgan, N. (2004). An overview of events management. In I. Yeoman *et al.* (eds), *Festival and Events Management*. Elsevier Butterworth-Heinemann.

Webb, T. (2001). *The Collaborative Games: The Story behind the Spectacle*. Pluto Press.

Chapter 2
Human resource planning

Learning objectives

After reading through this chapter you will be able to:

- **Provide and discuss definitions of human resource management**
- **Describe the strategic human resource planning role**
- **Illustrate how human resource planning is linked to the event purpose and goals**
- **Describe key human resource functions**
- **Discuss issues relating to integrating human resource functions across projects**
- **Conduct a human resource risk analysis.**

Introduction

Human resource management is much more than recruitment and selection of staff and volunteers; it is a wide-ranging activity, involving the long-term strategic development of the event organization. The expected outcome of this is a positive culture of commitment and co-operation developed in the process of managing the workforce. In the event business diverse nontraditional employment contracts and an extraordinarily complex workforce need to be integrated into one cohesive body working towards the same purpose and goals. For a mega event this collaboration needs to occur over a long and stressful planning period which can take four years or more. It is entirely conceivable that the planning team may become frustrated, particularly during periods when the media is critical about issues such as budget overruns, and alternative options (job and lifestyle changes) are being considered by members of the team. In fact, a serious consideration for every event human resource manager is the possibility that key staff will bail out shortly before an event in order to avoid competing with peers in the flooded employment market that often occurs soon after a large event. One can easily conceive of an event where the infrastructure is not complete and the venues are still being constructed in the final days before opening. Similarly, human resource strategies can fail to meet their objectives and the human side of the event can spiral into disaster very quickly. The human version of the wet concrete syndrome must be avoided at all costs; people must be confident and ready to meet the opening deadline.

Definition of human resource management

The range and variety of definitions for event management are matched by those for human resource management, which is problematic if a single definition is necessary, or indeed desirable. Maund (2001, p. 36) defines strategic human resource management as follows:

> *It is strategic human resource management which provides the context within which human resource management will work and will include the resourcing to carry out the plans, for example, in relation to employee development, the HRM specialist will consider training and development. Therefore, strategic human resource management is concerned with assisting the organization in achieving its objectives and gaining (or maintaining) its competitive edge through its objectives. These are informed by the mission of the organization – its purpose, what it wants to achieve for the stakeholders – as well as by the internal and external business environment.*

The above emphasis on the external business environment will be stressed in this chapter. A detailed labour force analysis is often required to identify whether sufficient numbers of skilled individuals are available for short-term employment with the event organization. Indeed, for many larger events, senior event professionals travel the world to meet the temporary recruitment needs of such event projects. While the need for specialist staff may be met overseas, the bulk of the labour force required for the very short period of event execution is typically large and unskilled. For this reason, consideration might be given to running the event during school and university holidays with a view to employing large numbers of students. This is only one of many considerations, which may include competitive forces complicating planning when workers are in short supply and casual staff are being double counted if they work for more than one security or catering company.

In the event environment, an additional challenge is the logistics of staff planning which may involve organizing uniforms, accreditation, transportation and meals. This is not unique to events such as World Cup Soccer. Events such as music festivals also need to give consideration to the logistics issues that do not face human resource professionals in the conventional business environment. For example, students volunteering for work at a festival may be asked to arrive at the venue at 5 am to assist in setting up the event. At this time of day, public transport systems are seldom working. Finishing very late at night, sometimes three hours or more after the event audience has left the site, presents the additional problem of safety. Food is an unusual topic to raise in a chapter on strategic planning, but it is an essential need which is costly to meet if 300 volunteers need two hot meals outside normal catering hours at a temporary venue. The logistics of staff planning is thus an additional feature of human resource management that needs to be stressed for the event environment.

These issues fall within the scope of leadership and logistics planning for the human resource manager. A strategic approach to human resource management means taking a leadership role in the development of the event organization and the execution of event plans. Furthermore, as mentioned above, logistics of staff planning is far more complex in this environment of temporary structures and transient teams than it is for human resource professionals in traditional environments. As Armstrong (2001, p. 33) suggests, 'the fundamental aim of strategic HRM is to generate strategic capability by ensuring that the organization has the skilled, committed and well-motivated employees it needs to achieve sustained competitive advantage'.

Strategic approach to HR planning

A strategic approach to human resources planning involves the following:

1 Formulating strategy, including an environmental assessment of the labour market, industrial relations framework and the level of expertise required. It involves decisions regarding outsourcing components of the project to other organizations, and working with stakeholders such as government bodies and sponsors.
2 Developing a flexible and responsive approach to dealing with HR issues as they emerge in the planning period and providing advice at strategic level.
3 Ensuring that the event organization's vision, goals and objectives are the starting point for all human resources planning, incorporating the values of the organization.
4 Facilitating integration across a wide range of projects, all working at a different pace towards the target date for the event.
5 Focusing on customer service, both internal and external, in all elements of planning and delivery.

Analysis of the labour market is essential. In Atlanta in 1996, staff shortages were reported in many businesses, including hotels. As a result, volunteers were poached, leading to an unacceptable attrition rate (rumours attribute this premature departure of volunteers to the baggy shorts they refused to wear, but that is probably a myth). If the event requires staff and volunteers to undertake police checks for accreditation purposes, volunteers become a valuable and employable commodity. According to Webb (2001), Games contracting employers in Atlanta found that they needed to recruit up to 4000 staff to be sure of having 1000 employees at the event. Knowing this, the Sydney 2000 organizers developed two key strategies: first, they recruited many volunteers from out of town, leaving the local labour force intact; second, a formal industrial agreement was reached for paid and contractor employees which rewarded them for assigned shift completion with a bonus hourly rate, paid only after the event.

For a large-scale event, an analysis of the skill requirements is an essential part of planning. Shortages of skilled staff such as chefs can be remedied through innovative approaches to menu planning and food storage (e.g. cook-chill). However, before specific solutions such as these are discussed, the impact of the event's staffing needs should be analysed in detail across the board, including the size of the labour pool, the knowledge and competence of those in the labour pool, the size and skill of a potential volunteer workforce, and the availability of contractor organizations to meet the short-term demands of providing event services.

The most significant role for human resource experts in event planning is that of integration. A major event comprises multiple projects with different timelines. Each of these has human resource components, including staffing, development of policies and procedures, training, performance management and recognition. In some cases, these are similar for all projects, while in others the project has specific human resource requirements. This effort needs to be integrated in order to develop a cohesive workforce while recognizing the unique challenges posed in some areas. This requires pro-active leadership by the human resources team. For example, the transportation team may commence operations much earlier than the catering team, yet both groups require induction training on commencement. Add to this a range of management training programmes and the complexity of the training schedule is immediately evident. Just-in-time training is different for multiple teams at different stages of event implementation.

The main strategic focus in the event environment is organizational design and effectiveness. The unique life cycle of an event provides a completely new environment for the traditional human resource practitioner, although in the areas of recruitment and staffing, training and development, employee relations, productivity management, and reward and recognition there are similarities. However, the event workforce goes through several phases: from a long planning period with relatively small numbers to a short operational and delivery period when potentially thousands of people are brought into the workforce. In this context, the human resource professional cannot afford to play a service and support role, but must instead act in a leadership and consultative role (Rothwell *et al.*, 1998).

For optimal human performance in this dynamic and challenging project-oriented environment, human resource management must have a strategic focus. This is not only the case for mega events, but also for events in the area of arts and entertainment as an example. A creative focus requires an innovative and flexible approach to human resource planning. This is particularly the case for an annual festival that needs to be sustainable over time.

Developing the event purpose

In all event planning the vision, mission statement or purpose is the overriding statement that defines the event. Due to the competing interests of various stakeholders and the potential for losing focus during planning, it is vital that the event organizer or committee has a clear and purposeful direction. In some cases, such as a celebrity concert performance, there is the undisguised motive of profit making; in others, such as a not-for-profit arts festival, the aim may be to achieve certain social objectives. Many community festivals wish to retain their authenticity and to avoid commercialization at any cost. Decisions regarding the event purpose guide all decision making, such as the source of funds, the design of the event programme, marketing strategies and human resource strategies, including the use or not of volunteers.

From the examples that follow, it is easy to see that the purpose will differ from one event to another:

> *The Chelsea Flower Show is still viewed as the most important event in the horticultural calendar. Garden designers from around the world compete for space at the most famous of flower shows. With new trends constantly appearing – illustrated in the changing face of garden design – it is certain that the Chelsea Flower Show will continue to mark this country's ever-changing horticultural history.*

The Chelsea Flower Show (www.rhs.org.uk/chelsea/history.asp) is run by the Royal Horticultural Society:

> *Established in 1804, the Royal Horticultural Society is now the UK's leading gardening charity dedicated to advancing horticulture and promoting good gardening. Our goal is to help people share a passion for plants, to encourage excellence in horticulture and inspire all those with an interest in gardening.*

From this short description, the main selection criteria for anyone working on the frontline with exhibitors and visitors would be horticultural expertise and a passion for the industry.

The purpose for the Asian Games (www.doha-2006.com/en/), which is on a much larger scale, is quite different:

> *The Asian Games are held every four years for the purpose of developing international relations and inter-cultural knowledge in Asia. The 15th Asian Games is not just a sporting event and the hosting of delegates, it is a window of opportunity through which Qatar has the opportunity to show the world its capabilities and the ideals for which it stands.*

In contrast, the objectives of the Vancouver International Readers and Writers Festival (www.writersfest.bc.ca), a registered nonprofit charitable organization, are:

- *To advance literacy by introducing young readers to the wonder of books.*
- *To deliver the world's best writers to festival audiences.*
- *To promote new and undiscovered British Columbian, Canadian and international writers.*

Finally, Special Olympics is an international organization dedicated to empowering individuals with an intellectual disability to become physically fit, productive and respected members of society through sports training and competition. Special Olympics offers children and adults with an intellectual disability year-round training and competition in 26 Olympic-type summer and winter sports. Special Olympics currently serves over 1.2 million people with an intellectual disability in more than 200 programmes in over 150 countries. The mission of Special Olympics (www.specialolympics.org) is:

> *To provide year-round sports training and athletic competition in a variety of Olympic-type sports for children and adults with intellectual disabilities, giving them continuing opportunities to develop physical fitness, demonstrate courage, experience joy, and participate in a sharing of gifts, skills and friendship with their families, other Special Olympics athletes and the community.*

As these examples illustrate, the diversity of event type is matched by the diversity of purpose, goals and objectives. In order to ensure that the appropriate people are on board, are trained and motivated, and are provided with the means to perform at the highest level, the human resource team must be involved in the strategic development of the event concept and in all aspects of operational planning. It is only with this involvement that the customer service levels expected will be delivered and will sit consistently with the event purpose.

Integrating planning across functions

With this in mind, integrating planning across functions is vitally important. This is difficult because these functional areas (FAs) work at different rates in preparation for the event and generally want to conduct recruitment, training and so on just in time to meet their needs. This may be ahead of many others. For example, one area which generally commences operations quite early is technology. This functional area meets all information technology requirements in the lead-up to the event, including building the event intranet and website. During the operational period their role may change to scoring and results reporting amongst other things. From this example alone, it can be seen how a job analysis for this functional area would reveal different phases of staffing and different staffing and training needs. The same process would be replicated across all functional areas such as transport or sponsorship.

Before going any further, it is essential to understand the concept of *functional area*, which is widely used in event management. Functional areas are the divisions within the event organization that carry responsibility for delivering the key infrastructure. In a traditional business these would be departments. This is illustrated in Figure 2.1, which shows that all areas work towards meeting the same deadline for delivery of their services. Along the way there are many 'which comes first?' questions of the chicken and egg variety.

Event organizations are extremely organic, shifting and changing as the implications of one decision impact on others. For example, a change in sponsor might impact on uniform design, production and delivery. As a result, accreditation might be asked to delay their schedule to match uniform issue. As Figure 2.1 indicates, some teams finalise their planning before others.

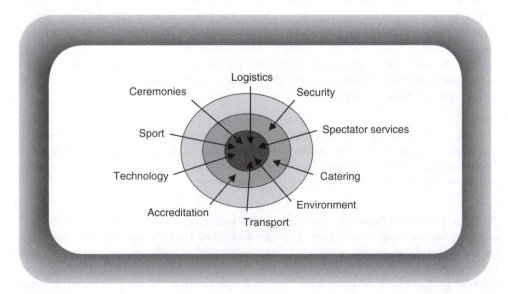

Figure 2.1   Functional areas, each working at a different pace towards a common deadline

While the Olympic Games has fifty-four functional areas, the key considerations for smaller events would be:

- Finance
- Legal
- Programme management
- Risk
- Workforce planning
- Procurement and logistics
- Technology
- Transport
- Security
- Accreditation
- Ceremonies
- Catering
- Cleaning and waste management
- Environment
- Ticketing
- Marketing
- Media
- Sponsorship
- Merchandising
- Sport/entertainment/production
- Medical
- Customer service.

While the functional areas for a mega sporting event, for example, play a primary role during the early planning phase, there comes a time when the venues are nearing completion and the venue team, generally including representatives of these functional areas, needs to be established. So, for example, catering would need to provide services to both the stadium and the tennis centre. At this point the organization structure of the event changes from a functional focus to a geographical or venue focus.

For most events, this change manifests as a shift to management of venues, zones, clusters or precincts, each of which operates almost autonomously. While the tradition of the Olympic Games is to call these *venue areas* (VAs) or *precincts*, this text will use the term *zone areas* (ZAs). Not every event is so large that the incumbent venue management team is eclipsed by a team appointed by the organizing committee. In most cases, the event organization works with the incumbent venue management team who might be full-time staff of a sporting complex.

Even much smaller events, such as a fun run, would operate on the basis of teams responsible for the start, the route and the finish, with a manager responsible for each. The geographical area is also most commonly known as a zone, so that in this case one would have a Manager – Start; Manager – Route; and Manager – Finish and Ceremonies.

This is a significant strategic shift to a 'matrix organization', which will be discussed in detail in the next chapter. Matrix structures are useful as they 'draw the members of their project teams from discipline groups ... These individuals are assigned to a project team and they will be responsible to the team leader for delivering the required results, but they will continue to be accountable generally to the head of their discipline for their overall performance and contribution' (Armstrong, 2001, p. 190). Figure 2.2 illustrates how a project manager responsible for risk and

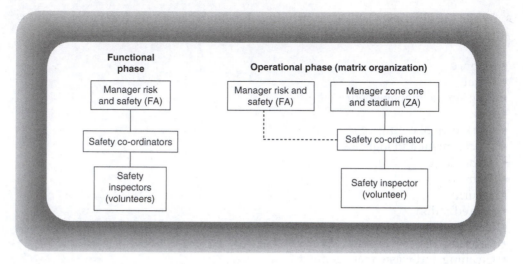

Figure 2.2 Evolution from functional area structure (left) to a matrix organization structure (right)

safety (a function) might be responsible for his or her team right up until shortly before the event, at which time staff will be allocated to zones (or geographical areas), reporting directly to the local manager and only indirectly to the Manager Risk and Safety for advice on specific issues. Thus the Safety Co-ordinator would no longer report directly to the Manager Risk and Safety but to the Manager of Zone One.

Evolution of the event organization

All events undergo evolutionary development, either as major single projects or as a series of smaller events, each with project characteristics. The Manchester Commonwealth Games project underwent several phases including:

- Strategic planning (four years)
- Operational planning (one year)
- Operational stage (six months)
- Delivery (three months)
- Wind up (four months).

At each stage of a project's development there is a different focus to planning and the structure of the organization can change. This is the case for events of all sizes and types. If the event is an annual event with a two-year planning cycle, then the event team will be doing several things concurrently for the two events, one in the strategic design phase and the other in the operational stage. This is illustrated in Figure 2.3 where, for example, the 2008 event may be in the early design phase even before the 2007 event is wound up. For an annual music event, for example, acts may need to be signed up more than a year out from the next event.

Toffler (1990) uses the term 'pulsating organization' to describe organizations that expand and contract. Hanlon and Cuskelly (2002), in their study of two major sporting events, make recommendations for management induction, which will be discussed in

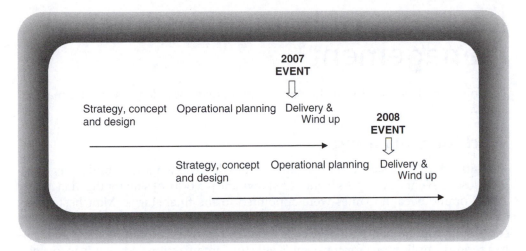

Figure 2.3   Timelines for an annual event at different stages

more detail in Chapter 9. The point is well made that organizations such as these have a special character compared with generic organizations which are much more stable.

The organizing committee

Shone and Parry (2004) suggest the organizational structure in Figure 2.4 for an event committee. Notable is the absence of anyone dedicated to the human resources role. This is quite common in smaller events. In most cases, this function becomes part of the job of the operations manager, venue manager, artistic director and the like. Each hires a team and manages their performance.

Shone and Parry suggest that, in addition to the above, a range of stakeholders might be invited to committee meetings, for example, representatives from the venue, licence holders, sponsors, police, first aid providers, fire service and the local council.

For larger events, however, a human resource specialist is highly recommended. This role might extend to workforce planning, contractor management, volunteer management, recruitment and training, occupational health and safety, uniforms, meals and the human resources policy.

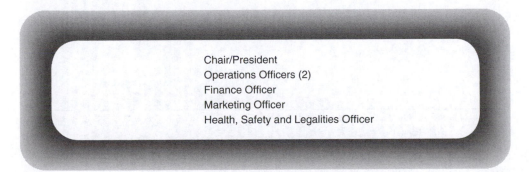

Figure 2.4   Organization structure for an event committee
(Shone, A. and Parry, B. (2004). *Successful Event Management*, 2nd edn, p. 66. Reproduced with permission of Learning.)

Key tasks of human resource management

The following key roles for the human resources team or delegates are summarized below.

Workforce planning

Recruitment of paid staff has to be timed optimally. The workforce builds very rapidly close to event delivery. As Figure 2.5 shows, the majority of staff for the Manchester 2002 Commonwealth Games were appointed in the final stages (Manchester City Council, 2003). Where an event is running over budget the temptation is to delay some staff appointments for weeks or months. However, as can be imagined, this has serious implications for the event's effective organization. While it is inconceivable that building the physical infrastructure of the event would be stopped, it seems that human resources can be a soft target for cost savings.

Case study 2.1

Growth in workforce – Manchester 2002 Commonwealth Games

The following graph illustrates the cumulative employment of staff for the Manchester 2002 Commonwealth Games. This provides a graphic illustration of the exponential growth of the workforce for large events.

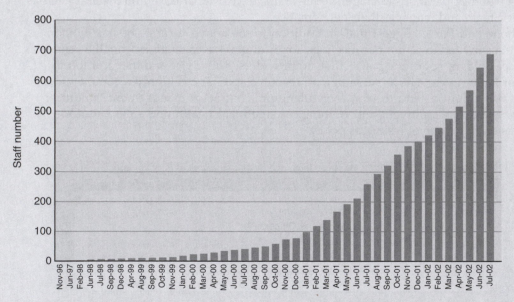

Figure 2.5   Cumulative employment of staff for the Manchester 2002 Olympic Games
(Manchester City Council (2003), Manchester Commonwealth Games Post Games Report; for further information see: www.gameslegacy.com)

Reflective practice 2.1
1 Every new employee needs induction training. What are the implications for human resources of this sharp workforce growth?
2 Compare the levels of team development and camaraderie with work colleagues at the two ends of the spectrum.

Organizational design

As mentioned previously, the organization's design is impacted by the project time-line, with significant key points at which the organizational structure may change dramatically to a matrix organizational structure. The involvement of a range of stakeholders and contractors is also significant and these need to be included when designing the structure and reporting relationships.

Contractor selection and management

Contractors make up almost half of the event workforce required for many events. This being the case, these contractors need to be selected with human resource considerations in mind, such as labour force, expertise, training, recognition and attrition. Contractors may include companies providing services such as equipment hire, lighting, sound, staging, catering, and security.

Volunteer planning

Volunteers play a vital role in many events, ranging from sporting events to street parades. Their involvement needs to be planned and budgeted for. Motivation of volunteers is critical to the success of the event as paid and unpaid staff contribute in many ways to the ambience created. Industrial issues can emerge if it is perceived that volunteers are taking the place of skilled, paid and experienced staff.

Recruitment and selection

Many events conduct recruitment and selection online, and some are heavily oversubscribed by volunteers. By asking applicants to make decisions on preferences for functional area, venue and shifts at this early stage, the organization of allocations can proceed more rapidly. Effective communication with staff and volunteers sets the tone for relationships with internal and external customers.

Training

Everyone working on the event site, whether front or back of house (behind the scenes), needs to be trained. This includes the entire workforce, for example, sponsor employees and emergency services. Visitors are likely to ask questions of everyone in uniform and each person plays a customer relations role. Training can play a role in promoting an event and can become an event in its own right. As a motivating force it is unparalleled.

Occupational health and safety

Concerns about safety dominate most current events, and an analysis of induction sessions shows that the majority of time is spent on this topic (Van der Wagen, unpublished thesis). Safety is a compulsory training component for everyone on site and needs to be documented. All employees need to be told about potential safety risks, how to report incidents and how to respond in an emergency.

Uniforms, accreditation, meals and transportation

All staff require uniforms and accreditation passes as well as meals and transportation. These are sometimes the responsibility of other functional areas, but may be part of the human resources role.

Human resources policy

Policies and procedures need to be written for all aspects of staff management, including a code of conduct and a disciplinary policy. Procedures for such aspects as incident reporting, shift allocation, redeployment, updating information, breaks and absence reporting need to be extremely detailed.

Job analysis

Job analysis, otherwise known as work breakdown structure, needs to be done for every element of the event down to its smallest detail. For larger events this is usually done by the human resources team, most often in collaboration with each functional area or venue. From a strategic viewpoint, the point at which the venue 'owns' the staff and all their related human resource issues is a consideration. While human resources, as a functional area, generally retains a consulting capacity, this is a staff, as opposed to a line, function.

Leadership and motivation

Staff shortages, attrition and lack of motivation are the stuff of nightmares for the event organizer. Focusing on organizational behaviour is essential, as is analysis of leadership and motivation in the context of the specific event, with programmes designed to reward and retain paid staff and volunteers.

Risk analysis

Risk analysis and contingency planning is commonplace in event management to anticipate issues of concern. For the 2002 Commonwealth Games, for example, staff shortages took third place in the list of top ten concerns (Manchester City Council, 2003).

Table 2.1 illustrates a human resources risk analysis for an event. This table shows identified risks, which are then judged according to likelihood and consequence, thus determining the level of risk. Consideration is then given to potential preventive measures and contingencies that could be put in place should the risk become a reality. From this table it is evident that staff shortages in one form or another are a serious concern and that plans would need to be developed for a redeployment team to fill any serious gaps. However, the highest risk in this analysis is mismanagement at senior level.

Let's take a look at Table 2.1 in more detail:

1 *Mismanagement.* This is listed as possible with major consequences, but can be prevented by effective planning and documenting meetings. Contingency planning for situations where planning is derailed may include negotiation, formal arbitration or appointment of a crisis management team.

Case study 2.2

Sizeable market in special events insurance

The following quote discusses the importance of insurance for special events. Note particularly that this coverage extends to mismanagement.

In a country that is extremely litigious and understandably obsessed with terrorism, special events insurance has become tremendously important for co-ordinators of events of all sizes. Virtually any event can result in suits from jittery spectators, vendors and performers. All-inclusive event coverage is now a necessity – and that necessity reaches way down to local events and right down into independent agents' hometowns.

Gone are the romantic days of Babe Ruth proudly indicating to the fans in the bleachers the ultimate destination of his intended home run. Now, millionaire athletes play for billionaire owners, and spectators who take offense at happenings on the field or in the stands may very well decide to roll the dice and try to share in the bounty.

Special events policies provide liability coverage and legal defense for claims of negligence based on mismanagement or acts of God such as weather or earthquakes. This can include improper security, failure to maintain safe equipment or, in some cases, weather that causes the cancellation of an event. However, legal liability is not just limited to organizations as large as the National Football League or Major League Baseball. Claims and lawsuits have been brought against wedding organizers, universities, private hosts, and those managing community events, making the market considerable. Large brokers deal with national sporting leagues, but it's the smaller agent who deals with local events such as rodeos or street fairs.

(Reprinted from the April 2004 issue of *Rough Notes* magazine with the permission of Rough Notes Company.)

Reflective practice 2.2

1 What are the types of risks discussed in this article?
2 What is an insurance broker?
3 What are some of the potential consequences of mismanagement at one of the smaller community events mentioned?

2 *Staff shortages.* This is listed as possible with moderate consequences. For some events the consequences could be more serious than indicated in Table 2.1, raising the risk to extreme. Preventing staff shortages can be tackled by careful workforce planning and implementing innovative recruitment strategies. Contingency plans include the use of employment agencies and incentives for new applicants.

3 *Loss of key personnel.* Depending on the seniority of the person concerned and their role, this possibility must be taken very seriously. Many events have one person

Table 2.1 Human resources risk analysis

Identified risk	Likelihood	Consequence	Level of risk	Prevention	Contingency
Mismanagement or misdirection by committee or executive staff	Possible	Major	Extreme	• Clarity in event purpose and aims • Documented meetings and actions • Maintenance of media support	• Negotiation • Formal arbitration • Restructure • Crisis management team • Press release
Unable to recruit critical staff with specific technical experience	Possible	Moderate	High	• Workforce planning • International recruitment • Database of applicants	• Use agencies, network of contacts, head hunt • Meet relocation expenses • Provide incentives
Key staff member resigns or becomes ill shortly before the event	Almost certain	Major	Extreme	• Document policy and procedure • Maintain records • Work in teams • Appoint assistants • Provide incentives for staying until closedown	• Restructure • Recover lost ground • Reshape plans • Reassign responsibility
Volunteer and staff attrition during the event	Almost certain	Moderate	Extreme	• Provide a reason to be there • Reward attendance • Acknowledge support	• Ensure rosters allow for attrition (inevitable) • Have a redeployment team

Risk	Consequence	Likelihood	Rating	Controls	Response
Contractor defaults on service immediately prior to or during the event	Major	Possible	Extreme	• Appoint contractors based on selection criteria, including past performance • Contracts to have penalty clauses • Work breakdown extremely detailed • Monitor activities	• Invoke penalties • Hire another contractor • Undertake work using own staff
Misconduct by staff member causes bad press	Major	Rare	High	• Code of conduct • Disciplinary policy • Counselling and dismissal processes	• Dismissal • Press release
Fatal safety incident resulting from inadequate staff selection and training	Catastrophic	Unlikely	Extreme	• Job analysis • Safety risk analysis • Selection based on experience and in some cases specific licences • Training in safety procedures • Documented procedures and signed checklists • Supervision	• Incident reporting system • First aid services • Communication system • Crisis management team • Press release
Non-compliance with industrial legislation	Minor	Unlikely	Low	• Assign responsibility for HR compliance • Monitor compliance, including contractors	• Resolve with authorities

who carries an enormous amount of information 'in their head'. The loss of this person (through illness or accident) can be mitigated by the organization by documenting plans, policies and procedures, and by working collaboratively. In the eventuality of this occurring, it would be necessary to restructure and reshape plans.

4 *Workforce attrition*. Attrition, or staff turnover, is almost a certainty. For this reason plans need to be made to take this into account. This risk can be reduced by providing incentives and implementing strategies for motivating staff. Many events plan for attrition by having a team specifically organized to fill such gaps, known as the redeployment team. These people can be assigned to new roles at a moment's notice.

5 *Contractor defaults*. Unfortunately, the event organizer is blamed for problems created by contractors or vendors. For example, if food runs out, the organizer is regarded as 'at fault'. Careful selection and appointment of contractors is an important preventative measure. Extremely detailed contracts with itemized specifications are essential. Penalties can also be included in the contract.

6 *Staff misconduct*. With a large workforce it is almost guaranteed that someone will behave badly, for example, by harassing athletes. Policies for misconduct and training in appropriate conduct are essential. While dismissal is unpleasant, there are occasions when it is quite appropriate to ask a person to leave the site, particularly if they are putting their own safety and the safety of others at risk.

7 *Safety incident*. This is an extreme risk, with potential fatal consequences. While the likelihood is low, planning must be undertaken to prevent safety incidents and to develop systems and procedures for dealing with near-misses and serious incidents, including effective communication systems and detailed emergency planning.

The Edinburgh International Festival was established in 1947. It is one of the most important cultural celebrations in the world. From the beginning the festival has presented programmes of classical music, opera, theatre and dance of the highest possible standard, involving the best artists in the world. From Case study 2.3 it is evident that the director of the festival should have vision and outstanding leadership in the field.

Case study 2.3

Visionary leadership for Edinburgh International Festival

Festival seeks new visionary and inspirational leader

The Council (board) of the Edinburgh International Festival today released details of the search for a successor to Brian McMaster, who will step down as Director of the Festival after his final Festival in 2006, following fifteen highly successful years.

The Festival Council is seeking a visionary and inspirational leader with a successful track record in managing major arts organizations and large-scale artistic events. The new Festival Director will be responsible for programming the 2007 Festival and beyond. Lesley Hinds, Chair of the Festival Council, and Lord Provost of the City of Edinburgh said today: 'The Director is the creative force at the centre of the Festival, shaping and driving a multi-dimensional programme each year that is innovative, challenging and world-class. We are looking for someone who has an in-depth knowledge of the arts that crosses boundaries and cultures and who has an international reputation for artistic vision and flair.'

(Reproduced with permission of Edinburgh International Festival; for further information see www.eif.co.uk/)

Reflective practice 2.3

1 What are some of the factors that have contributed to the success of the Edinburgh International Festival? Information can be obtained from their website (www.eif.co.uk/).
2 Discuss the importance of international (versus local) experience in the arts for someone appointed to this position.
3 If you were responsible for recruiting the Festival Director, how would you go about finding someone of this calibre?

Chapter summary and key points

This chapter has examined human resource management for events at a strategic level and has made a case for developing the role so that it is included at executive level in the event organization. For a successful event there are three major components: the programme of performance, the physical infrastructure and its operation, and the service provided to visitors in a vast number of ways. Professional human resource experts have a vital role to play in organizational development in the dynamic environment of event design, planning and delivery. In this chapter a number of key roles for human resources have been outlined and these will be elaborated on in later chapters.

Risk management principles can be applied to the strategic management of human resources. In fact, this is one of the most important early tasks. A risk assessment asks 'What could happen?' and looks at ways in which potential problems could be avoided or resolved. Problems might be negative (e.g. workplace accidents) or positive (e.g. too many volunteers). Each risk needs to be carefully evaluated in light of the external and internal event environment and plans put in place to deal with these staff-related contingencies.

Revision questions

1 Explain five ways in which a strategic approach can be taken to HR planning?
2 Integration of HR across a range of subprojects is necessary. Explain how this comes about.
3 Using an example, explain how the event purpose or mission drives planning for human resources implementation.
4 List and elaborate on ten key human resource management roles (functions) in the event organization.

References

Armstrong, M. (2001). *Human Resource Management*, 8th edn. Kogan Page Ltd.

Hanlon, C. and Cuskelly, G. (2002). Pulsating major sport event organizations: a framework for inducting managerial personnel. *Event Management*, **7**, 231–43.

Manchester City Council (2003). Manchester Commonwealth Games Post Games Report. Viewed 17 May 2006, www.gameslegacy.com.

Maund, L. (2001). *An Introduction to Human Resource Management*. Palgrave.

Rothwell, W., Prescott, R. and Taylor, M. (1998). *Strategic Human Resource Leader*. Davies-Black Publishing.

Shone, A. and Parry, B. (2004). *Successful Event Management*, 2nd edn. Thomson Learning.

Toffler, A. (1990). *Future Shock*. Bantam Books.

Van der Wagen, L. Contexts for Customer Service. Unpublished thesis. University of Technology, Sydney.

Webb, T. (2001). *The Collaborative Games: The Story behind the Spectacle*. Pluto Press.

Chapter 3
Event project planning

Learning objectives

After reading through this chapter you will be able to:

- Explain the reasons for application of project management principles to event management
- Discuss the topic of scope management in project design
- Analyse the evolutionary nature of the event organization
- Describe the responsibilities of functional area project teams
- Describe the responsibilities of zone area project teams.

Introduction

The previous chapters have looked at some of the unique characteristics of the event environment that provide challenges for managing people in this dynamic and sometimes highly creative environment. This chapter will take a project management perspective, using some of the terminology widely used as part of the Project Management Body of Knowledge (PMBOK™).

There is some debate about the suitability of this framework for event enterprises because they are creative and organic (Goldblatt, 2005a; O'Toole and Mikolaitis, 2002; Van der Wagen, 2005); however, it is important to recognize that the methodology and terminology of PMBOK™ are widely used in the event industry. This framework is illustrated in Figure 3.1. Tum *et al.* (2006) in their book on event operations management adopt a project management approach, the authors stating in the preface that 'each event is in fact a project, and the wealth of literature that is available on both operations and project management can be used to assist an event manager in the complex management of an event' (p. xxi).

Project management framework

A *project* is first and foremost a *temporary* endeavour undertaken to create a **unique** product or service (Project Management Institute, 2004). Temporary means that the

Project Management		
Project integration management • Project plan development • Project plan execution • Overall change control	**Project scope management** • Initiation • Scope planning • Scope definition • Scope verification • Scope change control	**Project time management** • Activity definition • Activity sequencing • Activity duration estimating • Schedule development • Schedule control
Project cost management • Resource planning • Cost estimating • Cost budgeting • Cost control	**Project quality management** • Quality planning • Quality assurance • Quality control	**Project human resource management** • Organizational planning • Staff acquisition • Team development
Project communications management • Communications planning • Information distribution • Performance reporting • Administrative closure	**Project risk management** • Risk identification • Risk qualification • Risk response development • Risk response control	**Project procurement management** • Procurement planning • Solicitation planning • Solicitation • Source selection • Contract administration • Contract close out

Figure 3.1 Overview of project management knowledge areas and project management processes, PMBOK™
(©1996 Project Management Institute, 130 South State Road, Upper Darby, PA 19082, USA; reproduced with permission)

project has a definite beginning and end, which is typical of most events. The predetermined end of the project drives most of the planning, and in the case of events the end is the culmination of the planning and comprises delivery of the event. In many other projects (such as engineering and software) the activity can peak earlier. The second feature of projects is their uniqueness. They may carry repetitive elements but this does not change the unique nature of the final product. For example, each Golf Masters championship is a unique event, and staging each contest is a project in its own right.

From a human resource perspective, it is well worth considering the role as that of *Project HRM*, with the emphasis on organizational planning, staff acquisition and team development that goes with every project. The terminology of PMBOK™ is useful, for example, the concept of *scope* can be used as the sum of the products and services provided as part of the project. If human resource management (or, more commonly, workforce planning) is a functional area (FA) providing specialized activities related to event staffing, a question of scope would be whether providing uniforms is one of the activities of this functional area. In the hot house of event planning, there is often much debate about the scope covered by functional areas. People are constantly trying to shift, reduce or expand responsibility. Some men and women are heard wailing 'it wasn't in my scope' on the way to the crying room (more on stress management later).

Using mega events as an example, human resources/workforce planning is not responsible for developing every job description; these lie within the scope of each functional area. In the same way that a project has to be delineated, the scope of each FA has to be defined in a logical way. Scope involves subdividing the project into deliverables: recruitment targets, training plans, policies and training sessions.

Events such as the Asian Games and Commonwealth Games follow the precedent set by the Olympic Games and offer three levels of training to the workforce:

1 Orientation training – general information about the event, its history and the event programme. This training is usually delivered on a large scale.
2 Venue training – this training is run at the venue (competition or noncompetition) and covers the layout of the site, emergency evacuation, incident reporting and the like.
3 Job specific training – this training is at small group or individual level, providing detailed information about the tasks to be performed.

This work breakdown provides a good example of how the scope of the training subproject is organized. In this case, orientation training would be the responsibility of human resources (a key deliverable), while the venue management team (with advice from HR) would plan and run venue training. Finally, job specific training would come within the scope of a particular functional area within the venue, for example, the merchandising team at the stadium.

Design before detail

Before project scope management commences, the main focus needs to be on the event design. As Brown and James (2004, p. 59) point out, 'design is essential to an event's success because it leads to improvement of the event at every level … Event design is the critical component, underpinning every other aspect of the event, and central to the event design are the core values of the event'. They list the design principles as: scale, shape, focus, timing and build. In many ways this part of the design relies on theatrical concepts and anticipates the audience response. The authors argue that while it is important to be systematic in planning, event managers often concern themselves too much with logistics and budget, leading to a 'one-dimensional' event. (For advice regarding the staging of an inspirational event, see Goldblatt (2005b) and Malouf (1999).)

It is important to be mindful of this concern as project management principles are implemented. While the tools and techniques of project management are useful, they should not dominate to the extent that they compromise creativity and hinder change. Finally, before looking at project management phases and organization charts, it is well worth highlighting this point in relation to human resource management – people can contribute to the event's design. Shone and Parry (2004) describe this as ambience and service. The way people dress and behave will determine to a

The set-up of an exhibition hall requires careful logistics planning

large degree the audience response. The most memorable event experiences are magical, and people make this magic.

Human Resource Project Management

Following the logic of project management, once the event project is initiated, scope planning begins. Typically, organizational planning follows several phases; in this case four stages have been illustrated: strategy, operations (functional), operations (venue/site), and implementation (event delivery). There is of course the final wrap-up stage (also known as closedown or divestment) during which reports are written, bills paid and contracts acquitted, but this has not been discussed below as there is usually only a small team remaining to complete these tasks. Evaluation of an event is vitally important, too, particularly the success of human resources strategies.

Stage 1 – strategic planning: concept and feasibility

At this early stage of event concept development, when ideas are tested for feasibility, the organization (which is usually a committee) is generally quite organic. Flexibility and role sharing are important features of this early phase when committee

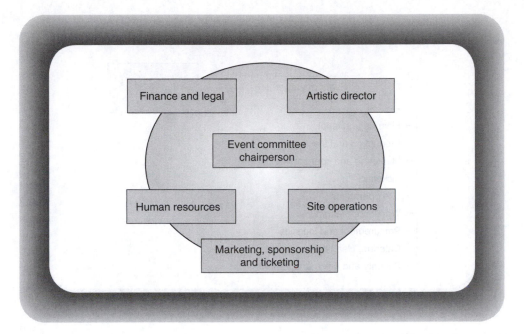

Figure 3.2 Event committee

members are in a creative frame of mind, although this has to be tempered with reality. This being the case, the structure can be illustrated with a circular diagram (see Figure 3.2).

As mentioned in the previous chapter, this phase would also include evaluation of the external and internal environment. For human resource management this would involve an analysis of labour force statistics, community attitudes towards volunteering, industrial relations issues, affirmative action programmes and so on.

Stage 2 – operational planning: functional focus

During the next phase of event planning each of the functional areas begins to set up the infrastructure for the event. The manager responsible for security and risk management would, for example, look at the scope of work involved in providing security services for the event. These might include searches at entry points, patrols, observation of the field of play, use of CCTV, and incident and reporting systems, requiring close liaison with a number of external stakeholders such as police, first aid providers and emergency services. At this stage a decision would be made about outsourcing security services and a contractor would be selected by tender. In order to tender the contract, the scope of work would have to be quite clear for the competing tendering parties.

In the simplified chart shown in Figure 3.3, the functional area managers would report to the event manager. A more sophisticated chart would also show the key stakeholders (perhaps in a different colour) such as sponsors, emergency services, etc. Relationship lines for stakeholders in the chart are just as important as reporting lines for paid staff. For example, sponsors are often vital to the success of an event and the event manager could decide that the naming rights sponsor has a direct relationship with him or her. The alternative would be for the marketing manager to deal with all sponsorship arrangements. It is most helpful to add these stakeholders to the chart, using dotted lines to show *relationship* rather than reporting.

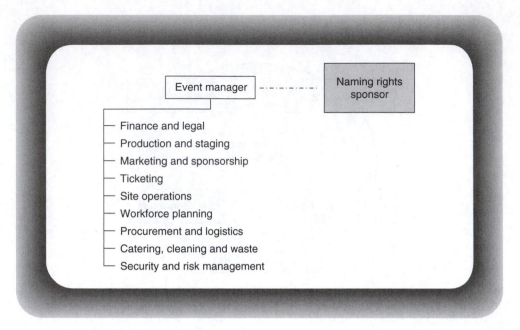

Figure 3.3 Functional area reporting

Stage 2 is part of operational planning. Each functional unit must decide what needs to be done to meet the strategic plan. Whereas the strategic plan focuses on *what* needs to be done, the operational plan deals with *how* it is to be done. An operational plan:

- is a description of how objectives will be achieved
- includes information about the resources that will be required
- indicates a timeline for project progress
- provides the basis for action planning at the next level down.

While there are advantages of using a functional structure such as the one illustrated in Figure 3.3, Bowdin, O'Toole, McDonnell and Allen (2001) point out that there are pitfalls associated with a functional structure. These include functional managers losing sight of the big picture and the organization's objectives while they focus on their own specializations; staff having little understanding of other functions, leading to lack of co-operation or integration; and heavy reliance on the event director to co-ordinate the activities of the functional areas.

In addition to co-ordinating activities within the event organizing workforce, the event director, or their delegate, must co-ordinate activities with external stakeholders. The Chelsea Flower Show will be used as an example to illustrate the roles of, and benefits accruing to, the various stakeholders:

- *Host organization.* Events such as the Chelsea Flower Show are often hosted by an association. In this case the Royal Horticultural Society (RHS) is the gardening charity host and the Chelsea Flower Show is just one of many events in their calendar of operations. The RHS has a wide scope of operation in its events.
- *Sponsors.* Most major events have several sponsors and these can range from a naming rights sponsor through to various levels of gold, silver and bronze sponsorship. Sponsors generally expect media exposure, hospitality at the event and

sales, if their merchandise is available to purchase on site. This is done in return for financial or value-in-kind support, where the sponsor provides, for example, the motor fleet, telecommunications system or the information technology services. In 2005 the Chelsea Flower Show sponsors included Merrill Lynch, Renault and BBC.

- *Broadcast organization.* For many international events, the broadcast element is critical as many more viewers watch these events than attend them. Broadcast rights are sold before the event, and for mega events this is the main source of income for the event after ticketing. The BBC is a sponsor and broadcaster for the Chelsea Flower Show.
- *Beneficiaries.* Where the event contributes substantially to a charity, the design of the event must be compatible with the charity's values. For the Chelsea Flower Show the main beneficiary is the Royal Hospital Chelsea, a home for old soldiers.
- *Exhibitors, concessions and other businesses.* An event may involve numerous exhibitors and provide commercial outlets for catering and retail sales. At the Chelsea show there are 450 commercial exhibitors.
- *Contractors.* Many event operational services, such as cleaning, waste management, lighting and sound, are provided by contractors. Hire companies provide temporary seating and many other elements of the event physical infrastructure.
- *Government.* Approvals are required for all manner of things including arrangements for transport, parking and traffic management.
- *Police, first aid and emergency services.* Working with these providers in the lead up to the event is vitally important as these services are the first point of call if there is a major accident or incident.
- *Community.* Liaison with the community is essential, as many small businesses enjoy increased trade during an event. Some government authorities have specific procedures for notifying the local community of the event and managing community relations.
- *Customers.* From a marketing viewpoint, analysis of consumer behaviour is part of the strategic marketing plan, which in turn leads to finalization of the event product, including sales and customer service.

Stage 3 – operational planning: zone, venue or precinct focus

As the event draws near and it becomes possible to see its physical layout, the structure moves to a geographical style, generally based on zones, venues or precincts. In the language of mega events this is known as 'venuization'. During this stage, a manager from the organizing committee 'takes over' the venue and installs the infrastructure (also known as the 'event overlay') for the upcoming event. If there is more than one sporting competition, for example, being held at the venue, this overlay might be changed from, say, gymnastics to basketball.

However, this occurrence is rare and the terminology is not suitable for smaller events where the incumbent venue manager typically retains his post. For example, for a music festival held in a park, the event director would work with the park manager at every stage of planning.

Figure 3.4 shows the layout/map of the Good Vibrations Music Festival and Figure 3.5 shows a simplified organizational structure for the execution phase of this event. As can be seen from Figure 3.5, when planning the organizational structure, Laundry, Good Vibrations and Roots stage would each require a manager, as would the food services and the amenities areas.

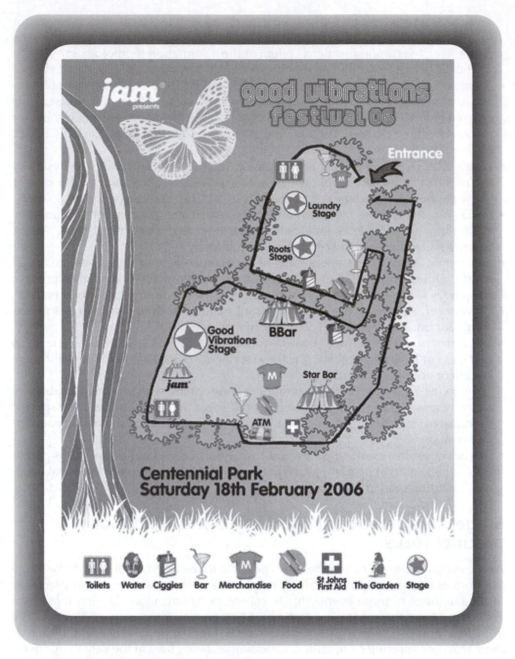

Figure 3.4 Map of Good Vibrations Festival
(Reproduced with permission of Jam®; for further information see www.jammusic.com.au)

As mentioned in the previous chapter, for the purposes of this text these project managers are known as zone area managers (ZAs). There are a number of reasons for this, the main one being that management of a physical area is logical from both an operational and a financial point of view. Imagine, for example, a show offering a commercial exhibition area, competition area, entertainment area and catering area. These areas would be labelled as clusters, precincts or zones and each would

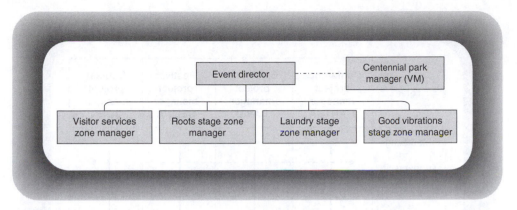

Figure 3.5   Zone managers reporting to the event director

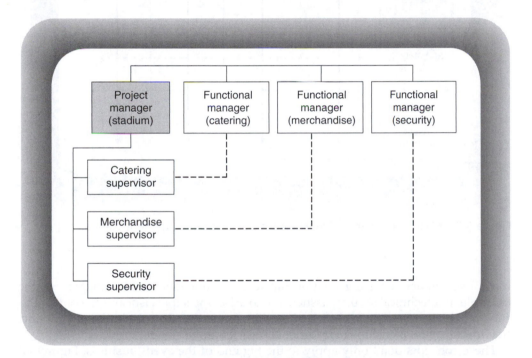

Figure 3.6   Matrix structure for zone area management (cross functional team)

become the responsibility of a zone area manager. This simplifies decision making and also allows for the use of cost centres for financial purposes. In this way costs, such as staffing, security and information technology, can be apportioned to the zone and their effectiveness evaluated post-event. In project management terms this is now a 'projectized' organization with projects comprising cross-functional teams.

Figure 3.6 shows a matrix organization in which the dominant manager is the manager responsible for all events at the stadium. On his team he has supervisors representing functional areas such as catering, merchandise and security. While each of these people has a direct reporting relationship to the stadium manager, they also

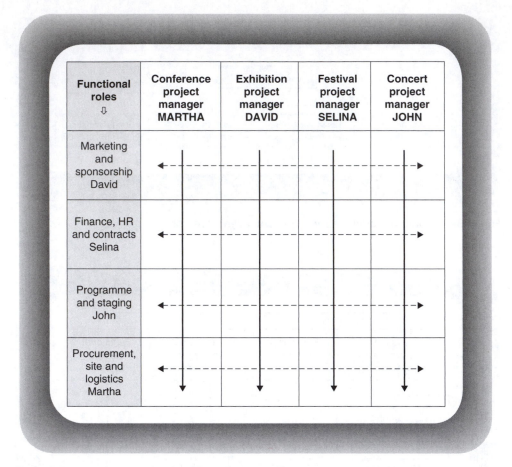

Figure 3.7 Matrix organization chart for a small event management company

have a secondary reporting relationship to their functional area manager. So, for example, if a technical security issue were to arise, the supervisor might contact the functional area manager in charge of security for advice. This is similar to staff and line reporting relationships in traditional business environments.

These concepts don't only apply to the big end of the event business. Figure 3.7 shows a very small event business comprising an owner/manager and four full-time members of staff, each a specialist in a particular functional area. This is also a matrix organization structure in that each person has dual roles. As can be seen from the chart, the dominant role for each person is that of project manager for one of the four events currently on the organization's agenda. These are a conference, an exhibition, a festival and a concert (these are used for illustrative purposes only as it would be unlikely that such a small business would diversify to this extent). As Figure 3.7 shows, each member of the team has a project management role but each also contributes his or her specialist expertise to the other events. Thus, for example, David is a marketing expert and provides this support across all events, while at the same time he has overall project management responsibility for the exhibition. Once again, the solid and dotted lines show reporting relationships – one ignores the bit where one reports to oneself!

Stage 4 – implementation: event delivery

Once the event is at the stage of implementation, a chart is needed to show everyone on site who is who. For this reason, every contractor needs to appear on the chart, as do all stakeholders, such as police. The chart, or a simplified parallel chart, needs also to show what to do when a minor incident or an emergency occurs. Generally there are shorter lines of communication if there is a crisis and this can be shown as an insert in a corner of the diagram.

From a human resources perspective, the important feature of such a chart is its value to the internal customers – all the people included in the event workforce. The event chart is a communications device and needs to be comprehensive as well as user friendly. As with maps of the event layout, professional design will ensure that these charts will be valuable and useful inclusions in the training manual.

Figure 3.8 shows an organization chart for a planning team prior to an event; Figure 3.9 shows a chart for the day of the same event for comparison.

Project deliverables for human resource functions

Looking at human resources from a project management perspective, there are a number of processes required to make the most of the people involved in the project. For a major one-off event the following deliverables would be seen as part of the human resources function. Each of these would be presented as a report or action plan.

For the whole workforce:

- External labour force analysis to identify shortages and skills gaps
- Review of relevant industrial legislation and compliance issues, such as equal employment opportunity (EEO)
- Job analysis based on work breakdown planning, including organization charts
- Job design and allocation of roles to paid and volunteer staff
- Training needs analysis ranging from general to specific knowledge
- Occupational health and safety programme
- Workforce database management and time recording system
- Workforce policies and procedures documentation
- Leadership, motivation and retention programme
- Communications plan
- HR budget
- Post-event evaluation report.

For paid event staff:

- Recruitment plan
- Induction schedule
- Training materials and schedule for delivery
- Payroll system
- Performance management system
- Recognition and severance programme

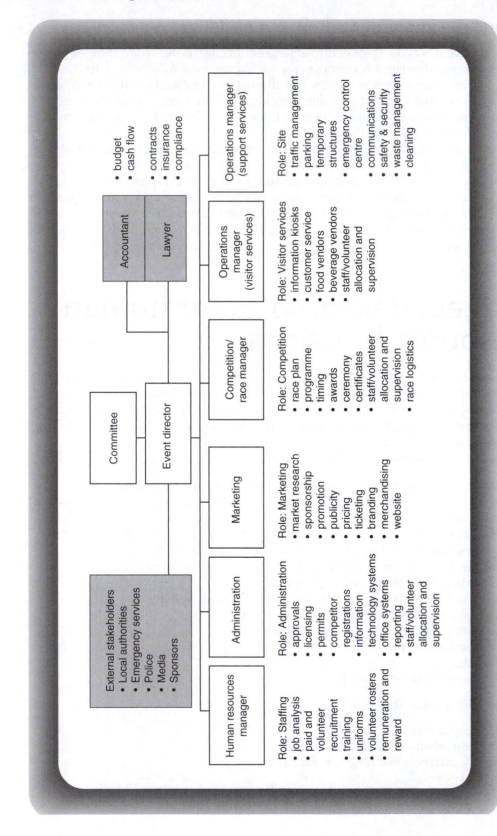

Figure 3.8 Organization chart during pre-event planning phase

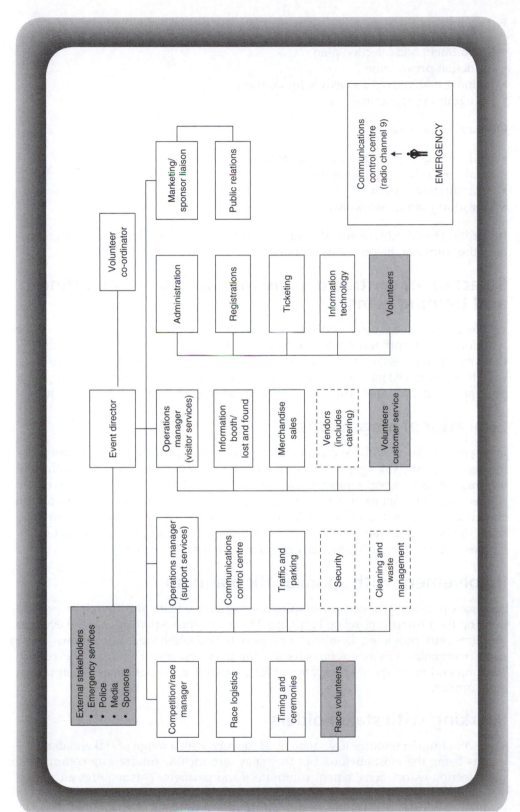

Figure 3.9 Organizational chart on day of event

For volunteers:

- Recruitment and selection plan
- Induction programme
- Training materials and schedule for delivery
- Recognition programme.

Optional involvement:

- Uniforms, design, manufacture, distribution
- Meals, including voucher system
- Accreditation system
- Transport plan for workforce.

In addition to the most obvious elements listed above, further demands may emerge over the course of the project as outlined below.

Selection of contractors and monitoring their staffing and training plans

As has already been mentioned, contract labour can form a large percentage of the workforce for events and for this reason this area needs close attention. Ultimately, these people will need to deliver seamless service to the event audience and thus need to be fully integrated into human resource planning for which training and recognition programmes are required. There are significant costs associated with these activities.

Educational programmes

In response to successful event bids, many governments provide funds to meet training needs identified by a gap analysis. This may be as simple as providing event-related information to transport employees working 'outside the fence' or it may involve a sophisticated programme of courses for upskilling. For example, training of apprentice chefs may be required or a plan may be necessary to import qualified people from overseas. Schools and universities are also keen to use major events in new curriculum initiatives and will approach the event organizer for assistance and support.

Involvement with sponsor HR planning

Sponsors frequently have their employees working on site and therefore need to develop their own event-related training. Moreover, some sponsors use the event to motivate staff, providing them with a range of tickets and hospitality options. These sponsor organizations may approach event human resources for advice in this regard. Training and motivational programmes for sponsor employees may need approval and support.

Working with stakeholders

The event human resource team may need to work with a range of stakeholders, the unions being the most obvious, but they may also include fundraising committees, volunteering associations, parent committees and partners. This requires an understanding of power and politics and an ability to exert influence to get things done in the interest of successful project completion, which is well illustrated in Case study 3.1.

Case study 3.1

Tour de France Grand Depart

Race against the clock for chance to take part in 2007 Tour de France

Following the announcement that London has won the right to host the 2007 Tour de France Grand Depart, applications from people wanting to play a key role in the world's greatest cycle race have come flooding in. Just five weeks since the route announcement, more than 1200 have signed up to marshalling the race in London and in Kent.

The incredible response that Transport for London (TfL), the co-ordinator of the event, has already received means that only a few hundred volunteer places are now left.

Volunteer marshals are being asked to help create a safe and enjoyable environment for the riders and spectators who will witness the Tour's first ever Grand Depart in the UK.

With almost 1000 junctions to marshal and three million people to help enjoy the race, approximately 2000 volunteers are needed to assist with managing crossing points, controlling and assisting the crowds of spectators, and ensuring that cars don't try to use closed roads.

Mick Hickford, Head of Special Projects at TfL, said: 'The Tour is not just the greatest cycle race but one of the greatest sporting events in the world and marshalling at the 2007 Grand Depart will be a unique opportunity for a whole generation of British cycling fans.'

'The fantastic response we have had to our call for volunteers demonstrates the incredible enthusiasm the British public has for hosting the start of the Tour de France.'

Robert Jefferies, Volunteer Support Officer at British Cycling, said: 'Volunteering is a brilliant way of getting involved in cycling and we will be giving specialist training for this role.

'British Cycling hopes that the opportunity to marshal during the British stages of the Tour de France in 2007 will encourage even more people to get involved with the sport in this country, whether as participants or supporters.'

(Reproduced with permission of Transport for London; for more information see www.tfl. gov.uk/tfl/press-centre/press-releases/press-releases-content.asp?prID=725)

Reflective practice 3.1

1 What are some of the project processes that need to be followed to stage the Grand Depart in London and Kent?
2 Who are some of the stakeholders involved in Tour de France?
3 How would project management principles assist with volunteer planning for this event?
4 Why is this such a popular volunteering opportunity?

Standards for event management

Standards are described by the International Organization for Standardization (ISO) as a series of guidelines that through widespread adoption become de facto regulations. Standards in their own right are not mandatory, and there is current ongoing discussion on this topic. Julia Rutherford Silvers (2005) suggests that the event industry needs to adopt voluntary consensus standards for event management but admits that in the United States it is a tall order to expect agreement on federal standards, much less international standards. This is the case in many countries.

The Event Management Body of Knowledge (EMBOK) is another international initiative, with the aim of developing a global curriculum framework for event management.

Despite difficulties associated with international agreement on common standards to cover the full scope of event management, there are three areas in which common practice is emerging across the globe. These are risk management, crowd management, and emergency planning. Readers were introduced to a risk analysis in the previous chapter.

National 'standards' on risk management first appeared in Australia and New Zealand in 1995, then in Canada in 1997 and in the United Kingdom in 2000. Other countries and regions (Europe) are currently studying similar standards and the International Standards Organization is preparing a list of common global definitions of risk management terms. The Australian and New Zealand AS/NZS 4360 Standard on Risk Management (2004 version) is widely used outside the Australasia region. Global concerns regarding crowd management are shared on the website (www.crowdsafe.com), with significant exchange between practitioners and researchers around the world. This website regularly features best practice legislation and guidelines. Planning for emergency evacuation in case of fire, for example, is also becoming increasingly consistent across the globe. The International Association of Emergency Managers provides the opportunity to become an accredited member.

When undertaking recruitment and training of event management personnel, it is essential to be mindful of the requirements of these standards.

For an organization working in an international arena this is particularly challenging. Studio Festi (see Case study 3.2) has most recently produced performances for the Olympic winter games in Torino and the opening of the Italian year in China. Each country has different legal requirements, standards and regulations, particularly for safety, which requires in-depth research when planning projects.

Case study 3.2

Studio Festi

Studio Festi is a well-known Italian organization that produces spectacular light shows. It has (over the last 20 years) produced breathtaking open-air performances in major cities around the world, including Tokyo, Madrid, Moscow and Sydney. This has involved outdoor lighting effects, mainly focusing on significant or historical buildings. Performances by air acrobats are often included.

Paris (France) – Galeries Lafayette
'Robe Lumière' Christmas of Light at Galleries Lafayette: for more than two months, from 6 November to 7 January, winter evenings and nights are lighted with 'Robe Lumière'. All across galleries facing Boulevard Haussmann, Festi is going to propose a new project of light's art, dedicated to Paris and Lafayette.

Something that elsewhere or usually is known as 'Christmas decoration', at Galeries Lafayette becomes a great project of Light's Art: a 'Robe Lumière' – original title of Festi's creation – ready to dress the historic and monumental 'admiral ship' of Lafayette for two months, transforming it into a new, great game of light's art: a dress, a stage costume, magic.

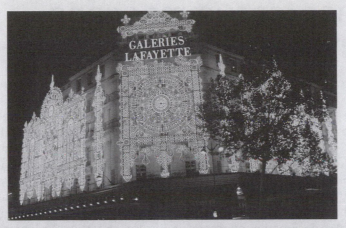

(Reproduced with permission of Studio Festi; for further information see www.studiofesti.com)

Reflective practice 3.2

1 Why would you describe this company's work as highly artistic?
2 How do you see project management principles applying to the design and operation of these shows?
3 From a human resource point of view, identify five challenges associated with staffing these events which travel the globe?
4 Identify three key deliverables for the person responsible for the human resource scope of these projects.

Chapter summary and key points

This chapter has introduced a number of project management concepts and has looked at the stages of an event project. Organizational design can vary for each of these phases, ranging from strategic planning through to operational planning and implementation. For the small, more collaborative type of event, no doubt the team is not conscious of these shifts in roles as the event draws near. However, even the smallest professional event company usually works on more than one project simultaneously and needs to use these planning tools.

In this deadline driven environment the work breakdown structure can contribute to, or inhibit, event planning. This structure needs to serve its purpose, assisting with the designation of responsibility for operational planning and facilitating a possible shift towards a different implementation structure. Ultimately, any diagram is a communication device and the human resource functional area contributes to and utilizes these diagrams for a range of purposes, including induction and training. Human resources play a vital role in managing transformation and change in the event environment.

Revision questions

1 How does an event (exhibition, conference, competition) meet the definition of a project?
2 List three types of training commonly delivered to the event workforce and explain who has responsibility for them.
3 Discuss the comment that 'using project management principles stifles creativity and limits flexibility, thus making events one-dimensional'.
4 Explain the concept of a matrix organization using an event example.
5 Provide examples of three standards relating to risk management or emergency planning.

References

Bowdin, G. A. J., O'Toole, W., McDonnell, I. and Allen, J. (2001). *Events Management*. Butterworth-Heinemann.

Brown, S. and James, J. (2004). Event design and management: ritual sacrifice?. In I. Yeoman *et al.* (eds), *Festival and Events Management: An International Arts and Culture Perspective*. Elsevier Butterworth-Heinemann.

Goldblatt, J. (2005a). An exploratory study of demand levels for EMBOK™. In *The Impacts of Events*. University of Technology, Sydney.

Goldblatt, J. J. (2005b). *Special Events: Event Leadership for a New World*, 4th edn. Wiley.

Malouf, L. (1999). *Behind the Scenes at Special Events: Flowers, Props and Design*. John Wiley.

O'Toole, W. and Mikolaitis, P. (2002). *Corporate Event Project Management*. Wiley.

Project Management Institute (2004). *A Guide to the Project Management Body of Knowledge: PMBOK Guide*, 3rd edn. Project Management Institute Inc.

Rutherford Silvers, J. (2005). *Standards: Fear or the Future?*. Mark Sonder Productions. Viewed 12 December 2005 (http://marksonderproductions.com/about/News/Feb05Standards.html).

Shone, A. and Parry, B. (2004). *Successful Event Management*, 2nd edn. Thomson Learning.

Tum, J., Norton, P. and Wright, J. (2006). *Management of Event Operations*. Elsevier Butterworth-Heinemann.

Van der Wagen, L. (2005). Olympic Games event leadership course design. In *The Impacts of Events*. University of Technology, Sydney.

Chapter 4
Managing volunteers

Learning objectives

After reading through this chapter you will be able to:

■ Describe the roles played by volunteers in the event workforce
■ Analyse the research on volunteer motivation
■ Evaluate when the use of volunteers is appropriate
■ Develop a code of conduct for managing volunteers
■ Develop strategies for volunteer recruitment
■ Provide a best practice example of volunteer management.

Introduction

While it would seem premature to introduce volunteering at this early stage of the text, best practice volunteer management is also best practice human resource management. Therefore, in order to create the appropriate context for activities such as recruitment, induction and training, this and the next chapter will deal briefly with two potential components of the event workforce: volunteers and contractors. Subsequent chapters on leadership, policy development, recognition and reward will thus apply to the combined workforce.

Incidentally, for mega events, the term 'inside the fence' is useful to identify the workforce as those people carrying event accreditation in the form of a badge or lanyard. For this type of event, therefore, the workforce might include paid staff, contractor employees, sponsor employees, volunteers, government officials and emergency services crews. All these people work within the event to make it successful, and it is the responsibility of the human resource department or the area managers to ensure that the workforce is cohesive and striving towards the same purpose: presenting flawless and integrated service to visitors (Byrne *et al.*, 2002).

For a mega event, there are also many people working 'outside the fence' to support the programme. These include staff working in hotels, restaurants, train stations and information centres. This is a useful clarification, as human resource departments in the mega event environment often have a role to play in analysing workforce requirements in these sectors where the event has an impact. Even in the case of smaller events, such as hallmark events, the event organizers are similarly concerned with service levels 'outside the fence' as well as inside, since all form part of the consumer's event experience. Event organizers are often asked to provide or approve training materials issued to personnel working in these service areas. The Beijing Olympic Games Organising Committee was pro-active to this end, releasing pre-Games training material on the Internet in 2005 for this event, which will be held in 2008. This included an introduction to China, and Beijing in particular, an overview of the Olympic Games and materials relating to training sites by facilities and regions (Beijing Olympic Committee, 2005).

Scope of volunteering

Volunteers can form a significant part of the event workforce. At the Winter Olympics held at Torino in 2006, for example, there were 25 000 volunteers, 5000 of whom were part of the ceremonies programme. Of these, 3500 worked as dancers, actors, gymnasts, acrobats and musicians, while 1500 worked behind the scenes as production assistants. For the Korean Jeonju International Film Festival (JIFF) 260 volunteers were divided into different teams, such as subtitles, ticket sales, information and traffic control. One of these volunteers, Kwak Won-hyeok, shares his experiences in Case study 4.1 (Giammarco, 2005).

Case study 4.1

Volunteers: a film festival's hidden strength

If you have ever attended a film festival in Korea, one of the things that may surprise you are the numbers of volunteer workers you will see. Of course, volunteers work at festivals around the world, but film festivals in Korea inspire thousands to apply for unpaid positions. At a recent film event in Europe, I asked a staff member if they could spare a volunteer to help me with something and he answered with a laugh, 'Sorry, but we don't have armies of volunteers like you have in Pusan.' So what is it that drives these people, usually students, to work at festivals for long hours and no pay? This year, one of my students, Kwak Won-hyeok, was working as a volunteer at the Jeonju International Film Festival so I took the opportunity to ask him about his experience.

Congratulations on being selected as a volunteer. I hear that the competition is pretty fierce.

Thanks, but actually, I wasn't selected at first. I was in China when the first round of selections were made so I was put on a waiting list. I just was lucky because some people who were originally selected weren't able to make it. The application process begins very early. The deadline for applying as a volunteer is in December. On the application we can select what part we are interested in doing like ticketing or information ... Then in early spring, we were interviewed. The interview lasted about 30 minutes. I had written on my application that I wanted to meet guests so part of my interview was in English and Chinese. I couldn't answer the questions in Chinese well – I have only studied the language since last winter.

What questions did they ask at the interview?

First they asked me about my experiences. I had mentioned that I was part of a leadership training programme and I am vice-president of my club at university. They also asked me why I had chosen to study English in England rather than another country. Finally, they asked me about what I thought of JIFF.

I was worried about that question because, even though I am from Jeonju, I had never attended the films screened at JIFF. I would always enjoy the downtown atmosphere while JIFF was going on, but I had never thought that I would be interested in the kind of films they show. This experience has changed that. I have been very surprised at how excited people get about these independent and short films and I hope to have the chance to start watching more of them.

What do you do as a volunteer?

Well, I was part of the foreign support team so my job was to pick up guests from the bus terminal and bring them to the hotel. Or to meet them at the hotels and take them to the guest center downtown. I also had to answer questions about Jeonju such as what to see or where and what to eat, manage the guests' interview schedules and take them to their appointments. JIFF had hired three taxis so we would call them whenever we needed.

It sounds like you got to meet many filmmakers

Well – not so many. Each of the volunteers in my team were in charge of seven or eight guests. I was in charge of some of the English speaking guests, but we had volunteers who could also speak Japanese, Chinese and French. Sosuke Ikematsu was probably the most popular out of all the guests among the volunteers. He was the little boy who appeared in The Last Samurai. He came with his mother and he was very bright and interested in everything. All the female volunteers wanted to show him around.

How many volunteers were there?

My team had twenty-six volunteers and five or six regular staff members. The whole festival had, I think, 260 volunteers divided into different teams like Subtitles, Ticket Sales, Information, and Traffic Control. I think I was lucky because some people on my team had to stay in the hotels or in the guest room just checking IDs. I was able to come and go if I was not needed, but we were on call constantly.

What hours did you work?

We began in the morning, usually about 10, and we were supposed to finish at 10 pm, but usually we were needed until about 12 midnight.

Those are long hours. What kind of benefits did JIFF provide for volunteers?

Well … they gave us W10 000 a day for lunch and dinner. (That's about US$10.) And we were able to go to the guest and press parties, I think there were five in all, but I was too tired by the end of the day to attend.

Well, you must have seen a lot of films

No! Volunteers can't watch the movies. Also, we weren't allowed to eat or drink with guests or press. They did have a special screening for volunteers of the short film M and a British animation called The Magic Roundabout. Those were the only movies I saw.

Wait. You don't get to see any movies, you work all day, and you can't spend much time with guests. What DO you get out of this experience?

I got to feel and experience the atmosphere of JIFF from a different perspective. It is a lot of fun but it's also a lot of work. I never realized what went into organizing and running a festival smoothly. Also, my team grew very close in the preparations before the festival and during our working days and I have made many valuable friendships. Also, the closer it got to the festival, the less important my reasons for *joining became. I got caught up in the excitement of making this festival a success and I really didn't mind that I couldn't watch the films. I felt a sense of satisfaction with the way things were going and I really value this experience.*

Is there anything that you would like to see improved or changed next year?

The only thing I would suggest is about organization. They need to give the volunteers in charge of guests a list of who is where. I was sometimes told to go to meet guests coming by shuttle bus from the airport, but I would have no idea who or how many people I was supposed to meet. I could only stand there with the JIFF sign and hope that they would find me.

(Reproduced with permission; for further information see http://koreanfilm.org/jiff05.html)

Reflective practice 4.1

1 Summarize the feelings of this volunteer towards the volunteering experience.
2 Explain how the volunteer's expectations in this situation might not be met.
3 This volunteer had one suggestion – explain what he meant.
4 Interview someone who has volunteered for an event and find out about their experiences. Then develop five recommendations for volunteer management.

Before exploring some specific event volunteering issues, it is useful to look at the status of volunteering in world communities as the volunteering ethic varies from country to country, and this has important implications for organizers of social impact events such as fundraisers, arts festivals and the like.

In the United States about 64.5 million persons, or 28.8 per cent of the civilian population aged 16 and over, volunteered through or for an organization at least once between September 2004 and September 2005. During the same year, 25 per cent of volunteers were men and about 33 per cent were women, about the same proportions as in the previous year. Women volunteered at a higher rate than men across age groups, education levels and other major characteristics. Among the different age groups, persons aged 35 to 44 were the most likely to volunteer, closely followed by 45- to 54-year olds (United States Department of Labor, 2005).

Interestingly, the rate of volunteering for employed persons was higher than for unemployed persons. Among employed persons, 31.1 per cent had volunteered during the year ending September 2005. By comparison, the volunteer rates of persons who were unemployed (26.4 per cent) or not in the labour force (24.4 per cent) were lower.

Table 4.1 provides additional information on the characteristics of volunteers in the United States from September 2002 to September 2005.

In Australia, 34 per cent of adults undertook voluntary work in the twelve months prior to an Australian Bureau of Statistics survey in 2002, with the rate of volunteering highest in the 35- to 44-year-old age group. Volunteering rates were lower in major cities than elsewhere.

In Canada, nonprofit and voluntary organizations employ over 2 million full-time equivalent (FTE) workers, two-thirds in paid positions and the remainder as volunteers. This represents about 12 per cent of the country's economically active population and about 13 per cent of its nonagricultural employment.

In an important Canadian study, voluntary organizations were classified according to service and expressive functions. *Service functions* involve the delivery of direct services

Table 4.1 Volunteers by selected characteristics, September 2002–2005 (Numbers in thousands) in the USA

Characteristic	September 2002		September 2003		September 2004		September 2005	
	Number	Per cent of population	Number	Per cent of population	Number	Per cent of population	Number	Per cent of population
Sex								
Total, both sexes	59 783	27.4	63 791	28.8	64 542	28.8	65 357	28.8
Men	24 706	23.6	26 805	25.1	27 011	25.0	27 370	25.0
Women	35 076	31.0	36 987	32.2	37 530	32.4	37 987	32.4
Age								
Total, 16 years and over	59 783	27.4	63 791	28.8	64 542	28.8	65 357	28.8
16 to 24 years	7 742	21.9	8 671	24.1	8 821	24.2	8 955	24.4
25 to 34 years	9 574	24.8	10 337	26.5	10 046	25.8	9 881	25.3
35 to 44 years	14 971	34.1	15 165	34.7	14 783	34.2	14 809	34.5
45 to 54 years	12 477	31.3	13 302	32.7	13 584	32.8	13 826	32.7
55 to 64 years	7 331	27.5	8 170	29.2	8 784	30.1	9 173	30.2
65 years and over	7 687	22.7	8 146	23.7	8 524	24.6	8 712	24.8
Employment status								
Civilian labour force	42 773	29.3	45 499	30.9	45 896	30.9	46 872	31.1
Employed	40 742	29.5	43 138	31.2	43 886	31.2	44 894	31.3
Full time (6)	32 210	28.3	33 599	29.6	34 237	29.6	35 225	29.8
Part time (7)	8 532	35.4	9 539	38.4	9 649	38.5	9 669	38.2
Unemployed	2 031	25.1	2 361	26.7	2 010	25.6	1 978	26.4
Not in the labour force	17 010	23.7	18 293	24.6	18 646	24.7	18 485	24.4

1 Beginning in 2003, persons who selected this race group only; persons who selected more than one race group are not included. Prior to 2003, persons who reported more than one race group were included in the group they identified as their main race.

2 Data for Asians were not tabulated in 2002.

3 Data refer to persons 25 years and over.

4 Includes high school diploma or equivalent.

5 Includes the categories, some college, no degree; and associate degree.

6 Usually work 35 hours or more a week at all jobs.

7 Usually work less than 35 hours a week at all jobs.

Note: Estimates for the above race groups (white, black or African American, and Asian) do not sum to totals because data are not presented for all races. In addition, persons whose ethnicity is identified as Hispanic or Latino may be of any race and, therefore, are classified by ethnicity as well as by race. Due to the introduction of revised population controls in January 2003, 2004, and 2005, estimated levels for 2003, 2004, and 2005 are not strictly comparable with each other or with those for 2002. See the Technical Note for further information. (United States Department of Labor (2005). Volunteering in the United States; for further information see www.bls.gov/news.release/volun.nr0.htm)

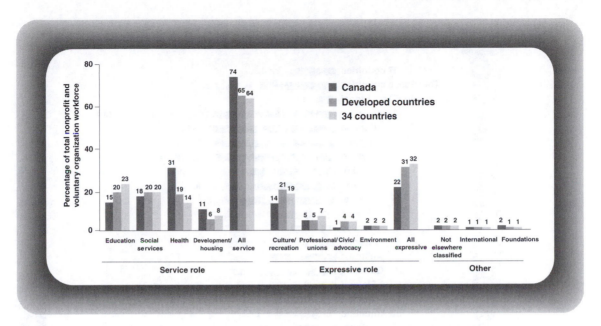

Figure 4.1 Composition of the nonprofit and voluntary organization workforce in Canada
(Reproduced with permission of Imagine Canada; for further information see www.nonprofitscan.ca/files/misc/jhu_report_en.pdf)

such as education, health, housing, economic development promotion, and the like. *Expressive functions* involve activities that provide avenues for the expression of cultural, spiritual, professional or policy values, interests and beliefs. Included here are cultural institutions, recreation groups, professional associations, advocacy groups, community organizations, environmental organizations, human rights groups and social movements. Most event volunteering would be classified as having an expressive function.

Figure 4.1 compares the composition of the nonprofit and voluntary organization workforce of Canada with that of other developed countries.

Hall *et al.* (2005, p. 11) also show that nonprofit and voluntary organizations are not simply places of employment:

> *What makes them significant are the functions they perform, and these functions are multiple. For one thing, these organizations deliver a variety of human services, from health care and education to social services and community development. Also important is the sector's advocacy role, its role in identifying unaddressed problems and bringing them to public attention, in protecting basic human rights, and in giving voice to a wide assortment of social, political, environmental and community interests and concerns. Beyond political and policy concerns, the nonprofit and voluntary sector also performs a broader expressive function, providing the vehicles through which an enormous variety of other sentiments and impulses – artistic, spiritual, cultural, occupational, social and recreational – also find expression. Opera companies, symphonies, soccer clubs, hobby associations, places of worship, fraternal societies, professional associations, book clubs, and youth groups are just some of the manifestations of this expressive function. Finally, nonprofit and voluntary organizations have also been credited with contributing to what scholars are increasingly coming to call 'social capital', those bonds of trust and reciprocity that seem to be crucial for a democracy and a market economy to function effectively. By establishing connections among individuals, involvement in associations teaches norms of co-operation that carry over into political and economic life.*

Figure 4.2 shows the top twenty countries in terms of nonprofit and voluntary workforce as a share of the economically active population.

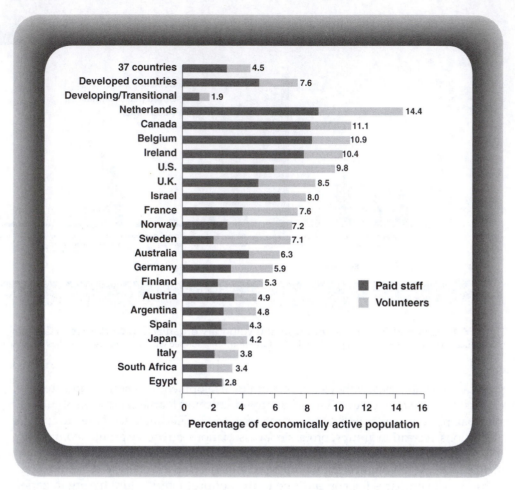

Figure 4.2 Nonprofit and voluntary organization workforce as a share of the economically active population by country
(Reproduced with permission of Imagine Canada; for further information see www.nonprofitscan.ca/files/misc/jhu_report_en.pdf)

In the United Kingdom, 22 million adults are involved in formal volunteering each year and 90 million hours of formal voluntary work takes place each week. Six out of ten volunteers say that volunteering gives them an opportunity to learn new skills. Half of all volunteers become involved because they were asked to help, and 90 per cent of the population agree with the notion that a society with volunteers shows a caring society (Institute for Volunteering).

These figures demonstrate a strong volunteering ethos in all four countries.

Volunteer motivation

A person's motivation for volunteering is closely linked to social interest and this in turn leads to satisfaction with the volunteering experience. As discussed above, volunteers

Commonwealth Games volunteer takes a break outside the Exhibition Centre in Melbourne
(Tim Clayton/Fairfaxphotos.com; reproduced with permission.)

may participate in service or expressive functions (Hall *et al.*, 2005). In both contexts, their desire is to see that relevant outcomes are achieved in line with the mission and purpose of the event. This is equally true of the event business in which many event organizations rely on volunteers.

The following quote from a United Nations report (2003) stresses the value of sports volunteering to the community and in doing so highlights many of the reasons why a volunteer contributes his or her time:

> *Once involved through sport, volunteers can then be mobilized to donate their time to other activities. Given that sport is a key site for volunteer involvement, sport should be used to promote volunteerism, especially among youth whose participation is a strong predictor of volunteering in later life. Volunteerism provides benefits to the individual, such as self-fulfilment, skill acquisition, increased understanding and social integration. It also benefits society, through impacts including economic growth, social welfare, community participation, generation of trust and reciprocity, and the broadening of social interaction through new networks. Consequently, volunteerism creates social capital, helping to build and consolidate social cohesion and stability. Sport is a key way to encourage volunteerism within societies and achieve the resulting social benefits. In the UK, the contribution made by volunteers to sport is estimated to be greater than government and lottery funding combined.*

Motivation is the one significant distinguishing difference between human resource management for volunteers and paid staff. Retention is a major issue for HR managers and needs to be addressed at all stages during recruitment, induction and training to ensure that volunteers have accurate expectations of the work and that the work will meet their needs. Volunteers generally have a much shorter commitment to the job and, in the case of a large event, it may not even be noticed if they leave before their allocated time has finished. While there would be repercussions for a paid employee who walked off the job, there are none for the volunteer. Ongoing communication at all stages, from recruitment to close of an event, is vitally important in ensuring that retention of volunteers does not become a problem for HR managers during the execution of an event (Byrne *et al.*, 2002).

During a detailed study of event volunteers participating in a regional marathon, Strigas and Newton Jackson (2003) conducted a factor analysis which produced a five-factor model for explaining motivation of event volunteers at this type of event:

1 *Material factor.* This includes incentives where the volunteer calculates the expected utility gain, which can include material rewards (such as goods and services) or social status that carries a material value. This may be represented by complimentary items, for example.
2 *Purposive factor.* Here the motives of volunteers were compatible with those of the event and the community: 'volunteering creates a better society'.
3 *Leisure factor.* In some cases, volunteering was seen as a leisure choice, an escape from everyday life and an opportunity to develop new interests.
4 *Egoistic factor.* Social interaction, networking and building self-esteem were motivations where the individual sought social contact as an affective incentive.
5 *External factor.* These factors were outside the individual's immediate control and linked to family traditions or course completion requirements.

In an analysis of motives and their importance, Strigas and Newton Jackson (2003) found the highest and lowest ranking reasons as illustrated in Table 4.2.

It would seem that there are often almost as many reasons to volunteer as there are volunteers. Many attempts have been made to analyse motivations according to demographic characteristics, but in a study of the motivational needs of adolescent volunteers, Schondel and Boehm (2000) found that there were similarities between the motivations of adolescents and those of adults and college students. These included helping others, social interaction and recognition of contributions. There were also differences, indicating that developmental stages of identity formation may influence motivation of this age group. Callow (2004) argues that the senior citizen segment is far from homogenous in its motives for, and behaviour towards, volunteering, which may have an impact on the effectiveness of recruitment campaigns.

Research efforts assist in clarifying and classifying the many and varied volunteer motivations. A consistent theme appears to be the importance of volunteers understanding the strategic purpose of the event and the important role that they will play in

Table 4.2   Highest and lowest ranking motives for volunteering for a sporting event

Highest ranking reasons	Lowest ranking reasons
• Volunteering creates a better society • Wanting to help make the event a success • Fun in volunteering for a marathon event • Putting something back into the community • Volunteering enables the organizational committee to provide more services for less money	• Wanting to gain some practical experience • Extra bonus/credit for volunteering from employer/school • Receiving complimentary items • Volunteering will look good on résumé • Volunteering makes person feel less lonely • Wanting to be recognized for doing this volunteer work

(Adapted from Strigas and Newton Jackson, 2003, p. 117)

its success. As discussed in the previous chapters, an event is a major project with multiple subprojects. Knowing that the project is temporal and finite is important both for volunteer and paid staff. If progress and tangible success are evident, then the whole team will be better motivated. This is illustrated in Case study 4.1: the volunteer does not see any of the films shown at the film festival but feels that, despite the lack of tangible reward, he has played an important role in the successful outcome of the project.

Leadership and motivation will be covered in detail in later chapters of this book, and in the remainder of the text the workforce will be discussed in the context of 'one team, one fence' (Byrne *et al.*, 2002), with occasional references to specific volunteer issues.

Deciding on the use of volunteers

Whether to involve volunteers in an event or not is a significant strategic decision. Volunteers are not 'free' as they need to be recruited, selected, trained, supervised, uniformed and fed. The total cost per volunteer, excluding management, for the Sydney 2000 Olympic Games was A$750 (Tourism Training Victoria, 2002).

There are many reasons why an event organization would recruit volunteers as a component of the workforce or, in some cases, as the complete workforce:

1 *Establishing the event.* Some events emerge as a result of the combined efforts of a group of individuals who have a cause-related reason to develop and run an event. These volunteers form a committee and the concept grows from there. Many music festivals start from small beginnings and grow over time, as do many historical celebrations.
2 *Expanding the workforce.* One of the most common reasons for involving volunteers is to expand the workforce in a cost-effective way. Without the contribution of volunteers many mega events and hallmark events would not be able to run in their present format as the contribution of volunteers is so significant in terms of the total hours contributed (for example, total volunteer hours for the Manchester Commonwealth Games were 1 260 000).
3 *Expanding the level of customer service.* Volunteers are primarily employed in customer contact roles and can contribute to the ambience of an event in important ways. At the Winter Olympics in Salt Lake City in 2002, for example, the level of service was so high that it attracted the interest of the media, including NBC's *Today Show* and the *Wall Street Journal* (Walker, 2002).
4 *Contributing to community spirit.* While it is true that events can contribute in important ways to developing community spirit, this is not typically the sole reason why an event is staffed by volunteers.
5 *Creating a social impact.* By using volunteers in a developmental role, thus improving their qualifications and employment prospects, events can have a long-term social impact. In South Africa, for example, events are widely regarded as part of 'capacity building'. The expectation of social impacts was also behind the bid for World Cup Soccer (see Case study 4.2).
6 *Contribution to diversity.* Event volunteers come from a remarkable range of backgrounds. This can be helpful in providing representative languages and cultures

for sporting competitions or world music festivals. Volunteers with diverse backgrounds also bring new ideas to problem situations that can be enlightening.

7 *Expanding the network.* Volunteers are often co-opted by family and friends. In this way the volunteering network can grow, leading to contacts with new sponsors and contractors.

8 *Belief in the ethos of volunteerism.* Some organizations have a strong belief in volunteerism, exhibited by their taking on volunteers and also by providing volunteers to work at events. This can lead to enhanced learning and organizational development.

While many of the above reasons are altruistic, it is essential for an organization to be honest about their reasons for recruiting volunteers. The motive of reducing labour costs is generally quite apparent to volunteers, and this can be stressed in recruitment efforts along the theme of 'we can't do this without you'.

Case study 4.2

Volunteers 2006™: Play a vital role at the football event in Germany!

One of the fundamental components of a successful 2006 FIFA World Cup™ is the passion, friendliness and helpfulness shown by volunteers. Foreign visitors form a lasting impression of the host nation from their frequent contacts with volunteers. Volunteers can expect to take away some unforgettable memories. They are offered a unique opportunity to play a crucial role at the 2006 FIFA World Cup™, experiencing the atmosphere at first hand in a number of interesting jobs. The importance of voluntary work to the community and its potential in Germany will be thrown into sharp relief by the enthusiastic efforts of our volunteers. We will recruit our team of volunteers for the 2006 FIFA World Cup™ over the course of the next few months. The unpaid helpers will play a pivotal role in bringing to life the official slogan of the 2006 FIFA World Cup™: 'A time to make friends™'.

(Reproduced with permission of FIFA World Cup Germany 2006; for further information see http://fifaworldcup.yahoo.com/06/en/o/volunteers/vpp.html)

Reflective practice 4.2

1 What would you identify as the primary reason for volunteering for the Soccer World Cup?
2 Do you think that volunteers for this event have realistic expectations of their event experience? Explain your reasoning.

Code of conduct for managing volunteers

Most professional event organizations have a code of conduct for managing volunteers and such guidelines are also provided by many volunteer associations. Following is a summary of the important elements of a code of conduct for organizations utilizing the services of volunteers.

The event organization will:

- Meet all legal obligations such as anti-discrimination legislation
- Provide a healthy and safe workplace
- Plan and document safe work practices
- Provide insurance cover for volunteer staff
- Provide clear and accurate information about how volunteer expectations will be met
- Provide orientation and training
- Avoid placing volunteers in positions more suitable for paid staff
- Treat volunteers as an integral part of the team
- Avoid placing volunteers in situations that are difficult or dangerous
- Provide meals, drinks and breaks as required
- Provide protection from the sun and the elements
- Provide adequate levels of supervision and support
- Define jobs and issue job descriptions or checklists
- Develop human resources policies and make these available to volunteers, including procedures for grievance resolution
- Acknowledge the rights of volunteers
- Offer opportunities for learning and development where possible
- Meet out-of-pocket expenses such as transportation
- Keep volunteers up to date with important information
- Constantly acknowledge the contribution of volunteers on both an individual and a group basis.

Long- and short-term volunteers

Volunteers contribute at various stages of an event project, including working as the organizing committee for many community events. In some event organizations this affiliation can last for years. For example, Cross Country Canada (2001) recognized the contribution of Tony Daffern for his lifetime commitment to the sport, including his many competition and organizational roles.

For larger annual events or mega events such as an Olympic Games, some volunteers come on board very early and stay with the planning group for an extended period. In Manchester these volunteers were known as Long Term Volunteers (LTVs) while in Sydney they were known as Pioneer Volunteers, both groups working with the respective organizing committees for a year or more. For events such as the Honda Classic, there are many veteran volunteers who have worked on this annual golf tournament every year over a long period (Coyne and Coyne, 2001). However, the majority of event volunteers work for a short time only, ranging from a few hours to a few days or weeks.

Source of volunteers

While recruitment is the topic of Chapter 8, it is useful to point out here that there are several specific contact points for finding volunteers, particularly those with relevant expertise and experience. Many of these associations work with event organizers in a partnership arrangement to ensure the success of the volunteering programme.

Volunteering associations

There are volunteering associations at local, state and national levels in most countries. Organizations such as AVA (Association for Volunteer Administration) in the United States and CSV (Community Services Volunteers) in the United Kingdom provide guidelines for volunteer management, statistics, and other publications and services.

Related associations

Many associations in the sporting arena support events by supplying qualified officials and judges; similarly in the arts, where organizations provide expertise in supporting exhibitions, competitions and concerts. In fact, many such associations provide grants to support events and can provide advice in relation to volunteer programmes.

Sponsor organizations

Sponsor organizations are often keen to have their staff involved in an event for the purpose of professional development or simply for the incentive that this provides to their staff.

Universities and colleges

Internship programmes and work experience programmes that form a compulsory course component are an invaluable source of volunteers, providing students who are interested in a particular field with valuable hands-on experience. Some students work for the event organization for a long period, participating fully in the planning process; others work for just a week or so on several events in order to widen the scope of their experience.

Special interest groups

Event volunteering can form part of an affirmative action programme. For example, a youth concert may be organized by a group of unemployed youths involved in a special programme.

Typical roles for volunteers at events

The outline of a code of conduct above stressed that the roles allocated to volunteers should not be roles that are typically paid jobs. If this were the case, it would certainly get the unions and other employee associations agitated. Using volunteer workers in paid jobs such as cleaning is regarded as exploitation.

Cuskelly and Auld (2000) have produced a guide to volunteer management which, among other things, presents a summary of comments from the national and state winners of the National Australia Bank Community Link Awards (see Table 4.3). One of the strongest themes emerging from this summary is the importance of workforce integration. Volunteers want to be treated the same as paid workers, feel part of the team and have their services recognized. Most importantly, they do not want to be taken for granted.

Table 4.3 Good practice advice for volunteer management

	Good practice advice	
	DO	*DON'T*
National winner Bicycle South Australia	• Provide written job descriptions for volunteers • Ensure training sessions are relevant • Acknowledge their achievements	• Neglect the recruitment of new volunteers • Ignore their interests • Treat them differently from paid staff
State winner Queensland Q-Rapid	• Identify clear paths for volunteers • Value each person's qualities, skills and efforts • Provide real responsibilities for volunteers through training	• Take people for granted • Provide ineffective information • Ignore volunteer services
State winner NSW Coonamble Rodeo Association	• Use time efficiently • Delegate according to skills • Openly discuss all issues	• Neglect to guide new volunteers • Forget to acknowledge contributors
State winner Victoria Kilmany Family Care	• Respect the role of volunteers • Ensure they have access to debriefing • Ensure that fun is part of the work	• Put barriers up to communication • Assume volunteers have all the required knowledge • Take anyone for granted
State winner Tasmania Tasmanian Trail Association	• Accept volunteers for what they can do • Listen to all viewpoints, including those of paid officials	• Lose patience • Be inflexible • Take anyone for granted
State winner WA Recreation and respite	• Include volunteers as part of the team • Listen to their ideas • Show appreciation of their efforts	• Overload volunteers with work • Isolate volunteers from staff • Put volunteers in difficult and dangerous situations
State winner ACT Australian Football International Youth Trophy	• Choose people according to their talents and desires • Involve those who can raise the group's profile • Make tasks enjoyable • Give positive feedback	• Give too few people too much work • Spring jobs on volunteers at the last minute • Assign jobs that are too difficult

(Reproduced with permission of the Australian Sports Commission)

Management of volunteer programmes

Volunteer programmes require careful planning and go well beyond recruitment and training. Volunteer management includes logistics: rosters, meals, uniforms, transportation, safety, and sometimes accommodation. Added to this is the need to develop recognition and reward programmes. Problem solving and communication are key elements during the operational phase.

While the topic of job descriptions will follow in Chapter 8, the example of a job description for a Human Resource Manager in Case study 4.3 demonstrates the volunteer management role in detail.

Case study 4.3

National Folk Festival – volunteer co-ordinator position

National Folk Festival

Human Resources & Administration Manager
Duty Statement & Selection Criteria

Position outline

Reports to: Festival Director
Position type: Full time
Salary range: $44 000–$50 000 p.a.
Duration: Two-year contract with scope for renewal

The Human Resources and Administration Manager reports to the Festival Director and is a key role within the management team. This is a key role both in the organisation of the festival as an annual event, and in the ongoing running of the festival as a company. The Human Resources and Administration Manager has responsibility for the efficient day-to-day running of the festival office, management of a dedicated volunteer budget, and the recruitment, maintenance and deployment of volunteers. Some of these duties are shared with the Production Manager.

The success of the National Folk Festival is built on its volunteer community. The volunteer team is one of the festival's most important resources and this position is crucial to the success of developing and maintaining volunteer morale. The successful applicant will be a strong advocate for volunteering in the community and will be expected to play a key advocacy role within the community on behalf of our festival volunteers.

Duties
Volunteer Programme
- Manage volunteer recruitment, rostering, training and deployment, including the identification of some 70 coordinators (across 45 teams) of major areas during the festival.
- Manage on-site volunteer support services such as volunteer reception and the volunteer kitchen.
- Build morale and motivation within the volunteer team.
- Manage coordinator recruitment and support.
- Implement, enforce and revise volunteer policies, ensuring that all procedures are documented and comply with risk management/organisational policy.
- Prepare and manage a budget for volunteer services, including volunteer training, co-ordinator meetings, debriefings and documentation of volunteer activities.
- Facilitate and organise volunteer and co-ordinator meetings, debriefings and social functions.
- Manage the preparation, publication and distribution of quarterly newsletters to some 1500 volunteers in conjunction with the Publications Manager.
- In areas where a coordinator has not been found, or is not functioning properly, act as contingency manager until a replacement is found.

Year-round administration
- In conjunction with the Festival Director, Production and Programme Manager, identify and develop timelines and checklists for the different streams of festival operations (i.e. performers, stalls, ticketing, marketing, etc.).
- As part of the management team be involved in the forward planning of the festival as a company and an annual event.
- Manage pre-festival volunteer teams, recruiting, training and deploying volunteers so as to meet projected timelines in any or all areas.
- Manage administration systems throughout the year, including large mail-outs, phones, fax, emails, stationery and volunteer staffing.
- Develop and improve advance purchase ticketing system.

Computing
- Assist in development of advance purchase ticketing database and systems.
- Assist in development of the master and volunteer databases.
- Assist in production of newsletters and forms.
- Manage data entry into all databases.

On-site (i.e. during the festival)
- Manage the reception and deployment of some 1100 volunteers.
- Liaise with coordinators to ensure their volunteer staffing needs are being met.
- Manage 'top up' volunteers for unforeseen emergencies, and no-shows in other areas.
- Act as contingency manager as and when required during the festival.

General
- Secretariat services to the Festival Board, including record keeping, minute taking and meeting organisation.

- Troubleshooting and problem solving, in any festival-related area, as necessary.
- Research, analysis and report preparation.
- As a team member attend regular staff meetings and follow up on requested actions.
- Manage the personnel functions for the festival, including worker's compensation, income tax and maintenance of personnel records.
- Other duties as requested by the Festival Director.

Selection criteria – essential

1 **Personal qualities.** The Human Resources and Administration Manager plays a critical role in the ongoing success of the National Folk Festival. The National Folk Festival is a dynamic and constantly evolving organisation. The Human Resources and Administration Manager needs to be adaptable and responsive to the needs of our volunteers and the strategic directions as set down by the Board.
   Communication skills. The successful applicant will have well-developed communication skills, being required to communicate professionally, efficiently and respectfully with volunteers, professional colleagues/stakeholders, sponsors and staff. This role requires highly developed negotiation and interpersonal skills. This position requires the ability to work with an enormous variety of people. The successful applicant will be able to communicate effectively with people from differing cultural and educational backgrounds and age groups. The role requires patience, tolerance, compassion and the ability to assert boundaries where appropriate. The Human Resources and Administration Manager will, on occasion, be required to speak publicly at conferences and forums.

2 **High level of initiative and motivation.** The nature of the position is often deadline-driven. It is important that the Human Resources and Administration Manager has the ability to remain calm and clear-headed in busy times and is self-motivated and able to work unsupervised.

3 **Ability to work within budget.** The Human Resources and Administration Manager will be given an annual budget. It is essential that the Human Resources and Administration Manager has the ability to operate within this budget. Operational budgetary areas include volunteer training, onsite volunteer kitchen, overall volunteer needs/services (e.g. stationery/equipment), volunteer activity documentation, newsletters and social functions.

4 **Demonstrated ability to work as a part of a team.** The success of the National Folk Festival past and future is dependent upon the hard work, commitment, skills and cohesiveness of its operational team. This team includes both paid staff and a large number of volunteers. The Human Resources and Administration Manager must have the demonstrated ability to work well in a team environment. This environment is collaborative and productive.

5 **Computer skills.** The Human Resources and Administration Manager is required to manage and maintain the volunteer database and to use and train volunteers in the use of the operating systems within the festival office. Knowledge and experience of Filemaker Pro (or similar database applications) and Microsoft Office products is essential as is computer literacy with Apple OSX and associated programmes.

Selection criteria – desired

6 **Areas of knowledge.** The National Folk Festival has gained a reputation as Australia's premier folk festival. Knowledge of and a demonstrated commitment to the National Folk Festival is important. Knowledge of the national folk scene and the key stakeholders would also be highly advantageous.

(Reproduced with permission of the National Folk Festival; for further information see www.folkfestival.asn.au/)

Reflective practice 4.3

1 Describe the primary purpose of the volunteer co-ordinator's role in a single sentence.
2 Discuss the following statement: 'The volunteer co-ordinator has to act as advocate for the volunteers in order to avoid them being exploited.'
3 Describe the planning activities that are undertaken by a volunteer co-ordinator.

Chapter summary and key points

This chapter has highlighted strategic decisions regarding the volunteer component of the event workforce. Volunteer motivations have been discussed in some detail with research studies indicating that there is a diverse range of reasons why people volunteer. Demographic and other forms of analysis show few consistent trends and therefore the event organizer has to acknowledge that for any event there will be a wide range of different motivations and expectations to be met. Acknowledgement and recognition of the important role that volunteers play appear to be significant factors in volunteer management in most studies, as does the event organization's expressed purpose of the event. Integration of a cohesive workforce is a priority, with one team 'inside the fence'. Everyone wants to feel the buzz, the sense of involvement in something big, something exciting and something that is going to be good.

Revision questions

1 Compare the volunteering rate in your community or country with those in this chapter.
2 Differentiate between service and expressive functions.
3 Investigate one mega event and discover the number of volunteers and the types of roles they have played.
4 List and explain five reasons why people volunteer for sporting events.
5 Provide a rationale for including volunteers at a specific event.
6 List and describe three sources of volunteers.

References

Australian Bureau of Statistics (2002). General social survey: summary results. Cat. no. 4159.0. Viewed 1 October 2005, www.abs.gov.au/Ausstats/abs@.nsf/2.6.4? OpenView.

Beijing Olympic Committee (2005). The pre-Games training guide. Viewed 10 June 2005, http://en.beijing-2008.org/71/76/column211637671.shtml.

Byrne, C., Houen, J. and Seaberg, M. (2002). One team. *Communication World*, 28–32.

Callow, M. (2004). Indentifying promotional appeals for targeting potential volunteers: an exploratory study on volunteering motives among retirees. *International Journal of Nonprofit and Voluntary Sector Marketing*, **9(3)**, 261–74.

Coyne, B. and Coyne, E. (2001). Getting, keeping and caring for unpaid volunteers for professional golf tournament events. *Human Resource Development International*, **4(2)**, 199–216.

Cross Country Canada (2001). CCC Volunteer Award Winners. Viewed 2 October 2005, www.cccski.com/main.asp?cmd=doc&ID=578&lan=0.

Cuskelly, G. and Auld, C. (2000). *Volunteer Management: A Guide to Good Practice*. Australian Sports Commission: Active Australia.

Giammarco, T. (2005). 2005 Jeonju International Film Festival Report. Viewed 1 October 2005, http://koreanfilm.org/jiff05.html.

Hall, M. *et al.* (2005). *The Canadian Nonprofit and Voluntary Sector in Comparative Perspective*. Imagine Canada.

Institute for Volunteering. Volunteering UK – key facts and figures. Viewed 1 October 2005, www.ivr.org.uk/facts.htm.

Schondel, C. and Boehm, K. (2000). Motivational needs of adolescent volunteers. *Adolescence*, **25(138)**, 335–44.

Strigas, A. and Newton Jackson, E. (2003). Motivation: volunteers to serve and succeed. *International Sports Journal*, **7(1)**, 111–23.

Tourism Training Victoria (2002). Strategic training issues for the 2006 Commonwealth Games. Viewed 17 May 2006, www.cecc.com.au/programs/resource_manager/accounts//ssv/CommGamesReport.pdf?view_file_btn=+View.

United Nations (2003). Sport for development and peace. Viewed 17 May 2006, www.un.org/themes/sport/index.htm.

United States Department of Labor (2005). Volunteering in the United States. Viewed 30 April 2005, www.bls.gov/news.release/volun.nr0.htm.

Walker, M. (2002). Going for gold. *TD*, May, 63–9. Viewed 17 May 2006, www.astd.org/astd/publications/td_magazine.

Chapter 5
Contractor management

Learning objectives

After reading through this chapter you will be able to:

- Explain the roles played by contractors in the event organization
- Discuss the role of human resource specialists in contractor management
- Identify some of the industrial relations issues emerging from the use of contractors
- Describe best practice in contractor management.

Introduction

Contractors make up a significant part of the labour force for most events, providing services such as staging, entertainment, technical production, ticketing, registration, catering, security, cleaning and waste management. For this reason, this component of the workforce is a major concern from a human resource perspective, necessitating the development of integrated internal and external customer relations (Rothwell *et al.*, 1998).

There are numerous and varied issues to consider here, including the different working conditions under which these contractors are employed, their health and safety on site, insurance and provision of meals.

In the event environment, integrating the efforts of these service teams is challenging, and for this reason it is essential that they are involved in event training, particularly induction or orientation training. From the consumer's perspective, everyone on site who is working has a customer service role to play and is a target for questions and complaints.

If the decision is made to take on volunteers, organizing committees can experience some backlash from potential contractor organizations and unions because they believe that the volunteers will take the place of paid staff. These organizations also argue that the volunteers are not appropriately trained or qualified for the work they are required to do. Ongoing and productive communication is therefore essential with these stakeholders.

Strategic decisions are generally made early as to which event services will be outsourced and which provided internally because there are many legislative considerations, such as appropriate licensing of riggers, forklift drivers, electricians and security staff. Insurance against workplace accidents is another important consideration with responsibility cascading downwards from the organizer to the smallest subcontractor. Contracts for event services are often renegotiated due to changing conditions in the event environment and this also needs to be taken into account in the planning stage (Allen *et al.*, 2005).

As Figures 5.1 and 5.2 illustrate, contractor staff comprises the biggest segment of the mega-event workforce – at the Sydney 2000 Olympic Games, 51 per cent, and at Athens 54 per cent.

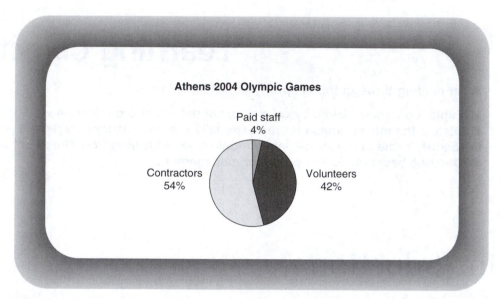

Figure 5.1 Athens 2004 workforce

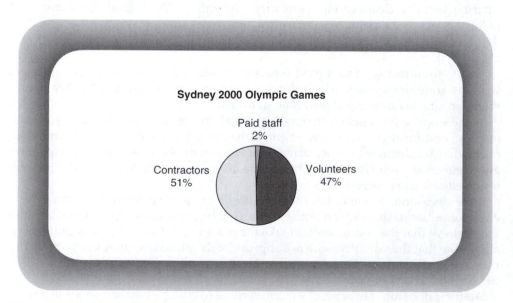

Figure 5.2 Sydney 2000 workforce

Common types of contractor services

The following services are most frequently contracted out to event services companies or suppliers. The list is not comprehensive, nor does it include suppliers of rental equipment or a multitude of different products.

Event design

Specialists in event design are briefed in the specifications required by an organization for a conference, awards ceremony, incentive or product launch, for example, develop the concept and cost it for the client.

Production

In a general sense, production means putting on the event – from concept through to implementation and evaluation. Sometimes production refers more narrowly to the performance component of the event.

Entertainment

Speakers, singers, dancers and musicians are just a few of the entertainers who might be contracted for an event. For a concert or music festival this is the core component of the event product and may involve promoters and agents. Entertainment contracts are complex and mostly include a 'rider', an attachment to the contract requiring additional payments by the event organizer (Allen *et al.*, 2005).

Lighting, sound, audiovisual and multimedia

All multimedia services can be outsourced, including the highly technical requirements of a sophisticated multimedia presentation. These services are often referred to as technical production.

Logistics

Organizing event operations may involve a logistics expert to transport and install all equipment and organize event elements such as crowd flow, communications, amenities, computer systems, sound and lighting systems, perimeter fencing etc., particularly in relation to temporary outdoor sites. Logistics may also be responsible for the transportation of performers and VIPs, as well as their equipment.

Registration

Large exhibitions generally use the services of a professional organization to take registrations online using specialized software and to take remaining registrations at the entry to the exhibition.

Décor

Décor requirements may include props, chair coverings, balloon art and flower arranging. In some cases, a themed event will require a complete design and build.

Printing

Printing requirements range from tickets to programmes, training materials and signs. Some events develop a 'look', which includes the colour scheme, logo, type font, etc., and this is used consistently across all printed material and signs.

Photography and video

Specialist photography and video services are common, with the results available in different formats and online after the event.

Staging

Preparing the performance space is a vitally important role and may include, for example, specific lighting effects and other stage design features. Staging can range from a simple stage and set to a state of the art, highly technical grand opening ceremony.

Catering

Most events require catering and there are numerous companies which provide these services, including menu planning, initiating appropriate food safety guidelines,

Cleaners sorting waste streams at a festival

and providing qualified and experienced staff. Catering can range from fast food to fine dining. In some cases, catering is allocated to concessions or stalls, in which case a separate contract is needed for each.

Cleaning and waste

Cleaning and waste management is a specialized service, particularly in the event environment where a waste management plan is almost compulsory for outdoor events. The waste output from Manchester is illustrated in Table 5.1.

Table 5.1 Waste streams and tonnages by venue – Manchester Commonwealth Games 2002 (11. 7. 2002–6. 8. 2002)

Venue	Residual	Cardboard	Plastic	Glass	Paper	Ferrous	Aluminium	Total
Sportcity	175.24	0.3	1	5.8	2.6			184.94
Velodrome	24	1.2		2.6	0.4			28.2
Belle Vue	28							28
Salford Quays	6							6
G-Mex	20			1.2	2.6			23.8
Aquatics	33.6							33.6
MEN Arena	16			1.5		31.09	3.11	17.5
Rivington	6.4							6.4
Bolton Arena	30.3			1.5				31.8
Wythenshawe Forum	11.2							11.2
Heaton Park	28							28
Athletes' Village	135.22	17.86	1	4.7	3.4			162.18
Bessemer Street	48.8	22.48	0.42	1.2				72.9
Town Hall	2							2
IBC Other	56.8				7.5			64.3
Total	**621.86**	**41.84**	**2.42**	**18.5**	**16.5**	**31.09**	**3.11**	**701.12**

(Manchester City Council (2003), Manchester Commonwealth Games Post Games Report; for further information see www. gameslegacy.com)

Security

Searching bags and premises and providing supervision of people (crowd management) and property are some of the roles of security staff, many of whom are trained for emergency management as well.

Recruitment

For the larger event, a recruitment company might be used to manage the process of recruitment of paid staff, including headhunting locally and overseas for appropriately experienced event professionals.

Training

Training is sometimes outsourced to a training organization. For example, Holmesglen TAFE in Victoria provided training for the Melbourne 2006 Commonwealth Games.

Responsibility for appointing contractors

For a small event, the organizer would find contractors on the Internet, in the *Yellow Pages* or through a recommendation. At the next level up in size, an expression of interest may be circulated by the organizers, for example, for the provision of catering services at a venue. This could lead to the appointment of preferred providers, thus excluding all other caterers from that venue, regardless of the type of event. Finally, the service can be put out to tender, leading to a formal selection process. In European Union (EU) countries there are rules about invitations to tender for event services, covering the amount awarded in the contract specifications and the process of selecting contractors.

Stages in contract management for event services

The process of contract negotiation through to service delivery and evaluation is outlined below, mainly from a human resource perspective:

1 *Project scope and work breakdown*
   Scope project, conduct job analysis
   Develop project specifications
   Conduct labour risk management analysis
   Review external labour force issues, numbers and expertise
   Develop human resource specifications, such as staffing guarantees and service level indicators
2 *Tendering and evaluating proposals*
   Evaluate tenders against criteria and weighting system
   Check references of applicants
   Evaluate tenderers' understanding of external and internal HR constraints on meeting service requirements
   Check compliance with industrial legislation and awards
   Determine ways to handle potential termination
   Negotiate outcomes and sign contracts
   Prepare for variations
3 *Lead-up phase*
   Develop and distribute operational manuals, procedures and checklists
   Organize participation in induction/orientation training
   Monitor delivery of job specific training by contractor
   Check roster planning
   Organize accreditation and uniforms
   Organize contractor staff meal requirements
   Check transport arrangements (this can be problematic for staff who need to travel extremely early or late)

4 *Event delivery phase*
   Implement operational planning
   Monitor service delivery
   Solve problems by trouble-shooting
   Communicate and motivate
   Monitor attrition
   Involve contractors in reward and recognition programmes
5 *Evaluate service provision*
   Check incident reports
   Evaluate service levels provided
   Develop recommendations
   Close out contract
   Send thank you letters and commendations

While human resource departments are generally not responsible for contract management, there is a need for HR input when outsourcing event services since contract employees are often the bulk of the labour force.

Industrial relations issues

One of the more complex aspects of contractor management is the problem of different working conditions under different industrial agreements. While it is the responsibility of the contractor organization, and not the event organizer, to manage this, it can nonetheless be problematic. In order to deliver seamless service at the Sydney 2000 Olympic Games, an industrial agreement (award) was developed that covered everyone employed on site ('inside the fence'). This had the advantage of enabling staff to cross over from one function to another and for all staff to be paid loyalty bonuses on completion of their allocated shifts. With all paid staff on the same wage scale, contractors were able to budget more accurately too.

Few events are able to create such agreement across the board. This leaves most event organizers and services suppliers with the headache of having to work with multiple workplace agreements. The following extract from the *Cleaning and Building Services Contractors (NSW) Award* (Australia) illustrates specific roles, rates of pay and a wide range of other conditions not shown here (40 other clauses) for cleaning employees (Office of Industrial Relations). One allowance is for cleaning offensive substances, which is quite understandable. From this it is immediately obvious that a more generic role description would lead to greater flexibility.

   Event Cleaning Stream

   (a) *Event cleaning means all work in or in connection with or incidental to the industries or industrial pursuits of cleaning, repair and maintenance services in or in connection with the staging of sporting, cultural, scientific, technological, agricultural or entertainment events and exhibitions of any nature. Event cleaning shall not include regular maintenance cleaning and shall be for a specific event and limited in duration to not more than three weeks.*

   (b) *'Event Services Employee Grade 1' means a casual employee who performs general cleaning duties before, during and after an event (as defined above), and shall include, but not be limited to, duties such as: operating hand-held powered equipment such as blowers, vacuum cleaners and polishers, wiping of seats, cleaning toilets used by the general public, picking up rubbish, vacuuming around and under* seats, sweeping under and around seats, vacuuming and cleaning table tops, and other work of a manual nature and is subject to direct supervision.

(c) 'Event Services Employee Grade 2' means a casual employee who performs cleaning duties before, during and after an event (as defined above) and who, in addition to performing, when required, all of the duties of a Grade 1 employee, drives/operates ride-on powered sweeping and scrubbing machines, mobile compaction units, vehicular rubbish collection; operates steam cleaning and pressure washing equipment; is responsible for the distribution and ordering of stores and supplies; is responsible for the supervision of Grade 1 employees in the performance of their duties; delivers on-the-job training and is subject to general supervision.

(d) 'Event Services Employee Grade 3' means a casual employee who, in addition to performing, when required, all of the duties of a Grade 1 or Grade 2 employee, is an operations trainer/work co-ordinator …

Table 3B – Wages – Event Services Stream (7(iii), (v))
The following rates shall take effect on and from the first full pay period to commence on or after 1 July 2004:

Total Hourly Rate Casual Employee	$
Rate 1: Monday to Friday	
Event Services Employee Level 1	17.41
Event Services Employee Level 2	18.29
Event Services Employee Level 3	19.66
Rate 2: Saturday, Sunday and Public Holiday	
Event Services Employee Level 1	24.46
Event Services Employee Level 2	25.75
Event Services Employee Level 3	27.80

As this award illustrates, a base level cleaner can do only manual cleaning and cannot operate cleaning equipment apart from blowers, vacuum cleaners and polishers. These classifications are extremely limiting, particularly when cleaning needs to be done between sessions, which means all hands on deck, including the supervisor.

Further, this award makes specific reference to the principal contractor contracting out to subcontractors who in turn must comply with these conditions. As mentioned previously, this is an important risk consideration. The event organization sits at the top of a pyramid of contractors, and thus carries responsibility right down the line. For this reason, contracts must include up-to-date insurance certificates for public liability and workers compensation.

During the Sydney 2000 Olympic Games there was close co-operation between the contractors/services providers, human resource department (workforce planning), the unions and the venue managers, with union representatives on site to resolve immediate issues. This level of co-operation was unprecedented for an event of this scale. As Webb points out, 'the Games organizers brought together the public and private sectors and the trade unions to create a unique set of industrial agreements that, over time, built mutual respect, trust, honesty and openness in the personal relationships between many of the key players.' He goes on to recommend that the following questions should be asked of contractors:

- Where is your information on workforce numbers and skills coming from?
- Your casuals, how will you hold onto them when they are also being recruited by others?
- How will you get people to work if travel time is longer?
- How many of your regular people won't be available

(Webb, 2001, p. 78)

In addition, we might ask what level of attrition is expected, as on any given day some staff will not turn up due to illness or other reasons.

Collaborative planning in partnership with suppliers is vitally important. This sounds easy in principle but, in practice, it is often the case that contractor organizations are appointed too late for this level of collaboration to occur.

Recruitment and training of contractor employees

Event organizers explain the problems associated with large events in tangible operational terms such as 'We had to hire every piece of technical equipment in the country and even had to fly in some components from overseas.' Human resource issues are similar. Very often the city does not have the required labour pool to meet the needs of a short-term event.

Catering contractor Spotless Services describes the problems of recruiting 8000 staff from a very shallow employment pool and the strategies used to meet labour shortages:

1 Borrowing competence. *This includes borrowing staff from their other international operations, and specific event placements for staff and students from colleges who may be on holidays during the event.*
2 Buying competence. *This involves recruiting people without experience and providing certified and government-funded training.*
3 Building competence. *Staff are seconded from other projects and provided with training to meet the needs of the new project.*

(Webb, 2001)

Recommendations from previous events also indicate that contractors gain considerable benefit from attending the same orientation and venue training as paid staff and volunteers. This is more likely to lead to a more cohesive workforce and seamless customer service. However, following the Commonwealth Games in Manchester some contractors expressed a need to have specific programme material to meet their needs: 'there was a bit of a sense of being "bolted-on" rather than "rusted-on" (Tourism Training Victoria, 2002).

In their study of major sporting event organizations, Hanlon and Cuskelly (2002) point out that contractor employee participation in generic event training needs to be spelled out within the tender brief, as this can add to labour costs for contractor organizations: 'in doing so, outsourcers would be more prepared for the high expectations and amount of induction time required' (p. 237). These authors also stress the importance of induction and onsite operational manuals as training resources in the event environment. Most events have an operational manual and these are frequently underutilized as a training resource.

Contract supervision

Goods and services specified in the contracts need to be monitored during the event by functional area managers. For example, the functional area manager for cleaning and waste management (a paid staff position) would have ongoing responsibility for cleaning contract management, including fine tuning as the event draws near.

Volunteers carrying checklists can be utilized to monitor levels of service by, for example, checking the cleanliness of event venues. If, as a result, the functional area manager has nothing to do during the event except monitor quality, this is an indication of good contract negotiation during the lead-up period. However, as Maund (2001) points out, it is important to acknowledge that contractor employees are not employees of the event organization; otherwise this can lead to uncertainty and confusion about reporting relationships. Issues relating to service standards need to be raised with the contracting organization (management and supervisors) and not directly with their staff on the ground.

Contract specifications and service standards

Writing the tender specification for an event supplier requires a detailed understanding of the service standards expected. In the catering area, for example, the types of meals and the number required are minimum requirements in the catering brief. There are different styles of food service (fast food to silver service) and vastly different levels of quality (ranging from a hot dog to an à la carte meal). The determination of service quality, in specific terms, is essential. Depending on the size of the event, and the degree to which planning has to occur prior to calls for tender, the level of work required in preparing the specifications will differ. For the smaller event, without formal tendering, the process of negotiating menus and services levels can be undertaken collaboratively. This, however, is one area in which misunderstandings can occur very easily. Is the menu to be à la carte or is it to be banquet style, i.e. two choices served to alternate guests? How many courses will there be? Is the food prepared from scratch or pre-prepared in frozen commercial quantities? Is a buffet a consideration? Is there provision for vegetarians? Is the alcohol billed on consumption or is it a fixed price? Can guests order spirits? Is the coffee filter or espresso?

Taylor (2005) suggests that the effect of tender procedures for catering in the public sector is to limit choices, leading to bidders coming in with low-cost and low-quality bids. Quality and cost configuration need to be evaluated in detail. For this reason, he suggests that this type of bid should be conducted in two rounds. This would certainly be recommended for the type of event at which food is an important feature, expensive and linked to the theme. A gala dinner is an example of an event at which the quality of the catering is vitally important. Where food is not central to an event, such as the provision of informal fast food, a contract containing specifications is still required, the most important being food hygiene planning if the event is to be held outdoors.

A catering contract for a food vendor at an outdoor site could include any of the following specifications:

- Menus and prices
- Staffing levels
- Food safety plans
- Waste management plans (recyclable cutlery and plates)

- Infrastructure requirements (water and power)
- Equipment brought on site.

Contract management is highly problematic if standards are not met. Therefore the more detailed the specification, the less likely that a misunderstanding will occur. For a one-off event, if the contractor does not deliver, then it is too late to find another! Menus should be tested and quantities discussed prior to the event.

The following detail should be included when drawing up contracts:

- *Written*. All agreements must be in writing. With most organizations this occurs as a matter of course in the early days of the negotiation. However, as the event draws near, small requests are added and things change. Contract variations must be clearly noted and agreed in writing.
- *Specifications*. The contract should clarify expectations on both sides so that products and services are clearly defined. As an event organizer you don't want to be embarrassed by a contract caterer who runs out of food. People will blame you! Furthermore, the event organization wants to hold the vendor fully responsible for the standard of product or service provided, which may include entertainment, décor, floral arrangements, seating, audiovisual, etc.
- *Insurances and licences*. As mentioned above, the contractor must carry the appropriate licences or permits and must have insurance. Verbal agreement on these matters is not sufficient; copies of workers compensation and public liability insurance policies should be provided by the contractor before contracts are signed.
- *Indemnification for damages*. The event organization needs to be indemnified against loss or damage caused by the contractor. For example, organizations responsible for outdoor parklands can issue severe fines for damage to grass and trees, and these fines will be passed on to the offending contractor. This should be made clear in the original specifications.
- *Payment terms*. Agreement on payment terms must be negotiated, including upfront payments prior to the event and completion payments after the event. Payments can take the form of commissions or percentages, such as a percentage of gross sales of merchandise. Rent may be charged to a vendor using space for a stall. Deposits may be required, refundable when the event is over, equipment has been removed and the site returned to pristine condition.
- *Regular meetings*. Ongoing positive negotiations conducted in good faith can lead to long-term business relationships. When problems emerge, they need to be resolved quickly. Positive working relationships in the lead-up to an event can reap rewards when extra commitment is needed.

McCabe *et al.* (2000) in their text on convention management suggest the following four ways in which service quality can differ:

1 Technical quality – what is delivered? This can include food, lighting and other technology.
2 Functional quality – how is it delivered? Are the staff trained and competent? Do the systems and procedures work?
3 Process quality – judged during service. Is every element integrated for seamless service from the customer perspective?
4 Output quality – after service is performed. This is the post-service customer evaluation, very often conducted by using questionnaires.

In summary, the management of contractors involves careful selection of suppliers, vendors, etc. Following this, contracts need to be negotiated, with clear specifications included. Ongoing positive relationships in the build-up to an event will have a payoff if problems occur, as integration and effort are often required from everyone on site in the last frantic moments. Case study 5.1 presents some of the issues from the contractor point of view. However, from the customer perspective, there is only one contact, the event organizer, who is responsible for all aspects of service provision. Besides, the customer is generally unaware that the operation is supported by a number of contractors harnessed for the duration of the event.

Case study 5.1

Game plan has silver lining for Aussies

Australia is cleaning up at the Olympics in more ways than one, writes Roy Masters in Athens.

Athens has twice the number of expected garbage trucks, carrying Olympic rubbish, but all are half full. It's an apt representation of the two major problems at the XXVIIIth Olympic Games: too much security and not enough people. The security protocol dictates trucks travelling between venues must reseal plastic sheeting with each new load and punch in a different code. It's easier to go straight to the tip. Loads are down because spectator attendance is the lowest in recent Olympic history, below Barcelona in 1992. Still, Cleanevent, the Melbourne company which heads a consortium handling the €50 million (A$85 million) cleaning contract, will do well out of Athens because of the bottom-line nature of the contract.

Not so fortunate is Concept Sports International, an Australian company which holds the merchandising rights to the Games. The 3500 sq m Super Store adjacent to the main Olympic Stadium sells merchandise from €500 sterling silver Greek worry beads to €1.50 pencil cases, all with the Olympic rings displayed, but no one can enter without a ticket.

Unlike Sydney, where people could freely wander around Homebush and buy merchandise, entry to the Athens Olympic precinct requires a pass to an event.

Often overlooked is the fact that Greece is a poor country by European standards and while people can't simply afford the IOC-levied ticket prices, they would like to buy the memorabilia. Enter the network of Australian businessmen whose companies basically present, guard, clean, accommodate, train, entertain and sell to anyone at the Athens Olympics. Gary March, chief executive and majority shareholder in CSI, says of the 'Aussie Mafia' which has helped get these Games up on time, and assist each other in the process: 'In true Greek fashion, they are talking about letting the people into the shop without an event ticket but I don't think they'll get their act together on time. Let's hope my Aussie mates can do something.'

The 70 000 people watching the track and field programme this week might not have seen close-ups of the action on two giant screens if the Aussie business brigade had not intervened. Greg Bowman, managing director of Great Big Events, has the contract to provide the announcer, music, video system, scoreboard operation and cuing the athlete introductions and medal ceremonies at eight venues, including the Olympic stadium. He was allocated a large control room at the stadium but the technical equipment used to operate the screens and sound system at the Opening Ceremony was in an outside broadcast van. Providing spectators with pictures of the athletics programme's simultaneous events – jumps and throws in the middle and running on the track – is not suitable via outside vans. 'It's essentially a TV production where you broadcast inside the stadium but managing to convince ATHOC (the

Athens Organizing Committee) that this is best done inside was not easy,' Bowman said. 'So I emailed and phoned my Australian colleagues here and managed to get it through the back door. The result is a room with a large state of the art digital console, a full display of monitors and technical equipment to manipulate the screen, integrated with the activities at the stadium.' Bowman describes his contract as 'not brilliant', but said: 'You've got to be in Athens for the ongoing business.'

He provided all the audio-visuals at the Sydney Olympics, Manchester Commonwealth Games, Rugby World Cup, Goodwill Games in Brisbane and has the contract for the 2006 Commonwealth Games in Melbourne. Cleanevent had the cleaning contract at the Atlanta, Sydney, Salt Lake City and Manchester Games and heads the Athens consortium with a Greek company and a Spanish company.

'We're in the senior advice role,' says Cleanevent part owner Craig Lovett. 'Because everything was running so late we walked into a construction zone. The main stadium was handed to us four days before the opening ceremony. Despite the attendance, we'll do in excess of one million man hours, employing 2500 workers, using €2.5 million worth of cleaning equipment. We'll shift 6500 tonnes of waste, less than Sydney. Sydney ate heaps but they drink more here. I wish the caterers would put up the price of a bottle of water (half a euro) because there are so many plastic bottles lying about. Forty per cent of the waste should be recyclable, down from 87 per cent in Sydney. There's enough tomato sauce being sold on their souvlakis to fill up an Olympic swimming pool.

(Masters, Roy (2004). Game plan has silver lining for Aussies. *The Sydney Morning Herald*, 23 August. Reproduced with permission.)

Reflective practice 5.1

1 This case study presents contractor viewpoints. Discuss the difficulties associated with predicting the labour force requirements for an event from the perspectives of both parties, the event organizer and the supplier.
2 Provide three suggestions for improved negotiation and collaboration between event organizers and contractors.

Chapter summary and key points

This chapter has looked at the role of contractors, or suppliers, in the event environment and has stressed that it is quite common for the number of contractors on site to exceed the number of staff employed by the event organization. An exhibition company, for example, is highly reliant on contractors to build the exhibition and manage registrations. In the process of appointing contractors there needs to be discussion about whether they have a reliable source of skilled labour. Contractor employees also require event specific training in order to fit comfortably into the event environment and answer questions from the general public. Cleaning staff, it could be argued, play a more important customer service role than many other staff on site. For this reason, in order to provide optimal service, everyone on site (including contractor employees) should undertake event-related training such as orientation training and venue training.

Revision questions

1 List and explain five examples of contractors/suppliers and the services they provide.
2 There are several phases in the management of contracts. Explain these briefly.
3 'The planning, selection and management of contractors is the role of the venue manager.' Discuss this statement in light of this chapter's suggestion that there is a role for human resources to play where multiple contractors are appointed and that their staff form a significant part of the workforce.

References

Allen, J., O'Toole, W., Harris, R. and McDonnell, I. (2005). *Festival and Special Event Management*, 3rd edn. John Wiley & Sons.

Hanlon, C. and Cuskelly, G. (2002). Pulsating major sport event organizations: a framework for inducting managerial personnel. *Event Management*, **7**, 231–43.

Maund, L. (2001). *An Introduction to Human Resource Management*. Palgrave.

McCabe, V., Poole, D., Weeks, N. and Leiper, N. (2000). *The Business and Management of Conventions*. John Wiley & Sons.

Office of Industrial Relations, NSW Department of Commerce. *Cleaning and Building Services Contractors (NSW) Award*, award code 116, serial C3860. Viewed 4 May 2006, www.industrialrelations.nsw.gov.au/awards/pathways/results.jsp?contentlist=true&contentlistresults=false&award_code=116.

Rothwell, W., Prescott, R. and Taylor, M. (1998). *Strategic Human Resource Leader*. Davies-Black Publishing.

Taylor, P. (2005). Do public sector contract catering tender procedures result in an auction for 'lemons'?. *International Journal of Public Sector Management*, **18(6)**, 484–97.

Tourism Training Victoria (2002). Strategic training issues for the 2006 Commonwealth Games.

Webb, T. (2001). *The Collaborative Games: The Story behind the Spectacle*. Pluto Press.

Chapter 6
Employment law and duty of care

Learning objectives

After reading through this chapter you will be able to:

■ Explain why a basic understanding of essential employment legislation is important
■ Discuss the statement 'a little knowledge is a dangerous thing' in this context
■ List and describe key employment laws and regulations
■ Explain the concept 'duty of care'
■ Apply knowledge of occupational health and safety legislation to the event workplace.

Introduction

This chapter will deal with employment legislation rather briefly for the potential scope of this subject. Employment laws, awards and regulations differ from country to country and from state to state. For this reason, general principles will be covered, with a cautionary recommendation that these issues be explored by managers locally and in depth.

Event organizers, regardless of the size of their events, need to pay close attention to the working conditions of everyone on site, with safety being the highest priority. A compulsory pre-event briefing is increasingly commonplace at today's events where safety issues are discussed and procedures for incident reporting and emergency evacuation are explained. For most, compulsory attendance (and in some cases the answering of a safety quiz) is required for all workers, including contract workers. This is the keystone of a risk management approach and essential for insurance purposes.

Duty of care is everyone's responsibility at every level as there are many examples of event fatalities at soccer matches and rock concerts. At least eleven people died and seventy-two were injured in a crowd trampling incident in South Korea in October 2005, reminiscent of the 1979 Who concert tragedy in Cincinnati, Ohio, at which eleven people died. Eight of those killed in South Korea were senior citizens or children, including one 12-year-old and a 76-year-old woman. People were waiting to enter a stadium in Sangju City for an evening concert when the doors did not open on time. In Australia in 1999 a race marshal was killed at the Melbourne Grand Prix.

Safety is important for both spectators and staff who could be caught up in crowd incidents such as fires and acts of terrorism. The lead-up to an event, called bump-in or build, is a time when risk is highest as there is always pressure to meet deadlines. Thirteen immigrant workers lost their lives on Athens' Olympic facilities, prompting outraged Greek unionists to draw comparisons with Sydney preparations that cost the life of only one building worker, 'What's happened is criminal in the truest sense of the word and it's been done in the name of profit,' said Giorgos Philiousis, president of the construction workers' union at the Athens 2004 Olympic Village. 'As the time got pressured with contractors chasing bonuses, and without serious health and safety measures, the number of accidents increased' (Workers Online, 2004, p. 216). According to unions there was also a high number of injuries. In contrast, Sydney's involvement of the unions in 2000 is illustrated in Case study 6.3 at the end of the chapter and is now regarded as a benchmark.

Thus, from a human resource perspective, a priority is the development of workforce safety policies and procedures and for this reason occupational health and safety (OHS) will be discussed in the chapter in some detail. Event organizers carry responsibility not only for their own workers (and volunteers) but for all workers on site.

Also covered in this chapter are the employment conditions of those on employment contracts with the event organization, as opposed to those on service contracts. These include equal employment opportunity (EEO), minimum wages and leave. Policies to deal with performance management, dismissal and grievance resolution will be covered in more detail in Chapters 11 and 13.

The role of unions is another topic for this chapter. In Sydney in 2000 there were 10 000 union members on site ('inside the fence') and 30 union organizers. A collaborative group of unions (calling themselves Union 2000) negotiated a special award for the Games which gave Olympic workers, on average, pay 15 per cent above normal award conditions. In addition, they received free transport, free meals and an attendance bonus of $1.50 for every hour worked, as was mentioned in the last chapter. The support of the unions is crucial to the success of mega events as the following quote about the London Olympic Games 2012 indicates (TUC, 2004). Note here, too, the reference to contractors:

> *If Britain's Olympic Games, hopefully to be held in London in 2012, are really to be the 'best Olympics the world has ever seen', then trade unions will have a vital role, building widespread support and mainstreaming quality throughout the organization and the delivery of the Games. History shows that winning the Games has not always been good news for a city and that cities have delivered the Games with varying degrees of success. It is widely agreed that the Sydney Olympics was an immense success and so it provides an exemplar which London would have to exceed if Lord Coe's promise of the best ever Games is to be realised. 'London 2012' has already acknowledged that working with unions was a secret to Sydney's success.*
>
> *At the TUC Congress in September, Lord Coe, Chairman of 'London 2012', expressed the organization's commitment to working closely with unions, saying: 'And if London is to win the bid, and deliver the 2012 Games, we need your support. We need your support in developing the strategies for the organizations that will successfully deliver the Games. Our aim must be to draw as much of the workforce from the local community, complemented by local training initiatives run by the London Development Agency and other partners. In setting up the London Organising Committee for the Olympic Games, we will develop a fair employment framework, policies to cover issues such as remuneration, terms and conditions, and health and safety. We will implement this ourselves and take it into account when evaluating tenders and awarding contracts. These should also be our guiding principles for our national sponsorships. We should never forget that Olympic Games do not happen without the selfless legion of volunteers. Sydney was a towering example of this, as was the Manchester Commonwealth Games. A London Games would require up to 70 000 volunteers. To maximise the opportunities available to them, we would set up a voluntary job programme and local job brokerage schemes so that people can develop transferable skills through voluntary work opportunities. Working in partnership with trade unions and developers we can ensure infrastructure is delivered on time, on budget and*

with appropriate levels of investment in skills, training, and health and safety, all enshrined in common prac-tice. I will also encourage Trade Union Representation on the new Organizing Committee and the development of a framework agreement in line with the experience of the Sydney Olympic Games. When we make our case to the IOC, we must be able to say we have the firm, unequivocal, enthusiastic backing of Government. We must also be able to demonstrate that we have the firm backing of trade unions and the firm backing of business. That too will strengthen our case.'

Legal context of employment

Event and human resource managers must be familiar with the legal context of employment. *Common law* is the law created by *judges* in their court decisions and is based on precedent. *Statute law* is law made in *parliament*, sometimes at various levels. Statute laws cover issues such as anti-discrimination, occupational health and safety, and minimum wages.

Common law

Two aspects of common law are most relevant to employment. *Contract law* covers all contractual relationships, specifically here, the contract of employment. When an employee accepts an offer of employment (oral or written), a contract of employment has been established. Under this contract, both the employer and the employee have certain rights and obligations. If there is a breach of contract, this must be taken up with the courts as common law is the jurisdiction of the court system. Under common law an employer must:

• Pay correct wages (including national minimum wage)
• Reimburse employees for work-related expenses
• Ensure a safe working environment suitable for the performance of the employee's duties
• Not act in a way that may seriously damage an employee's reputation or cause mental distress or humiliation
• Not act in a way that will damage the trust and confidence necessary for an employment relationship.

Some terms of a contract of employment may not be written down, but are implied by law or by custom and practice in the workplace. For example, the employer's duty to provide a safe, secure and healthy environment is implied by law into all contracts of employment.

An employee must:

• Obey the lawful and reasonable instructions of the employer
• Exercise due care in the performance of the work and do it competently
• Account to the employer for all moneys and property received while employed
• Make available to the employer any process or product invented by the employee in the course of employment
• Disclose to the employer information received by the employee relevant to the employer's business
• Be faithful to the employer's interests, for example, by not passing on to a competitor information about the employer's business or denigrating the employer's products and services.

The second important aspect of common law is that of *negligence*, under which employers owe their employees a *duty of care*. This involves providing a safe place of work and safe systems of work. If an employee is seriously injured he can make a common law claim for compensation, although this may be limited by statute in some countries. In doing so it must be shown that the employer did not take reasonable precautions to prevent such an accident.

Employment legislation: statute law

As mentioned above, legislation is created by parliamentary processes. There are many acts which cover such conditions as parental leave, mechanisms for dealing with industrial disputes, legitimacy of unions, provision of collective agreements or awards, workers' compensation and occupational health and safety. Some of these will be dealt with rather briefly, particularly the field of discrimination in which many countries have multiple acts.

Occupational health and safety

Occupational health and safety is a matter dealt with by statute law. While under common law, an employer has a duty of care, these acts go further requiring, for example, the appointment of safety committees and reporting of workplace accidents. Breaches can lead to investigation and fines.

In the United Kingdom, the *Health and Safety at Work Act* (HASAWA) requires all employers to protect the health, safety and welfare of their employees. Most countries, including the United States, Australia, New Zealand and South Africa, have legislation with similar provisions. This legislation covers all work practices. Employers

Building the stage for the 2006 Winter Olympic Games, and attendant safety risks

must make every effort to prevent injury or ill health at work, and generally, health and safety legislation also places duties on employers to protect the public whilst on their premises, as well as temporary staff and contract workers.

An employer should provide:

- A safe system of work
- A safe place of work
- Safe equipment, plant and machinery
- Safe and competent workers, because employers are also liable for the conduct of their staff and managers.

An employer should carry out risk assessments and take steps to eliminate or control any risks. Employees should be informed about all potential hazards associated with any work process, chemical substance or activity. Instruction, training and supervision are key elements of workplace safety. Note that employers' safety obligations extend to other workers on site (e.g. contractors and members of the public). There are some specific risks in the event industry which require particular attention. As Figure 6.1 shows, at the Manchester Commonwealth Games, injuries were the most common incident. These can occur because of use of incorrect equipment, because people are tired or because people are working in a highly pressured, unfamiliar environment.

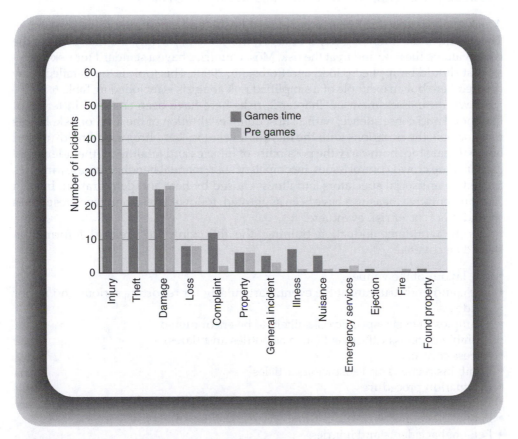

Figure 6.1 Pre Games and Games time incidents by incident type
(Manchester City Council (2003), Manchester Commonwealth Games Post Games Report; for further information see www.gameslegacy.com)

One common injury which can occur is through manual handling where a risk assessment is needed, based on the load and the person's capability. Personal protective clothing is required in some cases. Instructions and material data sheets should be provided for workers handling chemicals and equipment. Where employees require licensing, it should be checked that their licenses are up to date and relevant to the job at hand – this relates to the requirement that employees must be working with competent others.

In the event industry there are two critical times when safety is often compromised, at bump-in and at bump-out. At bump-in the organizer is usually pressed for time and it is not uncommon for installers to work around the clock. At the end of the show or exhibition, bump-out carries an even higher risk as everyone is exhausted. Special attention should be given to working hours and breaks because fatigue is a significant risk factor. In the European Community there are directives governing working times and these provide useful guidelines in any context:

- Forty-eight-hour maximum working week
- Four weeks' paid holiday
- Minimum daily rest periods of eleven hours
- Twenty-minute daily rest breaks after six hours' work, with young workers entitled to forty-five minutes if more than four and a half hours are worked
- A weekly rest period of twenty-four hours every seven days.

A risk analysis specifically for occupational health and safety should be conducted. This includes the following steps: establish the context; identify the risk; analyse the risk; evaluate the risk; and treat the risk. Most countries have a standard for risk analysis that should be applied (Hood and Rothstein, 2000). This topic is too detailed to be covered here but an example of a simplified risk analysis is included in Table 6.1.

As with the assessment in Chapter 2, risks here have been assessed in terms of likelihood and consequence, with a subsequent evaluation of the level of risk. In this risk analysis the situations with the highest level of risk are fire, armed hold-up and bomb threat since both carry the possibility of injuries and fatalities. Other identified risks include crowd control issues, incompetent staff, manual handling injuries, injuries caused by antisocial spectators and illness caused by heat and dehydration. In each case preventative measures have been suggested, followed by contingency responses should this type of risk eventuate.

During workforce induction training, the following OHS-related information should be covered:

- The layout of the venue
- The command structure at the event, particularly for reporting serious and minor incidents
- Examples of event-specific risks likely to be encountered
- Prohibited items at the event (such as bottles and flares)
- Access control
- Bomb inspections and suspicious articles
- Evacuation procedures
- Potential hazards and personal risks
- First aid treatment
- Personal accidents and injuries
- Accidents and injuries involving the public
- Duty of care and insurance.

Table 6.1 Sample occupational health and safety risk analysis

Type of risk	Level of risk	Prevention	Contingency
Incompetent or unqualified staff, e.g. driving forklift or skylarking	Major	• Ensure job specifications are accurate, including licensing requirements for specific roles • Conduct job-specific training based on job description and specifications • Conduct safety briefing before shift • Supervise and monitor workforce	• Remove worker or volunteer from task immediately • Investigate incident • Report incident • Implement disciplinary procedures if necessary
Inadequate procedures and instructions for crowd control	Catastrophic	• Fully document crowd measures • Assign responsibilities • Conduct training using scenarios • Brief staff • Conduct drills and simulations	• First aid treatment if required • Advise venue communications centre and enlist support • Investigate and report incidents
Hold-up during cash transfer	Catastrophic	• Prepare hold-up procedures • Copy instructions and post in key locations • Train staff in procedures	• Follow procedures to the letter • Investigate incident and report
Manual handling injury	Major	• Provide appropriate equipment • Ensure supervisors trained in OHS • Provide instructions during job-specific training regarding manual handling • Put up posters in staff areas	• First aid treatment • Investigate and report incident • Submit claim if necessary
Injury caused by antisocial spectators	Major	• Roster adequate security personnel • Limit alcohol consumption • Involve police	• First aid treatment • Contact police and security • Complete incident report
Bomb threat, fire or act of terrorism	Catastrophic	• Prepare procedures according to national standards • Train supervisors and staff • Rehearse procedures • Conduct searches	• Follow established emergency procedures, alerting venue communications centre
Exposure to extreme heat – dehydration	Moderate	• Provide water, hats and sunscreen • Warn staff and volunteers and ensure that they take necessary breaks • Explain symptoms of dehydration	• First aid treatment • Water and rest

As mentioned previously, some event organizations ask participants to complete a questionnaire to check their comprehension of safety information. If this is not done, at least an attendance register is essential to monitor who has and who has not done this training. Those who do not attend need to be provided with this information via email or a similar system. All the above information can be summarized in the form of a pocket guide.

There are numerous books on events and event safety covering risk management in more detail and providing guidelines for OHS risk management: Allen *et al.*, 2005; Bowdin *et al.*, 2001; Goldblatt, 1997, 2005; O'Toole and Mikolaitis, 2002.

Workers' compensation

Closely allied to occupational health and safety is workers' compensation. Under this legislation, employers are required to compensate employees for workplace accidents. In the United Kingdom, the United States and Australia, for example, as well as in other countries, this is no-fault legislation (also known as strict liability). The employee is compensated regardless of whether they have adequately taken care of themselves. Some acts specify specific sums for particular types of injury. In the past, an employee could claim negligence under common law as well and make a claim in the courts. In some countries efforts are underway to limit common law liability claims by setting limits or excluding the possibility entirely. In the United States, for example, the employee receives money and medical benefits in exchange for forfeiting the common law right to sue the employer. The employer benefits by receiving immunity from court actions against them by the employee in exchange for accepting liability that is limited and determined (see Case studies 6.1 and 6.2).

The general purpose of this legislation is to compensate for workplace accidents, injuries or fatalities. The acts that cover workers' compensation can vary and undergo frequent updates. Note that volunteers by definition are not workers and therefore generally do not come under the scope of workers' compensation insurance. They would be covered by the event organizer's public liability insurance or insurance taken out specifically to cover volunteers.

Case study 6.1

Workers' compensation

Workers' compensation laws provide a means of recovery for individuals injured during the course and scope of employment. Workers' compensation benefits are commonly reserved exclusively for injured 'employees' and their families. Several states, however, allow volunteers to utilize workers' compensation under some circumstances, while a few other states define 'employee' and/or 'employment' to include some classes of volunteers. Since workers' compensation laws vary from state to state, familiarity with the law of the state or states in which your organization operates is necessary to determine your obligation to purchase workers' compensation insurance.

The applicability of workers' compensation rules to volunteers depends on the wording of state statutes, some of which exclude nonprofits' employees as well as volunteers. The Arkansas statute, for example, expressly excludes from its definition of covered employment 'institutions maintained and operated wholly as public charities'. Idaho exempts from workers' compensation coverage 'employment which is not carried on by the employer for the sake of pecuniary gain.' Some states statutorily allow volunteer organizations the option of treating their volunteers as employees for purposes of workers' compensation.

In a few states, the question of whether a volunteer may receive workers' compensation benefits has been addressed by the courts. Some of these decisions hinge on whether the volunteer receives any form of compensation, such as a living allowance, stipend, room and board, benefits or even reimbursement for expenses. Other courts place little emphasis on whether or not the individual has been compensated, but look instead to the degree of control the employer exercises over the volunteer's service.

Although you may not want to pay workers' compensation premiums, covering volunteers under workers' compensation may offer a significant advantage if the option is available. In almost all states, individuals who elect to seek workers' compensation remedies cannot additionally attempt to recover damages through personal injury litigation against their employer. In these states, workers' compensation presents a tradeoff. Workers can recover under workers' compensation for work-related injuries without needing to prove the employer's fault; but their recoveries are more limited than a jury might award.

(Reproduced with permission of Nonprofit Risk Management Center; for more information see www.nonprofitrisk.org/csb/csb_mgv.htm)

Reflective practice 6.1
1 Summarize this article.
2 Give an example of a state, region or country that excludes volunteers from workers' compensation benefits.
3 Why is it vitally important that provision is made for volunteer insurance?

Conditions of employment

Industrial relations legislation can set up a framework for negotiating conditions of employment, which can vary widely from country to country and job to job. While some employees' conditions are extensively covered (particularly if their industry is unionized), other employees remain largely unprotected except, for example, by minimum wage rates and core statute legislation. In the case of union-negotiated contracts, awards and agreements, conditions of employment are spelled out in remarkable detail, covering special allowances, hours of work, casual and full-time rates of pay, etc. In Australia, there are moves afoot to reduce the number of conditions that form the minimum requirements for an Australian Workplace Agreement (AWA) in order to increase workforce 'flexibility'.

Equal opportunity and anti-discrimination legislation

Under most countries' laws, an employer cannot base employment, training and promotion decisions on personal characteristics that are not job related. These characteristics generally include:

- Age
- Race
- Sex
- Marital status
- Religion
- Country of origin
- Disability.

An interviewer isn't allowed to ask questions relating to these characteristics. Interview questions that aren't allowed include:

- Are you married? Are you planning to get married?
- Do you have children? Are you planning to have children?
- Will your children restrict your flexibility and availability?
- Where were you born?

This applies to volunteers as well. The reasons for rejecting an applicant must be job related.

Minimum wages and working time

The concept of minimum wages has already been mentioned. In the United States, the *Fair Labor Standards Act* (FLSA) sets minimum rates at federal level. This Act is very specific about working hours for young people (child labour). The Wage and Hour Division is responsible for administering and enforcing the minimum wage, overtime, and child labour provisions of the *Fair Labor Standards Act* and the *Family and Medical Leave Act* (FMLA). The FLSA requires that employees must receive at least the minimum wage and may not be employed for more than forty hours in a week without receiving at least one and a half times their regular rates of pay for the overtime hours.

Working hours for the United Kingdom were covered earlier, including break and rest times. From an event management perspective, working hours' rules provide challenges, as this can be a crisis environment in which people are working above and beyond expectations to stage the event, and generally they do this quite willingly. An employer must acknowledge, however, that this is not only a breach of guidelines but a serious risk. By allowing workers and enthusiastic teams to work unacceptable hours the employer is not displaying proper duty of care.

Leave

There are many different leave provisions: annual leave, parental leave, bereavement leave, etc. These may be covered by statute law or by employment contract, and variations from country to country are extensive.

Unions

The potential role of the unions has already been mentioned. Again, there are significant differences between countries such as the United States and the United Kingdom in the way in which unions and government work.

Discipline and dismissal

Disciplinary issues are more common than one would think in the event environment. Perhaps this is because there is less routine and control in terms of supervision. Workers and volunteers might harass athletes, celebrities or each other. Stories of major equipment disappearing are legendary. Many items are removed from the athletes' villages during closing ceremonies: taking home 'souvenirs' such as flags and other decorative items is commonplace. Many volunteers also feel the urge to take home memorabilia. One Sydney volunteer working in accreditation made himself a badge that would allow him into the athletes' village, but unfortunately he made it in the name of a popular and famous athlete and his identity was immediately questioned.

Policies in relation to misconduct and dismissal will be covered in Chapter 11.

In the majority of states in the United States, employees not working under an employment contract are deemed to be 'at will'. At-will employees may be terminated for any reason, so long as it's not illegal. There are numerous illegal reasons for termination. Typically such reasons fall into one of two large categories: illegal discrimination or illegal termination in violation of a public policy. Generally, employees who work under an employment contract can only be terminated for reasons specified in the contract. By contrast, Australia has unfair dismissal laws (currently the topic of debate and amendment), which cover dismissal and redundancy.

Registering attendance

One of the most problematic issues for event organizers and contractors is registering attendance of their staff and volunteers. This is particularly the case for people who may work across a number of precincts, signing on at one location and signing off at another. Clearly, a sophisticated, barcoded accreditation badge that can be scanned on entry and exit would solve this problem. Generally, however, most event budgets cannot accommodate such systems for temporary venues. The issue of signing on and off duty must be solved, however, as it is incumbent upon the event organizer to account for all personnel on site. Attendance registration for volunteers would form part of the procedural guidelines for managing volunteers.

As mentioned previously, insurance for volunteers is recommended (see Case study 6.2).

Case study 6.2

First insurance policies for Beijing 2008 Olympic Games volunteers underwritten

The PICC Property and Casualty Company Limited (PICC P&C) today underwrites the first batch of insurance policies for the Beijing 2008 Olympic Games volunteers, immediately after the insurance company has signed a partnership agreement with the Beijing Olympic organizers.

The policies cover personal accident and medical insurance for the thirty-six persons who work as pre-Games volunteers for the Beijing Organizing Committee for the Games of the XXIX Olympiad (BOCOG). The agreement, backed up by the new policies, constitutes the start-up of the partnership between PICC P&C and BOCOG.

The volunteers of the Beijing 2008 Olympic Volunteer Programme refer to those who provide services on a voluntary basis to the Olympic Games and Paralympic Games, to other people and to the society through their voluntary actions within the scope of the volunteer programme before and during the 2008 Olympic Games and Paralympic Games. It is estimated that at least 100 000 volunteers will be needed for the 2008 Olympic Games and the Paralympic Games. As a partner, PICC P&C vows to provide continued and outstanding services for BOCOG's pre-Games volunteers and Games-times volunteers.

(Beijing 2008, press release, 9 September 2005; for more information see http://en.beijing 2008.com/51/69/article211986951.shtml)

Validating suitability

In the process of assessing an individual's suitability for employment, there are a number of checks that might be done such as:

- Visa and other requirements for official employability status
- Licences and permits (e.g. to drive a forklift)
- Educational and other qualifications (e.g. responsible service of alcohol certificate, food safety training, first aid certificate). All of these need to be checked for currency
- Police check, mainly for mega events
- Working with children, training and register of child offenders
- References from past employers.

In all cases, the individual has to provide consent for the check to take place. This is commonly done by including a statement to this effect at the end of the application form, which the prospective employee or volunteer signs. This is also an important consideration when accepting applications online.

Offer letter

As mentioned previously, the employment offer is a contract like any other. Some important details need to be included such as:

- Position offered
- Compensation/pay
- Benefits
- Trial period
- Start and finish date (if project or temporary)
- Reference to the attached job description for duties and responsibilities
- Reference to the attached employee handbook for policies and rules
- Signatures of both parties.

In the case of volunteers, it is equally important to highlight the position as a voluntary position and include clear expectations of both sides.

Record keeping

Employee record keeping requires that the following information is maintained for auditing purposes (by the taxation department in particular). The period of time required for storing these records differs from region to region; however, seven years is a good guideline.

- Name
- Address
- Position held
- Hours or time card details
- Gross pay or earnings
- Deductions such as tax
- Record of leave due and taken.

It is also highly recommended that records of interview, training, evaluation and timekeeping are maintained for volunteers.

Rings of confidence

In his study of the 2000 Olympic Games, Tony Webb (2001) showed that the government and the unions reached a new level of co-operation, and goes on to explore a number of the lessons in more detail.

Industrial relations at the Games – how it worked on the ground

'It got to the point where we almost forgot sport was involved we were so caught up in dealing with the problems on the site.' Paul Howes, Unions 2000.

What the unions also learned was that for all of the planning some of the arrangements for the Games workforce would be found wanting during the Games operation. Two weeks before the Games the unions were given accreditation for an official at each venue, allowing direct contact with the workforce, and thirty-two union officials from five unions were rostered to provide coverage throughout the Games. In addition, members could access union support through a general call-centre number linked to a Unions 2000 office on site in the OCA building at Olympic Park. The plan was that unions would be in touch with the workforce and on call to identify and deal with any workplace or industrial relations problems that arose during the Games. In order to ensure efficient handling of disputes all officials involved went through a three-day training programme organized by the Labor Council and SOCOG. On site the rostered union officials had status on a par with venue staffing managers. The industrial structure envisaged by SOCOG was that each venue management would supervise the Games venue staff and volunteers allocated to that site. Contractor companies in the venue would have their own management and supervise their workers but report to the venue manager.

Fortunately a range of disputes in the twelve months leading up to the Games had helped in the building of trust between the unions, SOCOG and the companies. There had been:

* *Changes to the awards*
* *Issues over paid and volunteer workers for the Ceremonies*
* *The question of bonuses for bus drivers*
* *A major dispute over young people, some as young as fourteen, employed as vendors who were being defined as 'contractors' with full responsibility for self-employment*
* *The problem of New Zealand security workers recruited without licences or job guarantees*
* *Underpayment of wages at Bondi Beach Stadium.*

And a number of others.

All had been resolved satisfactorily and a large reservoir of trust and respect had been established. But nothing like the problems encountered during the Games had been anticipated.

Even before the Games some problems were apparent. The opening of the Games villages in June 2000 exposed a lack of understanding among staff of the systems, particularly payroll for workers. The unions assisted with presentations to supervisors and helped with the interpretation of the award. Within a few days of the Games Opening Ceremony, caterers struck problems. People were simply not purchasing food on the scale anticipated and the contractors proposed to lay off 1000 staff. Using the award provisions for flexible working the unions negotiated redeployment of some to other Games work. SOCOG staff used email networks to contact a number of industry groups, letting them know that there were people willing, keen and available, and asking if they needed any staff. These industry groups sent the message on to their members and within minutes SOCOG had emails from all over town saying they had openings for this or that number, skill etc. and a hot line of positions found many people work. For the remainder, the unions and caterers negotiated an across the board reduction of hours rather than layoffs so that no-one was without a job.

But above all the problem was with the payroll. Day in, day out there were problems with people not being paid, in some cases for weeks. It was not that these were unusual, complicated or difficult to resolve. It was the sheer unremitting volume and the knowledge that the problem was a generic one – that the systems were simply inadequate and could not be reorganized during the course of the Games.

In all the unions negotiated twelve major disputes, eight with 'real strike-potential', during the Games period that required intervention from SOCOG at a senior level, and dealt with over 2500 individual problems mainly over pay. The official procedure for dealing with issues through the venue manager was largely bypassed. Most problems were resolved directly with the companies involved. Many employers had people in place who were committed to resolving issues as they arose and networks of personal relations between the unions and these companies had been established. Some problems the unions stepped back from – judging that employers were acting with goodwill and working to deal with the issues.

One example might illustrate the nature of the collaboration. As part of the major problem we discussed earlier where caterers were laying off staff early in the Games, twenty workers in four bars in the Stadium threatened to walk out because three of their workmates had been laid off by the catering contractor Sodexho. Chris Christodoulou says:

> *It took three meetings, at 10 pm, 12 midnight and 5 am, along with help from John Quayle, from SOCOG – along with a few drinks in the bar near the Novotel with the key workers in the dispute to fix it.*

Paul Howes describes another:

> *There were just two food halls for some of our people to take their meal breaks. We had employers saying the meal break starts when they leave work and they would have to get back in twenty minutes. As you know everything was jam packed on the site so it could take that long just to get between the buildings. SOCOG overruled the companies, saying that it starts when they get to the food hall but, during the Games, there were long lines in the halls – it could take ten minutes to get served – so it was changed again – based on the principle that workers deserved a real break – they had to be fed properly – we gave flexibility on meal times and short breaks – and the companies gave back within a human relations principled framework. Nobody abused the system and morale stayed high.*

Overall the Games were a success, 'the best Games ever'. In the face of this the problems, large and small, pale into significance – unless that is, we wish to learn from both our successes and our failures in order to better understand:

- *What are the underlying components of the human relations framework that made this success possible?*
- *Which aspects were not in place in those 'near-disaster' areas and did their absence contribute to the problems?*
- *Why did these areas nevertheless succeed in spite of the problems?*
- *Whether any of these lessons might be useful in planning other major events or projects requiring collaboration between large groups of people in the future?*

(Extract from Webb, T. (2001). *The Collaborative Games*. Pluto Press, pp. 88–91. Reproduced with permission.)

Reflective practice 6.3
Answer the above questions for this case study.

Chapter summary and key points

While laws and regulations differ widely from country to country and state to state, effective human resource management requires close attention to these matters. The most important issues are working time and wages, followed by occupational health and safety on the event worksite. Events carry significant risks and a visit to (www. crowdsafe.com) will convince anyone that crowd management and safety are essential components of induction training, on-the-job training, briefings and debriefings. Duty of care requires responsible management of everyone on site, including visiting workers and volunteers. Duty of care also extends to the public.

A risk management analysis needs to be done on the issue of legal compliance as it applies to human resource management, covering all pertinent laws and regulations. This should be extended still further to cover the topic of occupational health and safety in detail as this is the one issue that dominates the minds of organizers and supervisors responsible for a temporary and often unskilled workforce.

Revision questions

1 Who has a contract of employment?
2 Is a volunteer covered by workers' compensation insurance?
3 What is duty of care?
4 What are the responsibilities of employers under OHS?
5 Referring to discrimination in employment, which characteristics are causes for complaint?

References

Allen, J., O'Toole, W., Harris, R. and McDonnell, I. (2005). *Festival and Special Event Management*, 3rd edn. John Wiley & Sons.

Bowdin, G. A. J., O'Toole, W., McDonnell, I. and Allen, J. (2001). *Events Management*. Butterworth-Heinemann.

Goldblatt, J. (1997). *Special Events*, 2nd edn. John Wiley and Sons Inc.

Goldblatt, J. J. (2005). *Special Events: Event Leadership for a New World*, 4th edn. Wiley.

Hood, C. and Rothstein, H. (2000). *Business Risk Management in Government: Pitfalls and Possibilities*, National Audit Office, London.

Manchester City Council (2003). Manchester Commonwealth Games Post Games Report. Viewed 17 May 2006, www.gameslegacy.com.

O'Toole, W. and Mikolaitis, P. (2002). *Corporate Event Project Management*. Wiley.

TUC (2004). Unions have a vital role in making London 2012 the best Olympic Games the world has ever seen. Viewed 12 October 2005, www.tuc.org.uk/ economy/tuc-9023-f0.cfm>.

Webb, T. (2001). *The Collaborative Games: The Story behind the Spectacle*. Pluto Press.

Workers Online (2004). Athens update: dying games. Viewed 12 October 2005, http://workers.labor.net.au/216/news85_athens.html.

Chapter 7

Job analysis

Learning objectives

After reading this chapter you will be able to:

- Explain the process of job analysis
- Evaluate the most appropriate ways in which to approach job analysis
- Develop job descriptions and person specifications
- Differentiate between different conditions of employment
- Explain why job descriptions are key elements of human resource planning.

Introduction

Job analysis is the process of collecting information in order to develop a comprehensive awareness about specific jobs, including job descriptions and person specifications. As this and the next chapter will show, job descriptions form the basis for recruitment and selection, as well as training and performance management. While some small event organizations are cavalier about their lack of human resource planning and have no written job descriptions, those event organizations that operate in professional and complex environments find that job descriptions are an invaluable part of planning. A job description can form the basis for recruitment of the most appropriate staff, provide guidelines to the individual accepting the position, form the basis for training plans and provide a foundation for performance management. For most individuals and organizations, job descriptions are invaluable – in the event business, job descriptions (like checklists) are part of the micro level planning that contributes to flawless performance.

What is job analysis?

Job analysis is the process of discovering the nature of jobs (Brannick and Levine, 2002) and for this to occur a systematic process is necessary. The outcomes of job analysis are primarily the job description and person specification for each role, including volunteers.

A *job description* is an outline of reporting relationships, tasks to be performed, job outcomes expected and working conditions. A *person specification* (also referred to as 'job requirements') provides details of the ideal candidate, including knowledge, skills and other attributes required to perform the above tasks.

In conjunction with project planning, the following questions might be asked as the job analysis process evolves:

- What is the primary purpose of the job?
- Is this job going to be performed by a paid staff member, a volunteer or a contractor?
- What are the tasks that need to be performed?
- What are the skills, knowledge and other attributes required?
- Are there any legislative considerations, such as requisite licences?
- When and where are the tasks performed?
- What are the reporting relationships?
- Which environmental factors need to be considered?
- Are specific job outcomes expected?
- Is the job likely to change during the course of the project?

As Figure 7.1 illustrates, the human resources strategic plan leads to the development of work breakdown structures, chunking the major project into smaller subprojects. These are then illustrated on charts and timelines. A labour force analysis is necessary to identify any gaps in supply or training and this in turn leads to identification of roles assigned to paid staff, volunteers and contractors. At this stage organizational charts can be developed.

The human resources operational plan has the objective of ensuring that all tasks are assigned and performed at the highest possible level. This involves recruitment, selection, training, workforce logistics management, performance management and recognition. All of these stages are supported by the foundation pillars of the human resources risk analysis; the human resources budget; policies and procedures; and detailed, systematic job analysis at every stage of the project.

Simple approaches to job analysis

There are whole textbooks on this topic and it is difficult to do it justice in a short space. The following approaches are simple ways in which job analysis can be done, resulting in person specifications and job descriptions. In the process, some thought must be given to job design, which takes into account the features of a job that make it rewarding, interesting and satisfying to the incumbent. For example, job rotation is one way in which volunteers' roles can be made more interesting, particularly if some are placed near the field of play and others not. However, job design is not a major consideration for any except paid roles in the event business. Even there, the short-term and varied nature of the work tends to ensure that jobs provide sufficient challenge. In most cases, the nature of the project (exhibition, festival, street parade, conference) tends to determine the tasks required, with little room to apply the job design principles evident in jobs for large, stable organizations in which motivation and career planning considerations are quite different.

Methods of job analysis are outlined below in brief.

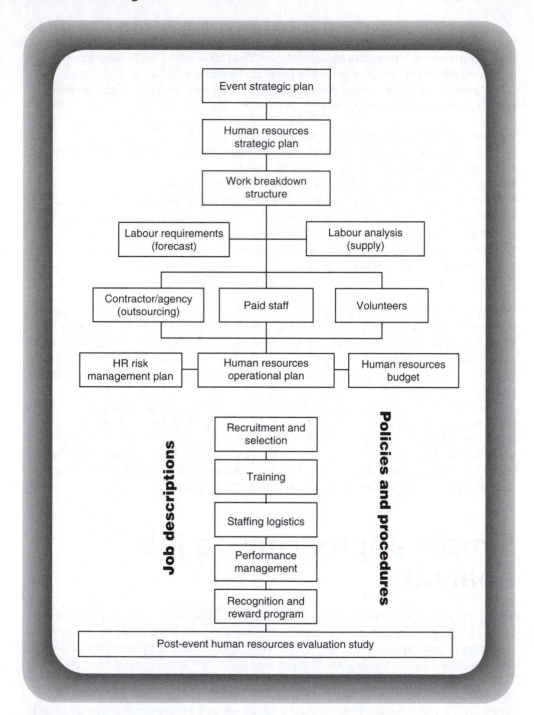

Figure 7.1 Strategic plan for human resource management

Project management processes

Chapter 3 looked at project management principles in some detail. This is one of the most common ways in which event organizations analyse the human resource requirements necessary to execute the overall plan. By breaking down the work into smaller and smaller subprojects it can ultimately be decided which tasks need to be performed in order to achieve the project outcomes. This is colloquially known as 'drilling down'.

Focus groups

Most event organizations are comprised of a group of experienced individuals at management level. Using their experience, a series of focus groups can be conducted which may abbreviate the detailed project planning identified above. This group can contribute something vital – they can identify the things that have worked and haven't worked in the past. Also, the members of the group have experience with employing their own staff, contractual arrangements with suppliers and volunteer management. Tapping into this experience, which may be local or international, is an essential part of job analysis.

Interviews

Individuals may have a wealth of ideas to contribute. As with the above approach, it is best to structure the sessions, using questions such as those described in the previous section to ensure that the discussion doesn't go off track.

Questionnaires

A simple format for job analysis is useful once the high-level planning has been completed. An example of a template for creating job descriptions in functional areas is shown in Figure 7.2.

Research

Industry research is another component of job analysis. Similar occupations and events may have similar roles. Legislative requirements, such as certification to serve alcohol, may be part of the person specification. Knowledge of food safety systems and procedures would be essential for catering supervisors.

Critical incidents

There is nothing more powerful than a critical incident analysis to point to planning deficiencies. Using this approach, the following questions would need to be asked:

- What went wrong/right?
- What were the contributing factors?

Job title, job summary, reporting relationships
Duties/responsibilities and job outcomes
Job environment/context, special requirements, equipment
Conditions of employment (paid, volunteer, term)

Figure 7.2 Template for developing job descriptions

- How did people performance contribute to the incident (in a positive or negative way)?
- How was this reflected in human resource management plans, policies and procedures (or not, as the case may be)?

For example, it may be found that an access control monitor has allowed people into an area who should not be there, leading to a security scare and bomb search. This could point to insufficient training for the access monitor and in turn should lead to a review of training materials and possibly the development of an assessment task to check volunteers' comprehension of the various codes on accreditation passes. More serious incidents such as injuries and accidents could result in more emphasis on control measures and thus more volunteers assigned to safety monitoring roles.

As Sanchez and Levine (2000) point out, job analysis is far from an exact science, regardless of the approach taken. Researchers of job analysis often evaluate the accuracy of the outcomes by analysing rater agreement. However, Sanchez and Levine propose that consequential validity is another way in which the outcomes of job analysis can be reviewed. Figure 7.1 shows the final stage of human resource management for an event as the evaluation report and it is here, post-event, that consequential validity of many elements of the human resources plan can be evaluated. By analysing critical incidents (and many of the not so critical ones) any deficiencies in job analysis, job design, recruitment and training can be highlighted.

Success factors are another consideration. The question asked could be 'How does this critical incident illustrate the success of our human resource programme?' If we take an incident, such as a volunteer going beyond the call of duty to assist a spectator who is feeling ill, or the part played by a security officer in providing information to visitors (one of whom turns out to be a visiting journalist), it is necessary to look back at their selection, training and motivation programmes to see how these members of the workforce were empowered to provide exceptional service.

Sanchez and Levine make the point that very detailed job analysis sometimes fails to lead to relevant selection procedures. Thus, while the process should be systematic, in the event environment heuristics (a little informed guesswork) has a role to play in the dynamic process of project planning. Indeed, the project management environment is often characterized by rapid change, competing demands and incomplete information (McCray *et al.*, 2002). However, when using heuristics it is important to acknowledge potential biases and apply appropriate measures to offset them.

Establishing conditions of employment

Part of job analysis involves establishing conditions of employment. In the event environment there are many different arrangements, with few staff working traditional jobs as full-time permanent employees. These conditions may include any or all of the following.

Paid employee

A person is an employee if a number of criteria are met. Essentially an employee agrees to 'serve': he or she agrees to follow directions. Control is therefore one of the primary criteria of the employment relationship. Another is the organization test whereby the employee works on the premises and uses all the tools and equipment of the employer. The employee is thus assimilated into the organization (Maund, 2001). Finally, 'consideration' is the payment of the employee for the hours worked so that money changes hands.

Full-time employee

Full-time staff work a full week, normally an eight-hour day over five days. However, legislation of a particular country or region, and industrial agreements, have an impact on this arrangement. Where such agreements exist, employees must be paid overtime if they exceed these hours. In practice, many event employees are very flexible and are responsive to the pressure and demands of the 'hot action', working long hours during set-up and running of an event.

Part-time employee

Part-time is where a person works a percentage of a full-time position, with associated benefits such as pay and leave on a pro-rata basis. Thus someone who works half the week is paid 50 per cent of the full-time wage for the same position and is entitled to half the annual leave and sick leave.

Permanent employee

A permanent employee has an open-ended relationship with the employer.

Temporary

Temporary positions are common in the event industry. For example, a paid volunteer co-ordinator might be employed for three months.

Casual

A casual employee works on an hourly basis. The pay rate reflects this, carrying loadings to compensate for the lack of sick leave or other leave. The hourly rate is thus higher than that for a permanent or temporary employee.

There are also other ways in which people might be employed to work on site:

Agency staff

Agency staff are somewhat complex as their employer is technically the agency that has hired them and is paying them. However, they do work in much the same way as employees, taking direction and participating fully in the organization. Despite this, they remain the employees of the agency.

Volunteers

Volunteers are not employees. They are not paid and are not able to access the benefits of employees. They are not covered by workers compensation. Where the position is unpaid this should be clearly stated on the job description and in all correspondence with the volunteer.

Contractors

An independent contractor does not fall within the definition of an employment relationship since he or she has control of an independent business and decides where, when and by whom the work should be done. The business is separate, and runs the risk of profit or loss. Tools and equipment belong to the contractor company. People employed by the independent contractor are answerable to their employer even if working on the event site.

While collectively everyone on site is described as being part of the 'event workforce', only a portion of these people are paid staff. Clarity about the basis for employment is essential for legal reasons. Anyone working as an employee of the event organization should be issued with an offer letter, which is essentially an employment contract.

Applying job analysis to human resource programmes

Many organizations see job descriptions as a formality, a paperwork requirement of the human resource department. Once completed, they are then disregarded. In the event business, job descriptions are vitally important and can contribute in many ways to the project's design and implementation. Managing the entire scope of people performance is the aim of the human resources operational plan, an example of which is illustrated in Figure 7.3. As Plekhanova (1998, p. 116) points out, 'most traditional approaches to process modelling do not provide an analysis of critical human resources and their impact(s) on project performance and output quality ... because they are concerned with resource availability and utilization, and do not provide study, analysis and management of resource *capabilities* and *compatibilities*'. While this author is discussing this topic in the context of software design, what he says could not be more pertinent to event management where '*people and their capabilities have a major impact on project performance and its quality*' (Plekhanova, 1998, p. 116).

The job description

A job description is a summary of the most important features of a job, including the general nature of the work performed (i.e. duties and responsibilities) and level of the work performed (i.e. skill, effort, responsibility and working conditions) (see Case study 7.1 on p. 115). A job description should describe and focus on the job itself and not on any specific individual who might fill the job.

There are four parts to a job description:

1 Identifies where the job fits within the organization and includes reporting relationships.
2 Describes the work performed, generally in the form of a list of duties or tasks. In many cases these duties can be clustered into groups of related items.

Job descriptions
The main feature is a list of duties and outcomes

⇩

Person specifications
Allow for the identification of the knowledge, skills and other
attributes of the ideal employee or volunteer

⇩

Training programmes
Gaps between the skills and knowledge of the appointee and the
requirements of the job role form part of a training plan

⇩

Performance appraisals
Performance can be measured against the duties and outcomes
listed in the job description

⇩

Disciplinary processes
Deficiencies in performance can be clearly identified in relation to clearly
set out duties and responsibilities

⇩

Post-event evaluation
Planning can be evaluated by asking selected individuals to identify
shortcomings in the original design of their position, roles and responsibilities

Figure 7.3   Developing a human resources operational plan

3 Describes the environment in which the person will work and any special requirements or limitations, including licensing and other mandatory requirements.
Machines, tools and equipment are also described here. And this part may describe
the context, such as outdoor work or shift work.
4 Describes the conditions of employment, including pay rate and period of
employment.

These are illustrated in the job description for an events co-ordinator in Figure 7.4.

The person specification

The person/job specification describes the ideal person for the job in terms of competencies relevant to the job description. In the sample job description in Figure 7.4
it is clear that the person is required to have experience in a similar event context, to
have developed budgets and to have used project planning software such as
Microsoft Project. All of these are directly relevant to the job role.

Charges of discrimination are unlikely to occur if the person specification includes
requirements that are not relevant to the job role as outlined in the job description. If

Job Description – Events Co-ordinator

Reports to: Executive Director

Summary

Plans, oversees and administers all aspects of events (conferences, workshops, board meetings, presentations and social events). Maintains the master calendar of events. Co-ordinates activities with administrative staff, and works with other staff members on events as appropriate.

Job responsibilities/tasks

1. Administers and oversees planning and execution of all organizational conferences, meetings and social events, both on site and off site
2. Identifies venues and suppliers of event services
3. Oversees and approves master calendar of events
4. Maintains a current, accurate and detailed project task timeline
5. Negotiates rates and contracts with venues and suppliers/vendors for a variety of services
6. Prepares budget and submits it for approval to Executive Committee
7. Monitors services to ensure contract terms are satisfied
8. Attends events to oversee activities and ensure details are handled as arranged
9. Issues invitations, monitors and co-ordinates replies
10. Arranges for travel and accommodation for event participants
11. Generates data reports on event activities as required
12. Co-ordinates in-house catering/hospitality

Job context

Extended hours and weekend hours may be required when running events.
Driving is necessary for occasional pick up and transportation of speakers and conference participants.

Conditions of employment

Full-time permanent (37.5 hours per week)
Salary level: Administrative staff, level three.

Figure 7.4 Job description – Events Co-ordinator

it can be seen that equal employment opportunity (EEO) principles have been applied, the recruitment and selection processes will survive scrutiny.

Most people writing person specifications have little difficulty with the sections on knowledge and skills (competencies) required. The difficulty is usually with the section called 'other attributes'. It is in this section that an inexperienced person is likely to list things like 'outgoing personality', 'organized and confident' or 'non-smoker'. First, these attributes are hard to judge objectively and, second, they are often hard to justify in relation to the specific job requirements. Certainly the criterion, nonsmoker, cannot be supported. While there may be office or venue areas in which there is no smoking, there is no reason that a person should be asked whether they smoke in other places or on other occasions. This section is the one where the law is most likely to be broken. Some unusual requirements seen by the author include: 'must be petit to fit into our uniform'; 'under 35'; 'good for public relations'; 'attractive'; 'muscular'; and 'fit looking'. Even a criterion 'interested in sport' may not be relevant to a volunteer working at a sporting event if they are working back of house

Person specification – Events Co-ordinator

Knowledge and experience

- Experience with event/meeting planning and co-ordination required at the same level
- Knowledge of event suppliers/vendors in the tourism and hospitality industry in the region, including venues, hotels, and food and beverage facilities
- Ability to organize travel, accommodation and hospitality for groups of 50 or more
- Experience negotiating contracts, primarily with hotels and event venues
- Experience in preparing budgets and allocating resources
- Proven ability to manage community volunteers, including recruitment and training
- Basic knowledge of audiovisual systems

Skills

- Computer programmes: all Microsoft office products, including Excel and Project
- Knowledge of special event planning software such as EventPro an advantage
- Driver's licence

Other attributes

- Able to handle multiple tasks simultaneously
- Attention to detail
- Ability to work under pressure and meet timelines
- Team player, ability to work with different people, flexible
- Able to work with minimal direction or supervision, highly motivated

Figure 7.5   Person/job specification – Events Co-ordinator

and nowhere near the field of play. Likewise, requirement of a driver's licence should not be included unless driving is an essential part of the job.

Examples of more appropriate 'other attributes' are shown in the sample person specification in Figure 7.5.

One final comment on the selection criteria included in the person specification: if it can be clearly shown that the event is themed and that the food and beverage staff are part of the theme, then selection of staff to fit the theme can be justified. For example, if the event included a Chinese banquet, décor and entertainment, it would be legal to select staff of Chinese appearance, with ability to speak this language, as would be done if hiring actors for a performance.

Using job descriptions as training and monitoring aids

Job descriptions can be used as the basis for employee and volunteer training. In fact, the volunteer job description can double as a checklist and control measure (see Figure 7.6), providing the volunteer with clear expectations of what the job entails and the supervisor with an outline for on-the-job training and measurement. Each task specified can be explained by the trainer and practised by the volunteer to ensure that the person knows what to do and feels confident.

Tasks	Times to be carried out	Record of daily inspection
Check access to electrical control box, in particular any blockages or obstructions	Hourly	
Check clearways/pathways, with particular attention to stairways to ensure that they aren't blocked	Twice per day	
Monitor cleanliness of staff areas, including canteen and change rooms	Twice per day	
Monitor use of recycling bins and report to kitchen supervisor if waste streams are contaminated	Hourly	
Monitor incident reporting system:	Three per day	

- Check that sufficient incident forms are provided for staff at staff entrance and staff canteen area
- Clear incident report form submission box and take forms to control centre
- Check signage for reporting major incidents or emergency evacuation

Figure 7.6   Job description used as training aid and control measure

Task: Maintains current, accurate and detailed project task timelines; reviews the timelines regularly with staff to determine completed tasks, pending tasks and task changes
Rating:
Comment:

Task: Negotiates rates and contracts with venues and suppliers/vendors for a variety of services
Rating:
Comment:

Figure 7.7   Appraisal of performance against job description

Using job descriptions as performance management tools

Some organizations use performance appraisal forms that are more general than specific. For example, the criteria by which the person is appraised may include 'quality of work' or 'ability to work in a team'. Consider instead how useful it would be to judge the individual's performance against the duties listed in the job description. For example, using the event co-ordinator's job description illustrated in Figure 7.4, the evaluation would look something like that illustrated in Figure 7.7.

A volunteer minder protects stilt walkers from sabotage

Case study 7.1

Writing job descriptions

Job title: Staging Assistant Bump-in and Bump-out

Job Summary
The volunteer will work with a team to put up tents, install seating, build stages and display kiosks. At the end of the festival the volunteer will work with a team to dismantle and remove all built items.

Reports to
Production Manager

Tasks
- Lifting and carrying equipment
- Moving heavy items
- Setting up tents and kiosks
- Building the stage
- Minor handyman tasks
- Putting up signage
- Other manual labour tasks

Shifts
Very early start on bump-in day of 4 am, working until 2 pm
Festival days 8 am to 4 pm
Bump-out 10 am to 4 pm

Conditions
Volunteer unpaid
Uniform and meals provided

Person specification/requirements
- Previous experience with this level of manual handling
- Handyman skills, mainly carpentry
- Basic occupational health and safety training

Experience in a festival environment would be an advantage.

Reflective practice 7.1
Develop similar job descriptions for two of the volunteer roles for the 2006 FIFA World Cup™ (see box) by expanding the list of duties and being specific about the job requirements and conditions of employment.

Volunteer roles for 2006 FIFA World Cup™

Accreditation
The accreditation department is responsible for providing personalized ID for all officials, teams, media representatives, service providers and local co-workers. This ID gives the bearer access to areas both at the stadium and off site.

Official accreditation is vital for optimal management of the sizeable organizational teams and staff required for the 2006 FIFA World Cup™. The ID will also provide proof of eligibility to enter official facilities.

Volunteers for this department will greet persons who have applied for ID at the accreditation centre, and will be responsible for the production and issuing of the identity document. Volunteers will also assist in distributing daily passes and in the 'problem solving' section in the event of issues arising regarding persons seeking accreditation. With very few exceptions, volunteers in accreditation work in specific, fixed locations near the stadium.

Information technology and telecommunication

Thousands of journalists will be filing reports around the world every day on TV and by email, telephone and fax from the 2006 FIFA World Cup™. To manage the enormous flow of data, we require a reliable and extensive IT and telecommunication network. In 2006 every press and media area requires around 500 PC workstations.

We need volunteers with relevant specialist skills to support the PC, network and telecommunication problem-solving effort. You will work in a wide variety of locations.

Fan service

During the 2006 FIFA World Cup™, Fan Embassies will be set up in the city centre of all FIFA World Cup Host Cities. These will be points of contacts that will provide fans with information on the city and the World Cup.

Fans come to the Fan Embassies to contact other fans but will also receive help if, for instance, they have lost their passport, couldn't book a return flight, etc. The volunteers that work here will be in constant touch with people from all over the world and will thus meet a lot of different cultures during this time.

Logistics

This department will plan, execute and control the logistical processes required to manage the transportation, delivery, storage and distribution operations. The logistics challenges include organizing, co-ordinating and controlling the setting up and dismantling of a number of temporary structures, and the punctual use of transportation and delivery routes to and from the stadiums.

Volunteers will be involved in all logistics processes, helping with loading and unloading and maintaining depots with essential temporary storage facilities, for example.

Volunteers will be deployed at one location throughout the tournaments and must be prepared to work flexible hours.

Marketing

Our task is to implement and protect the exclusive advertising rights of a total of fifteen Official Partners and six Official Suppliers. The areas around the stadiums must be maintained as competition-free zones, in which only these FIFA partners are permitted to advertise.

One of the major tasks assigned to marketing volunteers is to monitor the Official Partners' and Official Suppliers' advertising and ensuring no other advertising material is displayed in controlled areas.

Public relations media and communication

More than 12 000 journalists from around the world are expected to report from the 2006 FIFA World Cup™. A local Stadium Media Centre (SMC) will be established at each of the twelve stadiums. The International Media Centre (IMC) – the nerve centre and command post for TV stations around the world – will be located at the Munich Trade Fair.

Our goal is to provide excellent working conditions and a friendly atmosphere for the media.

Volunteers will be the first point of call for questions from media representatives. They will convey the latest information, give directions to the various media areas (main stand, press box, media conference, photographers' area, TV studios), give technical advice (for example on using ISDN and Internet connections) and help translate player reactions into all relevant languages.

The media centres will operate from a few days before the tournament and every day during the event, so volunteers in this area will be at work for several weeks.

Project management

Sports projects with the scope of the 2006 FIFA World Cup™, involving a lengthy planning phase, urgently require disciplined overall project leadership and a functioning communications structure. For the first time in the history of similar events, this will be managed via a Web-based umbrella controlling system (MS Project) encompassing every individual project, linked to regular status reporting. Targeted risk management will proceed along similar lines.

Volunteers will provide administrative support to the strategic and conceptual work undertaken by project managers at FIFA headquarters in Berlin throughout the tournament, and will contribute relevant previous experience to the overall project.

Guest service/security

The security department is responsible for implementing consistent security measures at all 2006 FIFA World Cup Host Cities. Our motto is: 'The necessary level of security with as few restrictions as possible.' Amongst other things, this involves a broad range of embassies and activities for fans to promote a peaceful and visitor-friendly atmosphere. Volunteers for this department will support security and law enforcement personnel, making themselves available as informal points of contact for all spectators. Volunteers will largely be deployed in stadiums and city centre areas.

Ticketing

The ticketing department co-ordinates all relevant processes related to match tickets, including seating plans, ordering and issuing tickets and stadium admission procedures for both events. By June 2006, all entry points at all FIFA World Cup stadiums will be equipped with electronic admission control systems.

Volunteers for this department will need to be familiar with ticket distribution and control procedures and how to operate the ticketing system.

A ticketing centre will be established at every location, coming into operation a few weeks before the tournament.

Transportation and traffic control

The transportation section is responsible for a smooth-running travel service for the teams and their support staff, the referees, the media, and a host of official FIFA guests, starting two weeks before the tournament and continuing until a few days after the Final.

We are responsible for all transfers within the twelve Host Cities, using a fleet of 800 Hyundai vehicles and more than 100 buses. Our responsibilities also include booking and organizing air and train travel within Germany, so we will maintain a presence at all FIFA hotels, railway stations and airports in every Host City. With so many passengers to be transported between so many locations, we will require an extensive and well co-ordinated organizational structure, both at the visible level and behind the scenes.

Volunteers will be assigned to a wide range of interesting tasks throughout this transportation network. As shuttle service drivers for our official guests from around the world, they will make an important contribution to the smooth running of the tournament. Wide-ranging support roles await volunteers working in our local travel co-ordination centres. Those with relevant experience will help maintain our vehicle fleet, or act as assistants to our professional transport managers. A handful of selected volunteers will provide a link between the professionals and the volunteer team as a whole.

Competition

The competition department is responsible for all activities directly relating to the smooth operation of the match schedule. Duties will include accompanying teams from their arrival until they depart, co-ordinating team training bases, maintaining regulations on match days, preparing and equipping training facilities and pitches, ensuring adequate medical support for teams, officials and spectators, doping control, and management of the refereeing team.

We are looking for volunteers with the skills to accompany teams from their hotels to the stadiums, and to support the managers responsible for referees and medical units in a broad range of activities.

Accommodation and tourism

The central task of the accommodation and tourism department is to prepare and maintain the ground for a visible, meaningful and realistic interpretation of the slogan 'A time to make friends™'. The OC 2006 FIFA World Cup has appointed '2006 FIFA World Cup™ Accommodation Services' to manage all matters relating to accommodation at the 2006 FIFA World Cup™. 'Accommodation Services' is responsible for ensuring a plentiful supply of appropriate, carefully targeted accommodation at fair prices for all visitor categories.

Volunteers will work as personal points of contact stationed in FIFA and OC 2006 FIFA World Cup hotels, and squad and team delegation headquarters, responsible for all organizational matters which may arise between the arrival and departure of the respective groups. Successfully breathing life into the slogan 'A time to make friends™' will require excellent interpersonal skills and expertise in hospitality.

Volunteer management

All activities relating to work carried out by volunteers during the 2006 FIFA World Cup™ will be co-ordinated and executed within the volunteer programme. Implementing the volunteer training sessions ahead of the tournaments, providing uniforms and leisure facilities for volunteers at Volunteer Centres during the tournament must themselves be planned and co-ordinated.

The primary task of volunteers for this department is to cater for the total of approximately 1000 volunteers at each location and support the volunteer manager in a smooth and efficient operation of the Volunteer Centre.

Volunteers for this section will be deployed at the stadiums or in the Volunteer Centres, which will open every day during the tournament.

(Reproduced with permission of 2006 FIFA World Cup™; for further information see http://fifaworldcup.yahoo.com/06/en/o/volunteers/vaap1.html#1)

Chapter summary and key points

This chapter has looked at the process of job analysis, the outcomes of which are the job descriptions and person specifications for paid and volunteer roles for an event. This process needs to be systematic but flexible since an event project generally evolves over time, with new priorities and even perhaps a new artistic direction. While the human resource department or event manager needs to oversee the process of job analysis, it is usually the direct manager (functional or zone manager) who develops the detail for each of the job descriptions. The Sydney 2000 Olympic Games plan resulted in 3500 job descriptions; however, smaller events would produce just a few. Job descriptions contribute in many ways to the next operational phases of recruitment, selection, training and performance management, which are covered in the following chapters.

Revision questions

1 What is job analysis?
2 What is a job description?
3 Explain the four parts of a job description using an example.
4 What is a person/job specification?
5 Discuss the statement 'job analysis is a waste of time if event plans are constantly changing'.
6 Explain why it is important to differentiate between paid, volunteer and contractor working conditions.

References

Brannick, M. and Levine, E. (2002). *Job Analysis*. Sage Publications.

Maund, L. (2001). *An Introduction to Human Resource Management*. Palgrave.

McCray, G., Purvis, R. and McCray, C. (2002). Project management under uncertainty: the impact of heuristics and biases. *Project Management Journal*, **33(1)**, 49–57.

Plekhanova, V. (1998). On project management scheduling where human resource is a critical variable. In *6th European Workshop on Software Process Technology*. Springer-Verlag.

Sanchez, J. and Levine, E. (2000). Accuracy or consequential validity: which is the better standard for job analysis data?. *Journal of Organizational Behaviour*, **21**, 809–18.

Part Two
Human resource operations: building the team

Part Two of this book looks at the operational elements of the human resources plan. For practitioners working on smaller events this is the part where things get done! Here we look at recruitment and selection, finding and choosing the right people, and then the major task of training is covered as three distinct components.

In this section we will also look at workforce logistics: feeding and clothing people, getting enough of them there on time, providing essential staff services and registering attendance. The later chapters in Part Two will cover two key elements of the human resources plan, leadership and motivation, the aim of which is to inspire and retain staff – even when the going gets tough. And last but not least we'll look at recognition and reward, which is an essential part of any volunteer programme.

Unfortunately, we can't have a party at the end of the book but that is often how the human resources operational plan folds up! Hugs and tears, plans for staff to stay in touch, a fine rosy glow, are the anticipated outcomes of every event, despite any crises and hardships that might occur along the way.

Chapter 8
Recruitment and selection

Learning objectives

After reading through this chapter you will be able to:

■ Define human resource needs
■ Source applicants
■ Select staff and volunteers
■ Maintain records of recruitment and selection
■ Ensure compliance with relevant legislation.

Introduction

This chapter will cover the processes of recruiting and selecting paid staff and volunteers, which is often fraught with difficulty. Some events are so popular that everyone wants to work there. For example, many thousands of people want to be on the field of play during an opening ceremony. During the Sydney 2000 Olympic Games there was one individual who called the organizing committee every day for over 1000 days to speak to anyone who would listen to him about his desire to be in this opening ceremony! For other event organizations it is quite the opposite: it is a real struggle to attract enough volunteers to sustain the event, particularly if it is a fundraiser.

Employing full-time temporary staff is another challenge, simply because the work is temporary. While event work has its intrinsic attraction, the event organization seldom offers permanency or a career path as would most traditional organizations. A convention centre is clearly able to sustain a group of permanent people at management level, but at the service end the staff cohort is almost always casual. Attracting volunteers to a rock concert is the easiest task in the world; it generally takes only one phone call and word spreads instantly. To advertise for volunteers would be insane, as the phones would ring around the clock for days.

Thus, an understanding of labour market forces, people's motivation and their interest level can assist a great deal when deciding how to approach recruitment.

Definitions of recruitment and selection

The terms recruitment and selection are often assumed to mean the same thing when in fact they do not. *Recruitment is the process of attracting potential candidates to the organization.* A successful recruitment campaign attracts a pool of candidates that is just large enough to handle. A campaign that is too successful is a disaster as each individual needs to be considered against the selection criteria. For example, a local council advertised an events manager's position and attracted 1000 applicants. Unfortunately, they were not specific about their requirements in terms of knowledge, skills and experience, and other pertinent criteria were missing. Therefore, they had to work through all the applications, some from people who had experience arranging school fetes and charity balls and others from council employees who had worked on the approvals process and had qualifications in this area only.

It is therefore essential to establish the appropriate criteria before advertising. How demanding the advertised requirements should be is a question of judgement; if too demanding it could result in too small a pool of applicants.

Selection is the process of choosing the most suitable candidates. It is here that equal employment opportunity (EEO) comes into full effect. The criteria by which candidates are chosen must be directly related to the position in question. A person must be offered the position on merit. The person specification is the document that supports the selection decisions.

Selection of volunteers is very difficult when jobs are fairly generic and there aren't many specific criteria, particularly if the interest level is high. If this is the case, the criteria should be expanded to include communications and customer service skills, experience in similar roles, knowledge of the city and region etc. All of these would support a spectator services role in an event environment. However, a volunteer cannot be discriminated against if they do not live in the area in which the event is held. As with all job requirements, the volunteer (or paid employee) must make his or her own decisions about transportation and accommodation.

Managing expectations is essential. If the job is routine, requires moving equipment or is away from the action, this needs to be explained beforehand. Some people will then remove themselves from the selection process because the position does not meet their expectations.

Defining human resource needs

The previous chapter on job analysis described the development of the master human resources plan, involving consideration of the number and type of people to be appointed and their start dates. In the event environment this is determined not only by need but also by the budget. It is not uncommon for appointments to be delayed until the last possible minute (or beyond it) in order to stay within budget. The commencement of recruitment thus needs to be approved by the responsible manager. This person will decide whether each position is necessary and whether it is in line with earlier planning. Specific requirements will be identified and the recruitment method and advertisements will be approved.

Issuing uniforms to volunteers

The process of recruitment and selection is illustrated in Figure 8.1. As this shows, once candidates have been sourced, they are selected against the criteria established in the person specification in a competitive process which identifies the best person or people for the job. Interviews are conducted, often by human resources personnel, and then by the direct supervisor. For very senior critical roles, such as artistic director, there is often a panel interview. Following this, references are checked and, for some events, a police check is done for accreditation purposes. Finally, the successful candidate is sent an offer letter which spells out the terms and conditions of their employment. It is also essential that unsuccessful candidates are advised in a timely manner.

In their study Arcodia and Axelson (2005) found that the top five skills mentioned in Australian advertisements for events managers were organizational/planning skills; general communication skills; team skills; customer service skills; and computer skills. These were closely followed by skill in building internal and external relationships. The top five attribute categories emerging from the study were motivated, flexible, positive, friendly, and committed/dedicated. One of the most interesting features of this study was the cataloguing of 355 job titles related to event management out of an analysis of 1002 job advertisements, some of which did not initially appear to have an association with event management.

Sourcing candidates

There are many ways in which people can be invited to apply for jobs, although success rates and costs differ markedly.

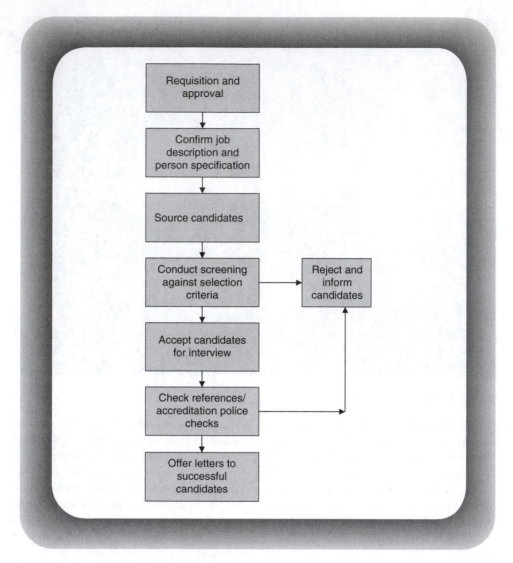

Figure 8.1 Recruitment and selection process

Referral by other employees

The most popular and cost-effective method of recruitment is to invite employees to make referrals (see Case study 8.1). It appears that their judgement of who might be a good prospective employee and their explanation of the duties involved in the position lead to realistic expectations and higher than average success rates. In some cases, there are incentives associated with this practice.

This is a core component of the recruitment practice of Cleanevent, a fast-growing international cleaning and waste management company which has been operating for seventeen years, employs over 10 000 people in permanent and casual positions, and has provided cleaning services for four Olympic Games, Wimbledon, the US Open and Formula One, to name just a few. Their human resources profile is exemplary and their website well worth visiting.

Case study 8.1

Referral as a source of applicants

Human resource managers from 70 area companies favour employee referrals to any other method when recruiting new workers, according to a recently released survey by the Southern Connecticut Chapter of the Society for Human Resource Management (SOCT SHRM). Nearly 70 per cent of respondents said they prefer their employees to refer new hires, while about 50 per cent said they also like to use regional-based websites, such as fairfieldcountyjobs.com, westchestercountyjobs.com and fairfieldcountyhelpwanted.com, to recruit workers. A close third in preference, with just fewer than 50 per cent, was national employment websites, such as monster.com, hotjobs.com and careerbuilder.com, followed by newspaper advertising a distant fourth, with about 22 per cent of HR managers using this method.

Perhaps the biggest surprise, however, was that employment agencies did not even receive 20 per cent support among managers, but David Lewis, vice president of SOCT SHRM, who conducted the survey with fellow vice president Will Brewer, said that agencies suffer partly from the current economic climate.

'The times we're in are directly reflected in this survey,' Lewis says. 'If this were 1999, when the job market was extremely tight, the results might be different. Back then, agencies were vital for finding good new hires. Nowadays, there are lots of potential employees out there.

'In addition, companies have been slashing HR budgets for the past few years so the managers of these departments are searching for less expensive ways to attract talent,' Lewis added. Using employment agencies can cost a firm thousands of dollars, but companies often pay between US$500 and US$2000 to employees for solid referrals that stay for six months or more, and the company still saves money.

(The Westchester County Business Journal, **44(43)**, 24 October 2005. Reproduced with permission.)

Reflective practice 8.1
1 Why do companies prefer referrals to other recruitment methods?
2 What job market conditions would lead to a swing to other methods?

Internet advertising on event or organization's website

Almost every major event advertises positions on their own website to encourage direct applications. Such sites are generally popular with consumers and cover all aspects of the event, including the programme and the organization. Events such as the Edinburgh Festival, Toronto Film Festival, Rio Carnivale and the Volvo Ocean Yacht Race are all examples of events that would attract potential candidates by virtue of their reputation. Conversely, recruitment is much more of a challenge for the smaller event for which it may be necessary to look for staff and volunteers among the local community.

Employment agencies and recruitment consultants

As the boxed article illustrates, employment agencies are seldom used but for the most difficult positions. However, there is an exception. Many world-class events appoint an employment agency as a service provider and sometimes sponsor, enabling them to meet staffing needs across a range of areas. For example, Adecco recruited and trained 20 000 volunteers for the 2006 Torino Winter Olympics following their success at the Hanover EXPO, Manchester Commonwealth Games and Sydney 2000 Olympic Games.

Newspaper advertising

Newspaper advertising remains one of the most common approaches to recruiting for mid-level and specialist positions such as conference organizers, production assistants, stage managers and sound technicians. By choosing the newspaper carefully, it is possible to limit the scope of applicants to the local area, or extend it to cover the whole nation.

Listing on job search engines

There are many different job search websites including seek.com and mycareer.com. Placement on this type of website is cost effective and easy to organize. The sites often provide a template for the candidate to enter key information, making it easier to find relevant data. Others provide the applicant with the opportunity to attach letters and résumés to the application. These websites are categorized as monster job boards or niche job boards. The latter is a board maintained by an event industry association, which is a much more targeted approach than placement on a monster job board.

Figure 8.2 provides an example of a website advertisement.

Associations and clubs

Volunteer associations are a first rate source of people and advice. Many sporting and music events are supported by associations and clubs, which play a vital role in their planning and organization. Qualified umpires and officials are essential for sporting events and they can be co-opted from such clubs. Networking with clubs and associations is the best and quickest way to find specialists in fields such as basketball, golf, blues music, etc.

Colleges and universities

These institutions are an exceptionally good source of volunteers and interns. If the event organization works closely with a university, the relationship can reap benefits for all parties. For example, BA (Hons) Event Management students within

---

Logistics & Operations Manager

Events & Logistics Management

Brilliant career opportunity

Prestigious sporting icon

Outstanding career opportunity to join the functions and events division of a well-known sporting institution. Reporting to the Food & Beverage Operations Manager, you will be responsible for the daily planning, purchasing, inventory control and distribution of food and beverage operations within this dynamic organization.

Click here to apply ⇨

Figure 8.2 Example of a website advertisement

the Tourism, Hospitality and Events (THE) School at Leeds Metropolitan University has a placement year in industry (Williamson, 2005). With this length of internship, there is no doubt that the intern is well placed to make a valuable contribution, applying knowledge gained in the lecture room. In Australia, colleges of technical and further education (TAFEs) are a common starting point for event recruitment drives.

Advertising positions

When developing an advertisement, whether it is to be used in a newspaper or on a college notice board, the purpose is the same: to attract the best candidates and reject those who are unsuitable. This requires a fine balance between selling the position in the most positive light and being quite clear about requirements and expectations. In the advertisement in Figure 8.3, there are two parts: one explains and sells the job in a positive light and the other states the selection criteria. If these are stated clearly, the individual can self-select by deciding whether or not they meet the minimum criteria.

When advertising in a newspaper, the placement of the advertisement is important. Some pages and places (e.g. the right-hand side) are better than others for visibility. The price per column centimetre will reflect this. In countries such as Australia hospitality positions are advertised in a separate section to the general classified job

---

Event Sponsorship Co-ordinator

We are a government agency with a brief to deliver high-profile events in the harbour area. We are looking for an exceptional person to drive our sponsorship programme, look after marketing and manage our ongoing relationships with business organizations. The position is challenging and requires someone with a strong track record in a competitive market.

Job details

- Deliver new sponsorship deals for our events
- Maintain and effectively manage current sponsor arrangements
- Manage marketing initiatives for current and new events
- Negotiate with other government agencies where required
- Manage and develop business and industry contacts

Selection criteria

- Previous demonstrated experience in sponsorship development and management in Arts and Entertainment
- Previous experience in negotiating and managing contractual relationships with key clients
- Project management skills, ability to meet tight deadlines
- Established relationships with key players in government and business
- Degree qualifications in Marketing, Business or Events Management
- Understanding of main legislative compliance issues for events

---

Figure 8.3 Example of a balanced advertisement

advertisements. This creates a dilemma when placing advertisements for event management positions, as many of them do not include any hospitality-related work. To play safe, some organizations place the advertisement in each of the two sections. Many event-specific websites include online magazines which also carry this type of advertisement (see www.specialevents.com.au).

Following are some tips for employment advertising:

1 Make sure that the main heading identifies the job.
2 Include the company name and contact details.
3 Explain and sell the paid or volunteer position.
4 Be clear about the selection criteria.
5 Describe the job context and conditions of employment.
6 Make sure that the wording meets EEO guidelines.

Using the Internet for recruitment

Michael Foster (2003) has written an excellent guide to recruiting on the Web. This is essential reading for anyone conducting a major recruitment drive using this method. Consistent with the earlier study which showed that 70 per cent of companies prefer to find new hires by employee referral, Foster suggests that positions should be widely advertised on the company intranet so that current employees are aware of vacant positions (and, of course, of any incentives for successful placement of their referred contacts).

When developing an online recruitment website, a facility for applicants to enter their data should be provided. This is absolutely essential for volunteers otherwise someone has to enter data for every written application.

Questions asked by the 2004 Athens Organizing Committee for the Olympic Games included:

• Name and contact details
• Educational background
• Occupation
• Field of studies (for students)
• Medical conditions (for consideration)
• Disability (in order to facilitate placement)
• Availability
• Languages (verbal and written).

The application then asks for experience and interests according to functional areas:

• Spectator services
• Security
• Doping control
• Venue staffing
• Transport
• Accreditation
• Village operations
• Press operations
• Technology
• Ticketing
• Venue management

- Medical services
- Sports (applicants could choose up to three sports, identifying their capacity: athlete, referee, instructor, club member).

For such positions the framework is quite rigid, giving the applicant little opportunity to go off track. For more senior positions, however, it is essential to allow for more free text or for submission of a résumé. The résumés are then stored in a digital database. From here they can be retrieved by using key search words. Text strings such as 'risk management', 'staging', 'Microsoft Project', 'conference planning' and 'crowd management' can be used to find applicants on the database. An automatic note of thanks should be generated for every application or résumé submission. The organization needs to think about the public relations role played out during a recruitment campaign. The biggest campaigns, generally both media and Internet based, generate a significant amount of interest in the event, which may also result in ticket sales. The profile of the organization, and the goodwill it generates, is a significant consideration in human resource planning and operations.

To drive traffic to jobs, the job centre webpage must be listed with key search engines such as Google and Yahoo! It needs to be registered separately from the main event website if you want to ensure that searches will lead applicants to your site. The design of the site is vitally important. As Foster (2003) suggests, keeping people engaged with interactive features is a good idea: 'the more they click, the more they stick'. This way people hang around the site for longer and their interests can be monitored by following the clicks, giving the web designer and the recruiter some insight into the profiles and interests of site visitors.

Figure 8.4 shows the total volunteer applications via the Internet and paper received by the Manchester Commonwealth Games from the launch of its recruitment programme in May 2001 to the end of the programme in August 2002. Figure 8.5 includes a good example of a volunteer application form.

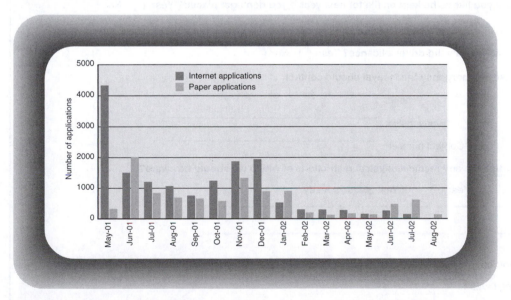

Figure 8.4 Total volunteer applications (paper v. Internet) by month for the Manchester Commonwealth Games
(Manchester City Council (2003), Manchester Commonwealth Games Post Games Report; for further information see www.gameslegacy.com)

Canmore Folk Music Festival
Volunteer Application Form

2005 Festival: July 30–August 1

*= Required Field

1. *Last name [＿＿＿＿] *First name [＿＿＿＿]

2. **Contact Information:**

    *Home phone: [＿＿＿＿] Cell phone: [＿＿＿＿]

    Business phone: [＿＿＿＿] Fax number: [＿＿＿＿]

3. **Email:** [＿＿＿＿]

4. *Address:

    Street [＿＿＿＿]

    City [＿＿＿＿]

    Province [＿＿＿＿] Postal code [＿＿＿＿]

5. **Have you volunteered for the festival before? Yes:** ○ **No:** ○

    If Yes, in which area? [＿＿＿＿]

    Who was your co-ordinator? [＿＿＿＿]

    What year(s)? [＿＿＿＿]

6. **Would you like to be kept on file for next year if you don't get placed? Yes:** ○ **No:** ○

    (*Note*: You must be available from Saturday to Monday of the festival in order to be placed as a volunteer)

7. **Do you have a valid driver's licence? Yes:** ○ **No:** ○

8. **In case of emergency the festival should contact:**

    *Name: [＿＿＿＿]

    *Relationship: [＿＿＿＿]

    *Contact number: [＿＿＿＿]

9. **Do you have any medical/physical restrictions of which we should be aware?**

    No: ○ **Yes:** ○ **If Yes, please specify**

    [＿＿＿＿]

    [＿＿＿＿]

10. **Do you have a valid first aid certificate? Yes:** ○ **No:** ○

    If Yes, level [＿＿＿＿]

Figure 8.5 Example of a volunteer application form
(www.canmorefolkfestival.com/volunteerform.html)

11. *Volunteer area: the following is a list of areas in which volunteers are needed. Please *indicate* your top 4 preferences in order of choice (1, 2, 3 and 4) *(Preference will be given to returning volunteers)*

   Note: The positions most needed by the festival are indicated with**.

**Children's area ☐	Floater ☐	**Site set-up/breakdown ☐
**Environment (recycling/park) ☐	Hospitality ☐	Transportation (requires class 4 licence) ☐
**Gate ☐	Parking ☐	Co-ordinator/ Co-ordinator Assistant ☐
Information booth ☐	**Security ☐	

12. *Age: (Select one)

   Under 16 ☐   16–17 ☐   18–24 ☐   25–60 ☐   Over 60 ☐

   Guardian contact information (req'd only for *Under 16*)

   APPLICANT'S AGE (if under 16): ☐

   GUARDIAN'S NAME: [   ]

   GUARDIAN'S PHONE: [   ]

13. *T-shirt size (Select one)

   Small ☐   **Medium** ☐   **Large** ☐   **X-Large** ☐   **XX-Large** ☐

14. *Volunteer Agreement: If accepted as a volunteer, I will adhere to the <u>volunteer code of ethics</u> and fulfil my responsibilities. I understand that if this is my first year volunteering, I may not be assigned my stated area(s) preference. I understand that I am committing myself to a minimum of eight hours festival volunteer work.

   I Agree ☐

   [   ]

   Print out the form[1] and mail to:
   Canmore Folk Music Festival
   Volunteer Co-ordinator
   PO Box 8098
   Canmore AB
   T1W 2T8

   [1]**Note**: *Please adjust your browser margins first (File -> Page Setup), and font size if necessary*, to ensure all questions fit on the page before sending to print. Include additional comments on separate page.

   Last Modified: 14 March 2005

Figure 8.5   *(Continued)*

Preparing for the interview

Once a number of applications have been received, they need to be sorted to see which meet the selection criteria. Candidates who are rejected should be advised immediately; those who make it to the next selection phase are usually interviewed.

Although there has been much debate about the validity of interviews for selection (De Cieri, 2003), they continue to be the mainstay of most human resource processes. One of the ways in which the validity of the interview can be improved is by asking all applicants the same carefully prepared questions. These questions should emerge from the job description and person specification. They should be 'behavioural' questions that reflect the person's past experience and not hypothetical questions about what they might do in the future. If we use the event sponsorship co-ordinator's position in Figure 8.3, the questions prepared for the interview could include:

Previous demonstrated experience in sponsorship development

Q: Describe the approach you took to securing sponsorship in your previous position

Previous experience in negotiating and managing contractual relationships with key clients

Q: Explain some of the problems and pitfalls you have experienced in managing contractual relationships with key clients.

Project management skills, ability to meet tight deadlines

Q: Describe a project you have managed where the critical path has been impacted by something unforeseen.

Established relationships with key players in government and business

Q: How have your relationships with government impacted on your role?

Degree qualifications in Marketing, Business or Events Management

Q: Why do you think your qualification is helpful in meeting the challenges of this position?

Understanding of main legislative compliance issues for events

Q: Can you identify legislation that impacts on arrangements with sponsors?

Conducting the interview

There are two main parts to the interview: explaining the job to the applicant and seeking information about how they meet the selection criteria. Most human resource professionals ask the questions first and explain the job later as this gives the person time to relax and absorb the information. By this time, the interviewer also has a fairly good idea of the person's likely success and can gauge how much time to spend in explanation. In some cases, of course, the interview turns into a sales pitch if the applicant is clearly outstanding and would be a potential asset to the organization.

In Case study 8.2, many of the keys to success and pitfalls of interviewing are discussed.

Case study 8.2

Interview for success and to avoid legal pitfalls

We all know how litigious our society has become in the area of employment-related issues. Every recruiter, hiring manager, executive and department manager must realize that asking the wrong questions or making improper inquiries can lead to discrimination or wrongful-discharge lawsuits, and these suits can be won or lost based on statements made during the interview process. Thus, it is important to incorporate risk management into your interviewing process to help minimize your firm's exposure to employment practices liability.

You, or your company, could be accused of asking improper questions or making discriminatory statements or comments that reflect bias. It is also possible to make assurances or promises during interviews that can be interpreted as binding contracts. Recognizing these potential danger areas is the best way to avoid saying the wrong thing during interviews.

To minimize the risk of discrimination lawsuits, it's important for interviewers to be familiar with topics that aren't permissible for questioning. For example, you shouldn't ask a female applicant detailed questions about her husband, children and family plans. Such questions can be used as proof of sex discrimination if a male applicant is selected for the position, or if the female is hired and later terminated. Older applicants shouldn't be asked about their ability to take instructions from younger supervisors.

It is also important to avoid making statements during the interview process that could be alleged to create a contract of employment. When describing the job avoid using terms like 'permanent', 'career job opportunity' or 'long term'.

Interviewers should also avoid making excessive assurances about job security. Avoid statements that employment will continue as long as the employee does a good job. For example, suppose that an applicant is told 'if you do a good job, there's no reason why you can't work here for the rest of your career.' The applicant accepts the job and six months later is laid off due to personnel cutbacks. This could lead to a breach of contract claim where the employee asserts that he or she can't be terminated unless it's proven that he or she didn't do a 'good job'. Courts have on occasion held that such promises made during interviews created contracts of employment.

Most companies have at least two people responsible for interviewing and hiring applicants. It's critical to have procedures to ensure consistency. Develop interviewing forms containing objective criteria to serve as checklists. They ensure consistency between interviewers, as well as create documentation to support the decision if a discrimination charge is later filed by an unsuccessful applicant.

Learn to assess job candidates on their merits. When developing evaluation criteria, break down broad subjective impressions to more objective factors.

(www.hireability.com/employers/articles/interview_for_success.html)

Reflective practice 8.2

1 This article provides some guidelines on questions that should not be asked in the employment interview (the same principles apply to volunteer recruitment). Explain why each of these questions is inappropriate.
2 Give three examples of behavioural interview questions more specifically related to event industry requirements.

Testing and evaluating candidates

There are many different types of tests that are used to test psychological attributes and general intelligence, as well as tests for specific skills such as word processing.

Psychological tests, despite their popularity, remain questionable in terms of validity and reliability, and there is much ongoing debate on this topic (Aiken, 2000; Cook and Cripps, 2005). Where used, the tests should be carried out by professionals qualified to conduct assessment and interpret results. It is typically an employment agency that performs this role. The test needs to be reliable, delivering consistent results over time, and valid in that it measures what it sets out to measure (construct validity). Finally, the results should have validity by predicting how well the individual will perform on the job (predictive validity).

References are another part of the selection process. While many employers are not prepared to make evaluative remarks due to legal and ethical problems, there is every reason why an employer should check the accuracy of the information provided in the candidate's résumé. According to the Society for Human Resource Management (2004):

- About 40 per cent of HR professionals report increasing the amount of time spent checking references for potential employees over the past three years.
- Of all organizations, 96 per cent conduct some kind of background or reference check on prospective hires.
- Almost 50 per cent of survey respondents reported that reference checks found inconsistencies in dates of previous employment, criminal records, former job titles and past salaries.

Maintaining records

It is essential to be aware that a selection decision may be challenged. For this reason, documentation should be maintained throughout the process of selection. This could include, for example, a rating scale when evaluating written applications and another when evaluating interview performance. Reference and background checks should also be fully documented. Employment on merit is the expectation and this can be justified long after the process if this has been done methodically. Comments made about applicants should not breach EEO guidelines.

Everyone who has been through a selection process knows how stressful it is. Since this is potentially the first stage of the person's psychological contract with the organization, first impressions count. An upbeat, positive and informative approach is essential.

Breaugh and Starke (2000) have done extensive reviews of recruitment research and have come up with the following conclusions:

> *Although one can view the existing recruitment literature as a hodgepodge of inconsistent results, we feel there are certain themes that emerge. For example, research on recruiters makes apparent the critical role these individuals can play both in terms of being informative and in terms of treating applicants in a personable fashion. These themes of informativeness and personable treatment also permeate other areas of*

recruitment research, such as research on the site visit and the timing of recruitment actions. The importance of providing realistic job information (e.g. via employee referrals or realistic job previews) has also been an important research theme in the recruitment literature. Another theme that emerged in our review of the literature is the importance of 'signals' that employers may unintentionally be sending to job applicants. For example, Rynes et al. (1991) showed that applicants used information with regard to recruiter friendliness and informativeness as an indicator of how a firm treated an employee (p. 27).

Case study 8.3

Edinburgh International Book Festival 2006

Job Description: Press Officer

Contract
Full-time temporary 30 May – 1 September 2006

Key dates
The 2006 Edinburgh International Festival runs 12–28 August.
The 2006 launch is on 15 June. Ticket sales open on 16 June.

Background
The Edinburgh International Book Festival began in 1983 and is now a key event in the August Festival season, celebrated annually in Scotland's capital city. Biennial at first, the Book Festival became a yearly celebration in 1997.

Throughout its 22-year history, the Book Festival has grown rapidly in size and scope to become the largest and most dynamic festival of its kind in the world. In its first year the Book Festival played host to just 30 'Meet the Author' events. Today, the Festival programmes over 600 events, which are enjoyed by people of all ages.

In 2001 Catherine Lockerbie, the Book Festival's fifth director, took the Festival to a new level by developing a high-profile debates and discussions series that is now one of the festival's hallmarks. Each year writers from all over the world gather to become part of this unique forum in which audience and author meet to exchange thoughts and opinions on some of the world's most pressing issues.

Running alongside the general programme is the highly acclaimed Children's Programme, which has grown to become a leading showcase for children's writers and illustrators. Incorporating workshops, storytelling, panel discussions, author events and book signings, the Children's Programme is popular with both the public and schools alike and now ranks as the world's premier books and reading event for young people.

The Book Festival receives just 18 per cent of its income from public funds (Scottish Arts Council, City of Edinburgh Council). An unusually high proportion of over 80 per cent of income is self-generated, raised from ticket sales, book sales and sponsorship. The Festival runs a unique independent book-selling operation, now a trading subsidiary, which has become increasingly important in the generation of revenue.

The Edinburgh International Book Festival is a VAT registered company limited by guarantee and has charitable status.

Press team
The Edinburgh International Book Festival Press Office comprises a Press Manager, a Press Officer and a Press and Marketing Assistant. The press team is very busy, working

long days and, during the festival itself, working a seven-day week. The press team will work at the Book Festival's offices in Charlotte Square in the lead-up to the festival, and on site in the Press Pod in Charlotte Square Gardens during the festival.

The Press Officer reports to the Press Manager and is responsible for:

1 being one of the main points of contact for all media enquiries in the lead-up to, and during, the Book Festival
2 proactively selling the Book Festival to targeted media sectors (including online channels) and regions and responding to all media enquiries
3 developing and nurturing strong two-way communication with these contacts to secure coverage/visits to the Book Festival in 2006 and future years
4 identifying and pitching strong news lines and clear feature angles (either generic or author-based). This will require a good working knowledge of the 2006 programme and the authors attending
5 maintaining an up-to-date database of journalists and publications
6 managing the media accreditation system and ticketing procedure
7 organizing the Book Festival press launch with the Press Manager and Marketing and PR Manager
8 liaising effectively with authors and authors' publicists as necessary
9 setting up, manning and helping to oversee the effective operation of the Press Pod – the service point for all media on site at the Book Festival
10 organizing photocalls and interview schedules in conjunction with the Press Manager and effectively supervising freelance and contracted photographers on site
11 overseeing television and broadcast crews on site
12 monitoring and archiving all coverage and chasing any outstanding copies of broadcast/print coverage for files
13 assisting the Joint Festivals Travel and Tourism Press Officer to maximize positive coverage in the travel media
14 regularly and proactively feeding Book Festival news to the Joint Festivals Web Content Coordinator and writing news stories and updates for the Book Festival website
15 along with all other staff, assisting with the clear-up of the Book Festival site and Press Pod – this will involve some moderate lifting and carrying
16 assisting the Press Manager prepare a debrief report evaluating the press operation during 2006 and making recommendations for 2007.

Person specification
The successful candidate will possess the following:

- Ideally, three years experience in an event-based PR role
- Excellent communication and organizational skills
- An enthusiastic personality with a flexible can-do attitude
- The ability to manage and report on projects and work under pressure to meet deadlines
- The ability to work effectively as part of a small team.

We are committed to making the Book Festival as accessible as possible to customers, participants and staff. If you have any specific access requirements or concerns, please let us know and we will do our best to meet your needs.

(Reproduced with permission of Edinburgh International Book Festival; for further information see www.edbookfest.co.uk)

Reflective practice 8.3

1 Discuss the best placement for this advertisement (e.g. newspapers, festival website, industry magazines). Which do you think would be most effective?
2 Develop a range of behavioural interview questions to match the position advertised. Which of these would you ask first?
3 Do you think educational qualifications would be relevant to this position?

Chapter summary and key points

This chapter has looked at two distinct processes, recruitment and selection. Recruitment attracts applicants to the organization, while selection is the process whereby the best of these is chosen and offered the jobs. Equal employment opportunity (EEO) needs to be applied at every step to ensure that only job-relevant selection criteria are used.

Recruitment for an event organization is often a public relations exercise too, as it raises awareness and impacts on the profile of the event. For these reasons, the recruitment process needs to be managed particularly well to prevent the oversubscribing of paid and volunteer positions. Smaller events have the opposite problem, and their approach has to be more targeted. By approaching clubs, associations, schools and colleges, many of these event planners find people they need who are well matched to the event type (sports, arts, community, etc.).

The validity of job interviews can be improved using behavioural interviewing techniques and asking the same questions of every candidate. Once the selection decision has been made and references checked, the person should be offered the position in writing.

Revision questions

1 Define recruitment.
2 Define selection.
3 Using a diagram, illustrate the staffing process.
4 List and describe the attributes of three primary sources of event employees.
5 List and describe the attributes of three primary sources of event volunteers.
6 Provide some simple guidelines for employment advertising.
7 Develop a job description and person specification for a volunteer working at an event information kiosk.
8 Using the above documents, prepare some questions for the volunteer interviews.

References

Aiken, L. R. (2000). *Psychological Testing and Assessment*, 10th edn. Allyn and Bacon.

Arcodia, C. and Axelson, M. (2005). A review of event management job advertisements in Australian newspapers. In *The Impacts of Events*. University of Technology, Sydney.

Branch, A. (2005). Do you know someone ...?, *The Westchester County Business Journal*, **44(33)**.

Breaugh, J. and Starke, M. (2000). Research on employee recruitment: so many studies, so many remaining questions. *Journal of Management*, **26(3)**, 405–34.

Cook, M. and Cripps, B. (2005). *Psychological Assessment in the Workplace: A Manager's Guide*. Wiley.

De Cieri, H. (2003). *Human Resource Management in Australia: Strategy, People, Performance*. McGraw-Hill.

Foster, M. (2003). *Recruiting on the Web*. McGraw-Hill.

Rynes, S., Bretz, R. and Gerhart, B. (1991). The importance of recruitment in job choice: a different way of looking. *Personnel Psychology*, **44**, 487–521.

Society for Human Resource Management (2004). *Reference and background checking survey report*. Denver.

Williamson, P. (2005). Event management students' reflections on their placement year: an examination of their critical experiences. In J. Allen (ed.), *International Event Research Conference 2005*. University of Technology, Sydney.

Chapter 9
Workforce training

Learning objectives

After reading through this chapter you will be able to:

■ Differentiate between the different types of training typically offered at major and mega events
■ Discuss the budget implications of volunteer training
■ Explain how to go about conducting a training needs analysis
■ Explain how the responsibility for training is split between functional areas
■ Identify key steps in designing Web-based training
■ Discuss whether leadership training is important in the event environment and how this might differ from the traditional business environment.

Introduction

Training an event workforce is quite a challenge. Work for the core management team starts months or even years before the event and so many different types of training may be necessary, the most common being project management, risk analysis and legislative awareness. The core planning team tends to be made up of a very diverse group, everyone coming from different backgrounds and industries. To make life even more complicated, there are rolling starts, with people coming on board right through to the event operational period. How much simpler it would be if the planning team were all to start at once!

The second lot of people requiring training comes on board just for the event itself, most starting work on day one just before the doors open. This group includes most volunteers, contract workers and a few casual paid staff. For a large event, this group would participate in one or more training sessions in the days or weeks before the event to give them a general overview of the event and information on the venue. Importantly, emergency and incident planning would usually be covered at this time.

Job-specific training can seldom be done before the venues have been hired and transformed in readiness for the event. For most events the build happens only the day before the event. Workers start several hours before the event audience arrives and training usually occurs on the job, just before the gates or doors open. Problems are then ironed out along the way. This situation dictates a higher than usual focus on pre-planning tasks and control measures before the event commences, as from that time on controlled chaos usually reigns. However, most problems are generally solved through a combination of common sense, commitment and goodwill, particularly if these values have been instilled prior to the event.

The training needs analysis

A training needs analysis is the basis for the training plan. It covers the training needs of both managers and the general workforce. The questions asked should include the following:

- What is the context for training?
- What are the profiles of the candidates undertaking training?
- How many people need to be trained?
- When and where do these people need to be trained?
- How could technology support the training?
- Who will be responsible for the various types of training?
- What approach should be taken (e.g. lecture, seminar, simulation) to each of these?
- Should training be outsourced to a contractor?
- What is the role of the trainer?
- Is assessment necessary?
- How will training be documented?
- What will it cost?
- Which aspects of training present the highest risk?
- How will the training be evaluated?

The training needs analysis can take many forms, from an informal approach where all functional and venue areas are responsible for their own training to a more formal approach where training needs are analysed across the organization. In this latter case, core training can be identified and delivery integrated across the board wherever possible.

Where a formal approach is taken, this can be done by document analysis, research into previous events and approaches to training, individual interviews, observation and focus groups. A pilot programme is recommended for feedback and fine tuning wherever possible, particularly for customer service training.

Prior to the Sydney 2000 Olympic Games there were two dilemmas (among many others): how to record attendance at large-scale orientation and venue training sessions where numbers in the audience ranged from 200 to 2000; and whether or not to provide refreshments. As trivial as these questions may seem, there were budget and logistical implications for both. A cup of tea and a biscuit for each volunteer attending training would cost in the region of $50 000, while attendance records would require manual registration and subsequent data entry or a more sophisticated barcode/identification card system. This seemed unnecessary as each person would receive an accreditation badge closer to the event, but this system was not yet operational.

Management training

The management team usually needs training to ensure that everyone is on the same wavelength. Training can be formal or informal, and run internally or outsourced to expert facilitators. Given the expertise of the management group, training has to be well delivered by someone experienced in adult learning and the event context. Because of the pressures of time faced by people in this role, a training room can be emptied after the coffee break if the learning is not relevant and meaningful to the group!

The following topics are indicative of material covered during induction training and later on during the planning period as needs emerge:

- History and purpose of the event, strategic plan
- Project management principles and techniques, including software
- Risk management for all aspects of the operation, including safety
- Legislative awareness, compliance issues
- Roles of stakeholders such as police, traffic authority, sponsors, etc.
- Cultural and disability awareness
- Recruitment and selection, including EEO
- Supervision/leadership (more on this later in the chapter)
- Operational planning, systems and procedures
- Contract negotiation, contractor management
- Delivering training at the venue or on the job for large and small audiences
- Customer service management.

This training can be delivered in a variety of formats, ranging from online tutorials (e.g. software use) to short sessions conducted by experts or visiting speakers during lunch periods. Conventional classroom training would seldom take more than a day. Depending on the size of the event, some of the above topics could be merged into one or more sessions.

Case study 9.1 illuminates the variety of skills gained by well-trained, committed volunteers.

Case study 9.1

European Sport and Youth Forum

Volunteering and active citizenship

We believe that volunteering in youth and sport plays an important role in developing the leaders of tomorrow. Participation in volunteering teaches responsibility, leadership skills, tolerance and democratic values. Volunteering should be recognized as a tool for combating social problems by the positive use of young people's energy, requiring involvement and challenging them to be active citizens within the local and European Community. Taking into account the advantages of volunteering, we recommend the following measures:

- *Invite Sport and Youth NGOs to consult at inter-governmental meetings*
- *Establish a policy of youth presence at executive committees dealing with youth- and sport-related decisions*

- *Support and develop existing Sport and Youth related networks at European level*
- *Educate volunteers by:*
  - *Including life skills subjects in primary education*
  - *Enabling experts to deliver courses and workshops in other European countries to promote best practice in Youth and Sport volunteering across Europe*
- *Create a European-recognized Voluntary Log-Book – which can be used by volunteers when applying for further education and employment*
- *Provide greater financial support within the 'Youth in Action' programme to cover volunteer expenses.*

Volunteers represent a low level investment but will produce a big effect. Therefore, we hope the above recommendations might be easily undertaken. Volunteering means active citizenship and we would appreciate your help to activate other citizens.

(For more information see European Youth and Sport Forum at www.euractiv.com)

Reflective practice 9.1

Discuss the following statement: 'Volunteer training in sport is an investment in citizenship and leadership development.'

General workforce training

Most major events follow the same formula for workforce training delivery as is illustrated in the example of the Commonwealth Games in Case study 9.2 at the end of the chapter. For all of the following events there were three types of training for the general workforce – orientation training, venue training, and job-specific training:

- Sydney 2000 Olympic Games
- Manchester 2002 Commonwealth Games
- Salt Lake City Winter Olympic Games 2002
- Asian Games Doha 2006
- Torino Winter Olympic Games 2006
- Melbourne Commonwealth Games 2006.

While these can be merged for smaller events, it is nonetheless worthwhile to look at each separately.

Orientation training

This training is a general introduction to the event, its history, mission, purpose, planning and programme. For sporting events it covers all the different sports and the different venues at which they will take place. For music events, this session would explain the different bands and stages; for an agricultural show it would cover the competition and commercial zones. There is usually a general introduction to customer service, disability awareness and cultural awareness. More than this, however, most orientation training is highly motivational, and this is achieved through the use of celebrity speakers, national songs and dance, music and inspiring words from key members of the organizing committee.

The two main aims are that people leaving the session are informed and inspired. This is an interesting point, as the discussion later in the chapter on web-based training will illustrate, since much of this information could be delivered online. The question is whether this approach would meet the psychological needs of volunteers, in particular, to feel included, involved and inspired.

Following are examples of the topics that might be covered in orientation training:

- Event overview
- Event history
- Event aims
- Symbols
- Organization
- Sponsors
- Event programme
- Event venues
- Performers or athletes
- Previous shows/events
- Workforce roles
- What to expect
- Commitment and expectations
- Customer service.

Venue training

As the title suggests, this type of training usually takes place at the venue or zone area to familiarize people with their working environment (a treasure hunt is a good way to do this) and their teams. Functional areas, teams and reporting relationships are discussed during this training and work groups get the opportunity to meet each other. The most significant part covers safety and emergency training, which is often venue specific. In some cases, orientation training and venue training can be combined as they were with the 1996 Atlanta Olympic Games.

Following are some of the topics that might be covered in venue training sessions:

- The event precinct (general area of operations)
- The event venue (performance location)
- Locations within the venue (e.g. stairs, lifts, exits, communications control)
- Functional areas represented at the venue (e.g. medical, accreditation, security)
- Accreditation zones/areas (who can go where)
- Safety of staff and visitors
- Emergency procedures
- Incident reporting
- Crowd control
- Recycling and waste management
- Staff procedures, check-in, meals, etc.
- Communicating in the team
- Staff rules
- Common questions customers will ask
- Venue management team and their support.

Workflow planning and training are essential for catering teams who work at a frantic pace

Job-specific training

This is very specific training for the particular job that the person is going to do. For the majority of roles this takes only an hour or two. However, there are some positions that require many hours of training in the lead-up to the event. This can sometimes be short-circuited using video or web-based multimedia for core training (e.g. in the use of two-way radios). Job-specific training will be covered in detail in the next chapter.

The issue raised in many event evaluation reports (Sydney 2000 Paralympic Games Post Games Report, 2001; Strategic training issues for the 2006 Commonwealth Games, 2002; Manchester Commonwealth Games Post Games Report, 2003) is the sequence in which this training is delivered. The order suggested in Figure 9.1 is most logical from the event organizer's perspective as it follows the general project plan of moving from the general to the specific. The information required for orientation training is generally available some time out, while venue overlays are only finalized shortly before the event and specific planning for particular jobs is finalized very late in the process, with small details requiring input from other functional areas.

From the volunteer's perspective, on the other hand, what they most urgently want to know is where they will work, what they will do, what they will wear, when they will start and finish, whether meals will be hot or cold, whether particular dietary needs will be met, and so on. Details such as rosters, meal voucher systems and locker allocation are seldom available right from the start. Thus, as Figure 9.1

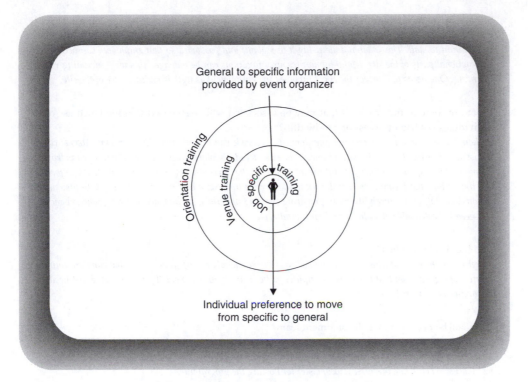

General to specific information provided by event organizer

Orientation training

Venue training

Job specific training

Individual preference to move from specific to general

Figure 9.1 Different preferences for order of job-specific training

shows, the event organizer needs to be mindful of the workforce's priority for personally relevant information over event history!

For the smaller event, all of this can be collapsed into a pre-event tour of the site and a briefing. Checklists and careful supervision will then ensure that things go smoothly.

Web-based training

Many of the above problems could of course be avoided if most of the training were delivered online. People would not need cups of tea, they would not have to travel or park, they would not need invitations or books or videos. Brandon Hall (1997) has written a primer on planning Web-based training for anyone working in training and development. This book provides outstanding advice for the design and development of this type of training but recommends specialist support for the finer details. He also suggests posing the following questions before setting off on this pathway:

Is this the best method of training?
While there are significant efficiencies associated with Web-based training, the most important question is whether the motivational content can be delivered using this medium. The informational content can definitely be provided on the Web, and with good instructional design this can become quite interactive. By monitoring use of the website, and the pathways people follow in navigating it, the organizing committee has a very accurate idea of the level of interest. Furthermore, the website can be used for conducting assessment on key topics such as occupational health and safety, thus demonstrating an adequate level of learning.

Should we do this in-house or outsource it?
Events with a website designed for ticket sales to the general public may be extended to provide training information to staff. This is often done using a user name and password so that employees can access the instructional parts of the site. Many human resource functions can be managed this way, including roster planning. One needs to consider the effort involved in development as well as maintenance of the site.

What are some of the problems that may be associated with Web-based training (such as some individuals not having access or bandwidth)?
Although most people have access to computers, at the very least through public libraries and Internet cafes, the issue of bandwidth is an important one. If the site includes sophisticated and memory hungry video, for example, this is going to prove difficult for many users. The alternative is burning the site to a CD format but this means that it cannot be maintained with the most up to date information available. One also needs to consider staff with a disability when preparing training materials, for instance, deciding whether materials need to be available in audio, large print, braille, etc.

Can the cost be justified?
A website with bells and whistles, one that has good instructional design, graphics etc. that can maintain the interest of a generation that has played computer games is likely to cost a small fortune, so the cost needs to be carefully considered.

Who will be needed on the development team?
The development team needs to include a project manager; an instructional designer who develops scripts and story boards; a programmer or author who can use the authoring tool; a graphic artist; writers or subject matter experts; and of course a webmaster for hosting the programme.

Are there issues with approving the content of Web information and graphics?
Major events often have an approved style for all communications including website, ticketing and signage. This includes font types and sizes, font colours, background colours, graphics etc. In addition to this sponsors and other stakeholders need to approve all logos and content relevant to their roles. The approvals process is arduous, statements about safety need to be checked by the relevant functional area, statements about meals need to be checked by catering, the list is endless. However this is not unique to Web-based training, it is just as big a task with print materials.

What level of interactivity will there be?
A website can be simply informative, with the user navigating their way through links to find the information they want to find. Alternatively, sophisticated design can guide learners through a process where interaction is indicative of learning. Asking how much multimedia is realistic is a related question, linked to design, outcomes and budget.

Is there any assessment planned?
This question is important for any type of training, whether Web-based or not. Will there be any assessment of how much learning has taken place? This is increasingly the case in the area of occupational health and safety. Even the smallest event these days is likely to issue a multiple choice test on safety with a requirement that everyone must score over 80 per cent. One such test had all the answers as (d) just to make it easy for most people and to eliminate those who were not listening and not very bright!

Who will have access to the training material?
This is a most interesting question. For many mega and hallmark events there are many people clamouring for information including sponsors, universities and organizations 'outside the tent'. They are serving the interests of the event and want to train their people. In a pre-emptive move the Beijing Organizing Committee for the Olympic Games launched their pre-Games training guide on their website a full three years before the event [see Figure 9.2]. This enabled all these parties to commence orientation type training a long way ahead.

CONTENTS		
Beijing Olympic Games Organizing Committee President Liu Qi's Message		⊕
Chinese Olympic Committee President Yuan Weimin's Message		
Prologue		
A. Introduction		⊕
Map of China: Administrative Regions	Map of China: Major Scenic Areas	
Map of Beijing	Introduction to China	
Introduction to Chinese Olympic Committee	Beijing Olympic Games Overview	
Attention		
B. Training sites and facilities by sport	⊕ 1st	⊕ 2nd
1. Athletics	2. Rowing	
3. Badminton	4. Baseball	
5. Basketball	6. Boxing etc. (28 sports)	
C. Training sites and facilities by region		
Beijing Municipality ⊕	Tianjin Municipality	⊕
Hebei Province ⊕	Shanxi Province	⊕
Liaoning Province ⊕	Heilongjiang Province	⊕
Qinghai Province ⊕	Etc. (25 regions)	
D. Others		⊕
Application Form	Key Contacts	
Acknowledgment		

Figure 9.2 Website training guide for the Beijing Olympic Games 2008 released three years prior to the Games
(Abbreviated version of website (2005), The Pre-Games Training Guide: The 29th Olympic Games China 2004–2008; for further information see http://en.beijing-2008.org/71/76/column211637671.shtml)

The decision regarding Web-based training is a difficult one if the event is a one-off occurrence. If, on the other hand, the event is held annually, then the investment made in training can be carried through to the following year (see Figure 9.3). Event organizations such as Cleanevent, mentioned in the last chapter, are well placed to develop Web-based human resource systems for training and rostering as they are involved in so many events year after year. The same would be true of an event catering company.

The role of technology in providing information to event staff so that they in turn can provide information to the event audience will be discussed in the next chapter where another question is asked: can information be made available to the workforce on the next generation of mobile phones (PDAs) acting as an extension of Web-based learning?

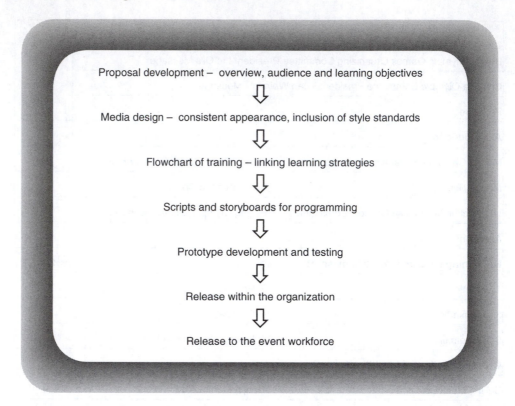

Proposal development – overview, audience and learning objectives

Media design – consistent appearance, inclusion of style standards

Flowchart of training – linking learning strategies

Scripts and storyboards for programming

Prototype development and testing

Release within the organization

Release to the event workforce

Figure 9.3 Stages of development for Web-based training

Leadership training

Leadership training has become a common feature of training for event supervisors and managers. The training aims are to develop workforce motivation and increase retention. One of the first of these programmes was developed for the 2000 Sydney Olympic Games in response to problems experienced in Atlanta in 1996, which included staff poaching, wage blowouts and volunteer attrition (Webb, 2001). While industrial relations initiatives were largely credited with the success that ensued, it was also widely accepted that recruitment, selection and training strategies also worked towards developing a sophisticated and well-trained workforce – according to Juan Antonio Samaranch, 'the best volunteers ever'.

The training needs analysis for event leadership for the 2000 Olympics included a literature review, analysis of previous event training materials, individual interviews and focus group sessions. The last of these were exceptionally useful, bringing a large number of experienced event professionals from around the world into one room to discuss the programme. The model illustrated in Figure 9.4 emerged directly from comments made by these experienced leaders. This in turn led to development of a video and a game to match the model. While subsequent models have been developed (e.g. Van der Wagen, 2004), the first model is discussed and illustrated here as a direct outcome of the training needs analysis for Sydney 2000:

*As a result of our research the model that we developed is called the 'Special Events Leadership Model'. One of the features of this model is the **contrasting nature of leadership roles**. In some situations, a leader has*

Figure 9.4 Event leadership model

to be directive and autocratic, such as in a crisis, and in others a leader needs to be collaborative and appreciative. This paradoxical and flexible approach seemed well suited to the dynamic event context.

*Another feature of the model is an illustration of roles as part of a circle **without sequential order**. In most organizations in which business is conducted over a longer time span, the processes of leadership are largely sequential, moving from planning through to organizing and controlling. In contrast, event leadership requires a **higher level of flexibility**. Three roles were specifically identified as being important, and these are **appreciating, managing time and stress, and energising**. These are not roles that are generally made explicit in traditional leadership texts.*

The quote that follows is an explanation of the concept of energising and the role it has to play in maintaining an upbeat atmosphere, which was one of the volunteers' main expectations (see also Figure 9.5). They would work hard, but they wanted to have fun too.

Energising

*One of the biggest challenges for most events is the creation of a celebratory atmosphere. Look at it like hosting a party – you are the host and have to look like you are enjoying yourself while you are working like crazy for everyone's enjoyment. **Both customers and team members look to you to take the initiative to build and maintain the atmosphere and create the ambience.** Many event staff say that one of their motivators is the opportunity to join in and enjoy the atmosphere. The positive buzz that this can create can be quickly destroyed through poor leadership. Energising is the most intangible leadership role but it is arguably the most important. Careful use of gestures, tone of voice and the building of the 'fun factors' is*

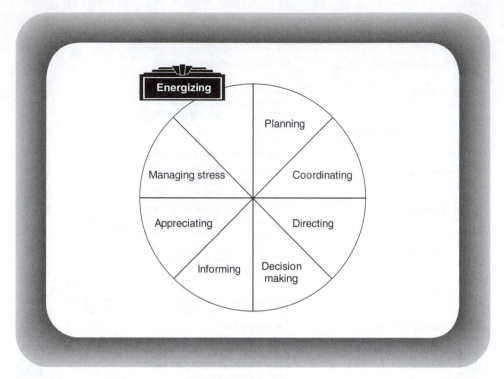

Figure 9.5   Energizing – an important aspect of event leadership
(TAFE NSW, Event leadership training, p. 4. Reproduced with permission.)

required to meet the expectations of all staff. For many of those involved fun is an essential motivator, and spontaneity, humour and high levels of energy are required. This is very different from traditional leadership roles within most business environments. Many energising strategies, as with appreciation strategies, can be planned in advance. Using icebreakers, games and jokes can help to create the right atmosphere.

Managing and co-ordinating the training programme

While for some events there is a specific functional area responsible for training, in many cases responsibility for training devolves to the supervisors. A marathon, for example, is unlikely to have more than one person assigned to the training role. A community children's festival might not have anyone in the role but expect training to simply evolve as the need arises. Learning would be largely an outcome of many planning meetings, and training would occur in the form of briefings before commencement.

Where it is a multi-venue, multi-session event, training requires much more attention. Typically, Human Resources or Training and Development (if there are such functional areas) would take overall responsibility for co-ordinating planning for the three workforce training sessions described earlier in this chapter, but would prepare and present only core components of the programme, including orientation. The event management team would be responsible for venue training, and supervisors for job-specific training. And sometimes training is outsourced, as it was for the volunteers in Case study 9.2.

Case study 9.2

Training for 600 roles

Commending the efforts of the Commonwealth Games volunteers

The enthusiasm of the volunteers can be felt right across Melbourne. Their vibrancy and friendliness is infectious, creating an awesome vibe in Melbourne and bringing the city to life. Their commitment is nothing short of inspiring.

They are the 13 500 unpaid volunteers of the Melbourne 2006 Commonwealth Games, and many have even come from interstate or returned from overseas to help make the Games a success. They have performed over 600 different roles, both sport-specific and generalist roles. For every role undertaken, training was provided by Holmesglen Institute of TAFE in everything from the specific skills associated with the role, to leadership and first aid, amongst many.

As a team, the volunteers have been providing the vital services that are crucial to running such a large international event, and it has been impossible not to witness the great work that they have been doing.

Senior officials, international guests and the public alike have all commended the high level of service provided throughout Games events particularly in areas for which most had previously no prior experience.

It is now our turn to show our appreciation for their extensive efforts.

The commitment of the volunteers to support the Games extends far beyond the eleven days of competition. Each volunteer has also contributed much of their time in training to perfect the part they would play. Melbourne 2006 and Holmesglen had initially identified that all volunteers should essentially share ten key qualities, being that they were Passionate, Determined, United, Confident, Adaptable, Respectful, Friendly, Fun, Proud, Professional.

The training programme was subsequently focused on incorporating these qualities into the roles being taught, ensuring the outstanding performances that we have been witness to over the last eleven days.

Despite the extensive commitment, the team of volunteers was only too happy to help out, citing the experience itself as being its own greatest reward. Even with such humility, Melbourne will be honoured to thank them with a tickertape parade on Monday, 27 March and all in and around this great city are encouraged to attend and say thank you.

Even if you can't make it, and you come across a volunteer, why not pass on the appreciation of the millions around the world who enjoyed the Melbourne 2006 Commonwealth Games as they are no doubt a big part of the success.

Thank you Volunteers, you've done us proud.

(Reproduced with permission of Holmesglen TAFE; for further information see www.holmesglen.vic.edu.au)

Reflective practice 9.2

1 What were the ten qualities shared by volunteers at the 2006 Commonwealth Games?
2 Why would an event outsource training, as it has here, to Holmesglen Institute of TAFE?
3 Most training for this event was face to face. Present a case for providing online training for the next Commonwealth Games.

Chapter summary and key points

This chapter has covered the full scope of workforce training, including management training, for the event planning team. This training can take many formats, and be formal or quite informal, as with small events. There is no doubt that a lot of experiential learning takes place in the planning of an event. This is aided in many ways by training, mentoring and learning through trial and error.

In order to prepare the workforce for the operational period there are typically three levels of training: orientation training, venue training, and job-specific training. The larger the event, the greater the time between the first training session and the start date of the event. For a mega event, the majority of training would occur approximately three months before the event. For a small music festival there may be a session a week before the event and some specific training given on arrival on the first day.

Event leadership training is an essential component for all supervisors, particularly those who have volunteers as their responsibility. The energy and commitment developed by event leaders translates into outstanding customer service.

Revision questions

1 List and expand on four training topics for managers involved in the event organization during the planning phase. For a specific event, identify which of these would be the highest priority.
2 Explain the three levels of training: orientation training, venue training, and job-specific training.
3 What are three of the logistical considerations associated with developing the overall training plan for the event organization?
4 Discuss why it is difficult to make a decision regarding online training for the event workforce.
5 What is the aim of event leadership training? Give an example of an event for which you think this type of training would be imperative.

References

Beijing Organising Committee for the Olympic Games (2005). The pre-Games training guide: the 29th Olympic Games China 2004–2008. Viewed 12 July 2005, http://en.beijing-2008.org/71/76/column211637671.shtml.

Hall, B. (1997). *Web-based Training Cookbook*. John Wiley.

Manchester City Council (2003). Manchester Commonwealth Games Post Games Report.

Sydney Paralympic Organising Committee (2001). Sydney 2000 Paralympic Games Post Games Report 2001. Olympic Co-ordination Authority. Viewed 20 December 2005, www.gamesinfo.com.au/postgames/pa/pg001301.htm.

Tourism Training Victoria (2002). Strategic training issues for the 2006 Commonwealth Games, Melbourne.

Van der Wagen, L. (2004). *Event Management*, 2nd edn. Pearson Education.

Webb, T. (2001). *The Collaborative Games: The Story behind the Spectacle*. Pluto Press.

Chapter 10
Job-specific training

Learning objectives

After reading through this chapter you will be able to:

- Plan job-specific training
- Link training to job requirements
- Deliver small group training
- Describe a range of training methods
- Evaluate training.

Introduction

Job-specific training is required for every event regardless of size. Each person on site needs to know what to do. In this chapter we will use the simple formula of plan, deliver, assess and evaluate training (see Figure 10.1). These four steps are the basic elements of small group and individual training for specific skills and knowledge.

Food safety training will be used as an example to illustrate job-specific training as it is a rare event that does not provide food as part of the event experience, whether provided by the event organization's caterers or a contractor. In each case, food safety planning and food safety training still must be carried out. The starting point for developing job-specific training is the job description and, if available, the pertinent parts of the project plan. These enable the trainer to take the first step, preparing for one-to-one or group instruction.

Planning training

Planning is one of the most crucial parts of training. It involves breaking down the task into elements, deciding how best to explain and demonstrate these elements and then obtaining feedback from the learner about their progress. While this sounds easy, Burns points out 'the act of training does not lend itself well to techniques, formulas, dogma or event logic; it is a dynamic process of interaction between humans that unfolds over time and is dependent on the elegant execution of complex skills' (Burns, 2000, p. 31). While this seems a contradiction of the opening remarks in this

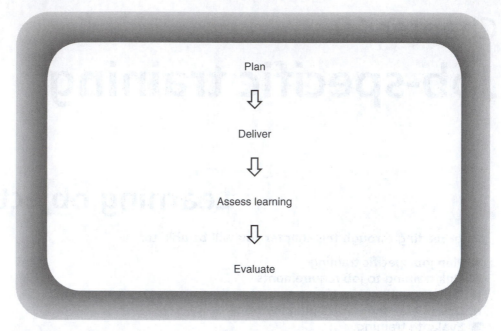

Figure 10.1 Formula for training people for specific jobs

chapter, even the most spontaneous of trainers would agree that their dynamic approach to meeting audience needs is based on a plan. This plan provides the bedrock for training: identifying learning outcomes. Thus, while the trainer might deviate, expand or become side-tracked, it is ultimately necessary to work back to the learning outcomes in the training plan and make sure that these, as a minimum, are achieved.

Placing ourselves in the position of event catering co-ordinator, we can see from the extract that follows that there is a role to play in training staff in food safety (State Government of Victoria, Australia, Department of Human Services, 2006). This is replicated across nearly every functional area. However, in this case there are regulations that have to be met, making this training vitally important.

> *When your organization holds an event where there will be food sold – for instance, a fete, sausage sizzle or cake stall – you will need to appoint an Event Co-ordinator. It is the role of the Event Co-ordinator to ensure that all food handlers at the event, whether they are volunteers or paid workers, understand the relevant food safety and safe food handling practices for the tasks which they are to be carrying out. To communicate such information to all food handlers, the Event Co-ordinator will have to conduct training or group discussions about food safety before the event.*
>
> *The Event Co-ordinator must be familiar with the following:*
>
> - *The Food Safety Program for the event*
> - *Safe food-handling practices*
> - *Personal hygiene – for instance, correct washing and drying of hands*
> - *Efficient cleaning procedures*
> - *Safe food preparation*
> - *Correct storage and transportation of food*
> - *How to conduct temperature checks*
> - *Safe food display.*

Ice-cream vendors being briefed in the rain

Having seen a specific example of a clearly identified training need, let us look at the training needs analysis for other roles and tasks before returning to this example of food safety training.

The training needs analysis for job-specific training generally needs to be facilitated by the event co-ordinator. This is done by discussing training with the relevant functional area or zone area supervisor.

The following questions are a guide for a training needs analysis:

1 What is the job title?
2 Who is responsible for conducting this training?
3 How many people are going to do this job (individual or group)?
4 What are the skills required?
5 What is the knowledge required?
6 What are the training objectives or learning outcomes?
7 How much does this person/group already know?
8 Are there any special requirements such as accredited training?
9 Having reviewed the common training modules (e.g. orientation training, customer service, OHS awareness), what are the remaining training objectives for this specific job?
10 What training method will be used (small group training, one-to-one training, self-directed training)?
11 When and where will training take place?
12 How long will it take?

13 Is equipment required?

14 What training materials are needed, including print materials?

15 Will there be any form of assessment?

16 How difficult is this likely to be for the participants?

17 How critical is this training to the success of the event?

The most important of these questions is number six: what are the training objectives or learning outcomes? A training objective (or learning outcome) states what the person can do or should know on completion of training, generally beginning with a verb. For example: 'On completion of training the catering assistant will be able to *prevent* food poisoning by *practising* good personal hygiene.' Another example would be: 'On completion of training the customer services officer will be able to *explain* the layout of the event site and *provide* directions to services and facilities.'

Once the overall job training plan has been developed, instruction needs to be planned in detail, including the particular steps that the trainer would follow. For the training objective, 'practising good personal hygiene', the State Government of Victoria, Australia, Department of Human Services (2006) recommends that the following skills and knowledge are required:

Objective: *Prevent food poisoning by practising good personal hygiene:*
Demonstrable skills *(these would be covered by demonstration and practice):*

- *Wear clean protective clothing, like an apron.*
- *Thoroughly wash and dry your hands before handling food.*
- *Dry your hands with clean towels, disposable paper towels or under an air dryer.*
- *Use disposable gloves.*

Knowledge *(these would be covered by explanation, example and questioning):*

- *Never smoke, chew gum, spit, change a baby's nappy or eat in a food handling or food storage area.*
- *Never cough or sneeze over food or where food is prepared or stored.*
- *Keep your spare clothes and other personal items away from where food is stored and prepared.*
- *If you have long hair, tie it back or cover it.*
- *Keep your nails short so they are easy to clean; don't wear nail polish which can chip into the food.*
- *Avoid wearing jewellery, only plain banded rings and sleeper earrings.*
- *If you have cuts or wounds, make sure they are completely covered by a waterproof wound strip or bandage. Use brightly coloured wound strips, so they can be easily seen if they fall off.*
- *Wear disposable gloves over the top of the wound strip if you have wounds on your hands.*
- *Change disposable gloves regularly.*
- *Don't handle food if you feel unwell, advise your supervisor.*
- *Follow the event Food Safety Program.*
- *Follow the advice given by the Food Safety Supervisor.*
- *Be trained in safe food handling (this to follow in detail).*

As Figure 10.2 illustrates, once the training objectives or learning outcomes have been developed, planning can commence. However, it is necessary to be mindful of the participants' prior skills and knowledge to ensure that they are not being taught something they already know. Performance deficiencies, such as not wearing gloves while preparing food, may be a result of laziness and poor supervision, not a lack of knowledge.

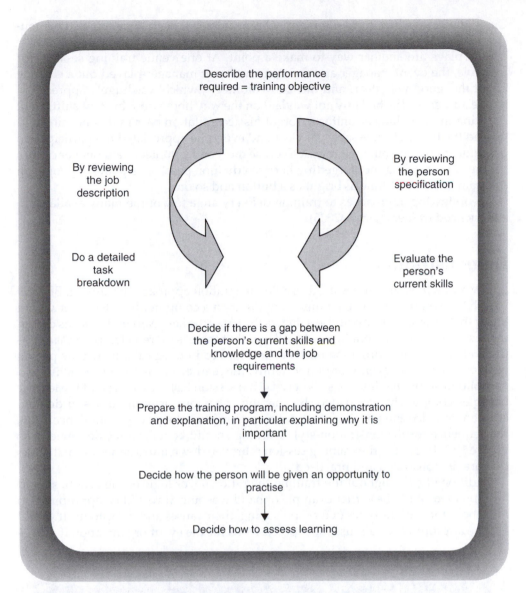

Describe the performance
required = training objective

By reviewing
the job
description

By reviewing
the person
specification

Do a detailed
task
breakdown

Evaluate the
person's
current skills

Decide if there is a gap between
the person's current skills and
knowledge and the job
requirements

Prepare the training program, including demonstration
and explanation, in particular explaining why it is
important

Decide how the person will be given an opportunity to
practise

Decide how to assess learning

Figure 10.2   Planning and delivering training

Training delivery

A training session for food safety is most effectively delivered using demonstration and practice, explanations, questions and answers. Following is an example of a demonstration of how hands should be washed prior to handling food. While it may be self-evident that people should wash their hands, do they do it properly? A test of this is to put zinc cream (the sort cricketers wear on their noses) on participants' hands and ask them to wash them. It is surprising how long it takes and how thorough one has to be to do it properly. This results in an indelible lesson, and hopefully no indelible zinc on the hands! Imaginative presentation is always appreciated.

Using the zinc (which comes in many vibrant colours), the trainer can also demonstrate how the 'germs' are transferred to utensils, plates, pot handles, etc.

Role plays are another way to make a point. At one venue training session, for example, the event manager and the event assistant manager played out a charade about the 'good volunteer' and the 'bad volunteer', which was hugely appreciated by the audience. The bad guy got waylaid on the way home from his first shift, went drinking in his volunteer uniform, forgot his accreditation pass in the morning and missed the train. The message was clear and everyone appreciated the participation of senior staff acting out their roles. Of course the 'good volunteer' laid out her clothes for the next morning (not forgetting her accreditation pass), was polite to people on the train, arrived on time as bright as a button and so on.

The following approaches to training delivery are a few of the many available to experienced trainers (Jarvis, 2005).

Demonstration

'Show and tell' is sometimes used as a demonstration approach to training. But any elderly person who has been 'taught' anything on a computer by a teenager would know that watching someone else's fingers fly across the keyboard with screens changing faster than you can blink, would tell you that there is more to learning than simply watching. The information needs to be chunked into logical bits that the person can cope with and, even more importantly, the learner needs time to practise and consolidate at regular intervals. Otherwise the session just falls apart and the learner becomes completely overloaded. By shaping behaviour using modules of demonstration, practice and revision, the learner is more likely to grow in confidence. Thus the sequence for demonstration-style learning should be tell, show, do, review. As Figure 10.3 illustrates, the training session is broken down into a series of small tasks that are demonstrated and practised.

Additionally, throughout the training the rationale, or logic of the action, should be explained. With the earlier example of hand washing, it would be appropriate to talk about the various types of food poisoning, their causes and symptoms. It would also be appropriate to discuss the repercussions for the event organization if a large

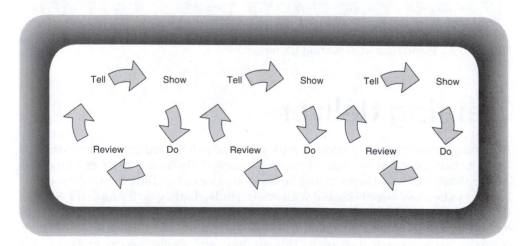

Figure 10.3 Explaining, practising and consolidating training

number of people suffered from food poisoning. It is a very serious issue: for example, 200 Russian train travellers were hospitalized and another 450 treated after they had visited a festival (200 festival visitors hospitalized with food poisoning in Southern Russia, 2005).

Lecture

This training approach is best suited to a large audience. Most commonly it is used to explain emergency and evacuation procedures using demonstrations of the fire alarms, the preparatory alarm, 'please evacuate as directed by the fire wardens', and finally the rising tone 'woop woop' instructing all to evacuate. This training is usually delivered by the fire department or someone appropriately qualified.

Mentoring

Mentoring is used at management level to build expertise. An individual is assigned a mentor who monitors their learning, providing suggestions and provocation to stimulate learning. At lower skill levels, the buddy system is a sound approach to skills training, providing that the buddy is doing their job correctly and can explain why it is important. In the high-pressure event environment it is important to monitor this role as the training may deteriorate as it is passed on from one person to another. Checklists or diagrams can be helpful in preventing this occurrence.

Brainstorming

The creative field of event concept development and the unique features of event planning lend themselves well to brainstorming as an approach to learning. As plans become more and more specific, it is important to ensure that people are not locked in, but instead are stimulated to think of new and better ways to do things. According to Beckett and Hager (2002), organic learning needs to grow explicitly. They suggest three questions to bear in mind during hot action:

- What are we doing?
- Why are we doing it?
- What comes next?

These three questions can be immensely valuable as a focus for learning, for evolving plans, and for visionary and creative responses to complex problems.

Debate

While debating appears to be a very formal training method, when used in an energetic and humorous way it can emphasize two positions, highlighting sensitivity to differences in fact or opinion. For example, the topic of waste management and recycling as it is typically covered at event briefings can be quite a dry topic. An energetic debate on the merits of maintaining waste streams (and the associated costs) and against (Why bother?) could be highly entertaining and get the message across.

Presentation

Presentations by visiting speakers such as police and first aid supervisors, sometimes as a segment of a programme, can contribute enormously to effective training. Likewise, an experienced volunteer with inspirational stories can raise the level of enthusiasm dramatically. If the presentation is followed by questions, they can also be used as an assessment approach to consolidate learning, enabling participants to explore and defend their learning.

Role play

This acting technique can be used to good effect in customer relations, disability and cultural awareness training. For example, it is clearly a most appropriate way to train staff working on the information booth at an event.

Group discussion

Group discussions can promote inclusiveness providing that they are run democratically, giving everyone a chance to participate. They also need to have a clear goal. Occupational health and safety committees can be run along these lines, although principles of effective meetings need to be applied, including minutes and agreements on emerging actions.

Guided discussion – conversational learning

This much more sophisticated idea is pitched at higher management levels: 'The role of the OD/HRD professional in conversational learning focuses on creating space for conversation, inviting different voices into the conversation, and cultivating a safe space for deliberation about difficult but meaningful issues' (Baker *et al.*, 2002, p. 204). As these authors point out, this type of conversation can occur in a face-to-face interaction or through technology. Risk management planning or discussion about emerging threats to the organization or running of the event would be appropriate topics for conversational learning. Here the outcomes would be less clear-cut and the issues more nebulous.

Case studies

Problem-based case studies have been widely used in medicine (Fish and Coles, 1998), and more recently in nursing (Tomey, 2003). Case studies are an effective way for participants to become involved in realistic and problematic situations, away from the pressure of the real situation. This type of experiential learning is likely to foster learning on a higher order level, such as critical thinking. In the event environment, problem-based case studies for customer service are particularly useful.

Simulations – experiential learning

In the mega event business it is typical to run a series of 'test events', which are a training ground for event staff, most particularly those responsible for managing the competition. For example, the Nordic Skiing World Cup held in January 2005 was a test event for the Winter Olympic Games in Torino in 2006. This is as close a simulation as you can get!

Many trainers use a combination of techniques. For example, following a test event, a brainstorming session could be held to iron out procedures and finalize job descriptions for specific roles. Specific incidents that occurred could be part of a group discussion. A visiting speaker (such as a competition manager) could make a presentation or a volunteer could talk about their experience. A trainer needs to be attentive to the needs of the audience and remain highly responsive to their feedback. This usually comes in the form of enthusiastic participation, ranging from doodling through to text messaging.

There are a number of ways in which a trainer can obtain feedback during delivery to make sure that the session is on track and meeting audience needs:

- Ask the group how many would like to step through the information again.
- Provide a self-check quiz and find out what people scored (1–5, 6–10, 11–15, etc.).
- Reinforce information by providing a framework (such as a flow chart) for learners to complete during the presentation.
- Ask learners to check their skills by practising with a procedure checklist and then without one.
- Leave out a key step on a list of steps and see how many can remember what to do.
- Ask learners to rate their skill level against your learning outcomes.
- Find out which parts are not clear.
- Find out which parts are perceived by learners to be most important.
- Ask specific questions.
- Use both closed and open questions.
- Ask if there are any questions.
- Use a matching exercise to check understanding.
- Ask learners to check one another when trying out a skill.
- Provide self-check procedures, diagrams and lists to take home so that learners can check themselves.
- Develop a rating scale, or barometer, to check confidence at the start and finish of training.

Training assessment

The term 'assessment' is generally used in the context of assessing the learner, while evaluation focuses on the overall success (or otherwise) of the training programme, which will be discussed in the next section. Some of the suggestions for obtaining feedback listed in the last section are also assessment methods – ways in which the trainer can test understanding and skills. Observation and questioning are the two main methods of assessing a learner's progress.

Few events have the luxury of allowing novices to practise in real-time situations; most can only observe and correct staff and volunteers on the job. There are, however, some reasons why assessment may be required. The most significant of these is for risk management and insurance purposes. It may therefore be useful to be able to demonstrate that each person on site (including contractors) has undergone training and assessment in occupational health and safety on site and is familiar with evacuation plans.

Case study 10.1 indicates the importance of volunteer training.

Case study 10.1

California Traditional Music Society Festival

What can I volunteer for?

There are MANY different types of jobs for which we need volunteers at the festival ranging from parking lot crew, to working in the instrument check room (<u>click here to see a complete list of jobs and their descriptions</u>). There are also many different options for WHEN you volunteer. <u>To see a full list of the potential shift days and times, click here.</u>

Skills and training

Most festival volunteer jobs do not require specialized skills (there are a few exceptions and will be noted). All new volunteers must be trained by the Area Co-ordinator who is responsible for making sure their area runs smoothly. Training occurs at one of two group meetings at the festival site in June before the festival (either Sunday, 5 June 2005 or Saturday, 18 June 2005).

Volunteer obligations

Volunteers are one of the mainstays of this festival – without their dedication and effort, we could not put the festival on each year. Each volunteer represents the 'face' of CTMS, and thereby is an ambassador for our organization. CTMS expects that they will be enthusiastic, friendly, helpful and professional at all times during their volunteer shifts. It will be important to report on time and ready to work to all shifts to which you have been assigned. In addition, volunteers are required to:

- *Sign and return one copy of their Festival Volunteer Contract as soon as possible after receiving it.*
- *Attend one of the training meetings held at the festival site (Soka University). Bring lunch and plan to meet for approximately three hours. Attendance at one meeting is mandatory for all new volunteers and indicates a volunteer's commitment to completing their job assignment. Individuals who miss the training meetings and do not communicate with their Area Co-ordinator are subject to being replaced.*

(Reproduced with permission of California Traditional Music Society Festival; for more information see www.ctmsfolkmusic.org/volunteer/festival/default.asp)

Reflective practice 10.1

Given three hours to train a group of festival volunteers prior to set-up of the event site, which topics would you cover in the training?

Training evaluation

Where briefings and training sessions are planned and prepared prior to an event, it is a good idea to run a pilot session to evaluate the effectiveness of the programme to see that it is fit for the purpose. A focus group can be invited to the session to critique it and make suggestions for improvement. However, in the mega event environment of the Olympic Games, for example, this can sometimes lead to deficiencies in the final programme as a result of endless cycles of change and review by multiple stakeholders (Van der Wagen, 2005).

Figure 10.4 provides a format for evaluation of a training session.

Presentation	Learning
Please rate the following on a scale of 1–5 (with 1 the least successful and 5 the most successful)	
Planning – room set-up and materials [ ] [ ] [ ] [ ] [ ]	Posed questions and used other ways to check learning [ ] [ ] [ ] [ ] [ ]
Purpose/objectives – clearly explained, people welcomed [ ] [ ] [ ] [ ] [ ]	Practice/application – given with guidance for learners [ ] [ ] [ ] [ ] [ ]
Process (session outline) – clearly explained [ ] [ ] [ ] [ ] [ ]	Practice/application – occurred independently for learners [ ] [ ] [ ] [ ] [ ]
Presentation – in small steps, logical, just enough information [ ] [ ] [ ] [ ] [ ]	Provided learners with support such as diagrams and checklists [ ] [ ] [ ] [ ] [ ]
Presentation – easy to hear, interesting and well paced [ ] [ ] [ ] [ ] [ ]	Problems solved if needed [ ] [ ] [ ] [ ] [ ]
Presentation – supported with visuals [ ] [ ] [ ] [ ] [ ]	Purpose/objectives – reviewed and closed with learners confident [ ] [ ] [ ] [ ] [ ]

Figure 10.4   Evaluation of pilot training programme by focus group

There are a number of other ways in which training can be evaluated, and this information should be included in the final event report. However, it is necessary to be aware that there are many variables at play and clear-cut research into the merits, benefits and outcomes of training is not easily achieved. Despite this, those responsible for training prior to a successful event like to claim that the success was a direct result of their efforts (Van der Wagen, 2005), as do many other functional areas and stakeholders! Despite the difficulty associated with conducting scientific research in this complex area of social interaction, a post-event evaluation report is immensely valuable for events that follow. Qualitative data, in the form of quotes and case studies, are a useful legacy.

Training participant feedback sheets

These feedback sheets are given to participants immediately after the training session requesting feedback very similar to that illustrated in Figure 10.4. In the human resource development (HRD) world, these are known as 'happy sheets' as they indicate how happy participants felt about the session. Note of course that they do not accurately indicate how much everyone learned.

Pre- and post-event interviews

A longitudinal study can be done, interviewing staff and volunteers pre- and post-event. This qualitative approach can also be matched with a quantitative skills rating sheet. To achieve research results that are valid and reliable would need careful planning, including selection of an appropriate sample group.

Mystery people studies

Evaluation of the effectiveness of training can also be conducted by using mystery customers, staff members and volunteers armed with key observation points and questions. These 'mystery shoppers' are much more aware of what they are looking for and may, for example, ask specific questions to evaluate responses on the job. The mystery customer may be primed to simulate heat exhaustion, for example, to evaluate the actions/responses of staff or volunteers. A mystery volunteer would likewise be well attuned to contextual factors and to the needs, expectations and experiences of their volunteer associates, including their satisfaction with the information provided during training, the skills needed and utilized, and unanticipated issues arising on the job.

On-the-job surveys and observation

Researchers armed with questionnaires can visit members of the event workforce and interview them on the job. They can also use observation techniques to evaluate skills in customer service, crowd management and information provision.

Critical incident analysis

This research methodology is used in many different circumstances. It is very valuable in that it uses one critical incident to highlight deficiencies in planning or execution. Likewise, it emphasizes successes, which are just as important a legacy of an event. Essentially, the questions are 'what worked' and 'what didn't work', with a specific example and an explanation for the reasons.

Case study 10.2 illustrates the approach taken in a critical incident focus group.

Case study 10.2

What worked? What didn't work?

The aim is to describe two incidents that illustrate positive and negative outcomes of the project with a view to developing recommendations for improvements in training for the next event or for future similar projects.

Please note: The focus for this evaluation is training, and ultimately effective on-job performance as a result of training. An incident such as a personality clash between members of a project team is not relevant since it could be generalised to all projects. However, an incident such as a workplace accident as a result of poor training (or no training) would be more relevant. And feedback from a volunteer who had travelled 120 km to attend training and felt that commitment to her role was reaffirmed through the motivational elements of the training would likewise be relevant to future training.

Please answer the following questions:

---

1 Please describe a negative incident (relevant to training effectiveness).

2 Why do you think this occurred?

3 What can we learn from this (to improve training effectiveness)?

***

4 Please describe a positive incident (relevant to training effectiveness).

5 Why do you think this occurred?

6 What can we learn from this (to improve training effectiveness)?

***

7 Do you have any other recommendations on training provided to the workforce for future events?

8 Do you have any other recommendations for future related projects?

Reflective practice 10.2
1 What is critical incident analysis?
2 Why is this approach useful for training evaluation?
3 Describe an alternative approach to training evaluation in detail.

Post-event management evaluation focus groups

There is another type of focus group that can be used for event evaluation, which is much more open ended, with general feedback about human resource strategies, including training. A number of focus groups could be arranged, including the following people:

- Event management/organizing committee
- Human resources and human resource development (trainers)
- Functional and zone area managers
- Supervisors
- Paid staff
- Volunteers.

For a smaller event, a focus group with each of the above representatives would be adequate.

Post-event analysis of risk planning and incident reports

Finally, it is essential that risk management plans for human resource management and training are revisited after the event to evaluate their accuracy. The risk ratings may or may not have been accurate, and there may be issues that emerged that were not anticipated at all.

Incident reports are another rich source of information about training effectiveness, particularly in the area of safety and customer service.

The training evaluation report

The following recommendations were made following the Paralympic Games in 2000 (Sydney Paralympic Organising Committee, 2001) for which training was conducted by TAFE NSW as an official provider:

- *Negotiate the training contract for all staff (paid, volunteer and contractor) and both Games in one contract, rather than separately.*
- *Provide adequate administrative back-up to the training consultants – a heavy administrative workload is involved including formatting of hundreds of documents and up to 100–150 phone calls a day. A desirable ratio would be one administrator for every three consultants.*
- *Negotiate contracts on the basis of materials to be produced, rather than a headcount. The Olympic and Paralympic headcount changed numerous times.*
- *Consider the needs of staff with a disability when preparing training materials, for instance, whether materials need to be available in audio, large print, Braille, etc.*
- *Develop a media relations strategy around the commencement of Games training as positive coverage will be a motivational boost, especially for volunteers.*
- *Consider ensuring that copyright of training materials resides with the organizing committee, not the training provider, as this will help future organizers.*
- *Clarify the training requirements as soon as possible and processes of associated agencies, e.g. transport, security, broadcasters, etc. to ensure consistency and avoid gaps.*
- *Consider holding job-specific training before orientation and venue training. Most people wanted to know the specifics of their job well before the training started. As well, much job-specific training could have occurred during the first two rostered shifts.*

Kraiger *et al.* (2004) take a much more strategic approach to training evaluation, suggesting that the first step is to develop a theory of impact. In doing so, business results that matter are linked to the knowledge and skills to do the job. Second, they suggest that the focus of the evaluation should be on evidence – evidence to show that training has been a success. Third, to claim success, the effects of training must be isolated, which is very difficult to do. Finally, as suggested throughout this and the previous chapter, it must be clear who is accountable for training. As these authors point out, 'research on training effectiveness suggests that training has its greatest impact when all parties in the organization share responsibility for identifying training needs, ensuring that trainees have the time and opportunity to focus on training, and have the opportunity and support to apply and practise trained skills on the job' (p. 347).

Completion of the task at the end of Case study 10.3 will test understanding of the material contained in this chapter.

Case study 10.3

Training for an exhibition project

This is a plan for installing an exhibition stand:

1. *Plan exhibition*
    1.1. Obtain requirements from marketing
    1.2. Agree on build materials

2. *Assemble equipment*
    2.1. Identify current stock of build materials
    2.2. Reserve required stock
    2.3. Generate list of equipment to be procured
    2.4. Identify suppliers
    2.5. Negotiate price and delivery
    2.6. Raise and approve purchase orders
    2.7. Place orders with suppliers
    2.8. Deliver materials
    2.9. Check materials and store materials

3. *Build exhibition stand*
    3.1. Ship exhibition materials
    3.2. Unpack materials
    3.3. Build stands
    3.4. Fit electrics
    3.5 Fit audio visual
    3.6. Check stand
    3.7. Install sales and marketing brochures, posters, etc.

4. *Dismantle exhibition stand*
    4.1. Remove audiovisual equipment
    4.2. Dismantle electrics
    4.3. Pack up materials
    4.4. Ship to base

Reflective practice 10.3

For Stage 2 of this project, 'assemble equipment', you need to develop a training plan, which should include the following information:

1 Learning outcomes/training objectives
2 Training method/s
3 Equipment required
4 Demonstrable skills, including break down into steps
5 Knowledge (hint – don't forget OHS)
6 Assessment – key points for observation and questions to ask.

Chapter summary and key points

Job-specific training is arguably the most important part of preparing an event workforce. This is where people learn how to use two-way radios, how to set up athletic equipment, who to admit at the VIP entrance, and how to provide customers with the information they need. For this to work successfully, jobs need to be broken down into tasks and basic knowledge, which form the basis for the training plan. A number of training methods can be used, such as demonstrations, case studies and brainstorming, and at the end of the training it must be evident that the trainees are competent to undertake their specific event roles. Evaluating the success of the training project is helpful and informative for subsequent events. Workforce morale is closely linked to the level of confidence employees and volunteers have in their ability to put on a good show.

Revision questions

1 What are the four steps in small group and individual training for specific skills? Explain the steps.
2 Using two specific events, can you identify at least three areas in which skills training will be required?
3 What are four different approaches to training delivery? Summarize these approaches.
4 Discuss the following statement: 'There is no point in evaluating training post event as the event is over and will never be replicated.'

References

200 festival visitors hospitalized with food poisoning in Southern Russia (2005). *mosnews.com*, 6 November 2005. Viewed 8 May 2006, http://mosnews.com/news/2005/11/06/passengerspoisoned.shtml.

Baker, A. C., Kolb, D. A. and Jensen, P. J. (2002). *Conversational Learning: An Experiential Approach to Knowledge Creation*. Quorum Books.

Beckett, D. and Hager, P. J. (2002). Life, work and learning: practice in postmodernity. *Routledge International Studies in the Philosophy of Education*, **14**. Routledge.

Burns, S. (2000). *Artistry in Training*. Woodslane Press.

Fish, D. and Coles, C. (1998). *Developing Professional Judgement in Health Care: Learning through the Critical Appreciation of Practice*. Butterworth-Heinemann.

Jarvis, M. (2005). *The Psychology of Effective Learning and Teaching*. Nelson Thornes.

Kraiger, K., McLinden, D. and Casper, W. (2004). Collaborative planning for training impact. *Human Resource Management*, **43(4)**, 337–51.

State Government of Victoria, Australia, Department of Human Services (2006). Food safety. Viewed 8 May 2006, www.health.vic.gov.au/foodsafety/.

Sydney Paralympic Organising Committee (2001). Sydney 2000 Paralympic Games Post Games Report 2001. Viewed 20 December 2005, www.gamesinfo.com.au/postgames/pa/pg001301.htm.

ibid., www.gamesinfo.com.au/postgames/pa/pg001301.htm.

Tomey, A. (2003). Learning with cases. *Journal of Continuing Education in Nursing*, **34(1)**, 34–8.

Van der Wagen, L. (2005). Olympic Games event leadership course design. In: *The Impacts of Events*, University of Technology, Sydney.

Chapter 11
Workforce policies and procedures

Learning objectives

After reading through this chapter you will be able to:

- List a number of areas of human resource management in which policies are required
- Provide examples of procedures that support these policies
- Discuss ethical and unethical human resource practices
- Describe logistical challenges for workforce planning.

Introduction

The logistics associated with having the right people doing the right thing at the right time are challenging as events generally run for a very short time. Staff and volunteers need their rosters, they need uniforms, they need food, and they need somewhere to sit during their breaks. Among the most common complaints from volunteers are those concerning the most elementary of needs, for example, being left on a gate collecting tickets for too long without being 'relieved' or given a drink.

Getting people into place and assigning work is the first hurdle. The next is to make sure that they are appropriately cared for in terms of their physical and emotional needs, such as having a supervisor stop by from time to time to talk to those working in isolated positions. The third hurdle is to make sure that the conduct of staff and volunteers is beyond reproach. This requires careful supervision, and in rare cases it may require asking the person to leave.

Developing policies and procedures to deal with such eventualities will mean that every event you participate in is more likely to run smoothly.

Policy planning

A *policy* is an *intended course of action* for an organization. A *procedure* is more specific, detailing the *steps* involved in seeing through the intent of the policy. For example, there may be a policy that every contractor should attend a safety induction session prior to working on site. To implement this policy, a record of attendance at these briefings would be necessary and a procedure would also be needed for contractors assigned at the very last minute. An example might be to have them go to staff check-in and be issued with a short booklet or watch a three-minute video presentation, much as they do in many fast food outlets with high staff turnovers.

UK Sports (2005) have an outstanding guide to ethics in their planning guidelines for major sporting events in which there are a number of points to be taken into consideration in the development of policy guidelines for human resource management, as follows.

Data protection and privacy

Good standards should be in place for protection of personal data, which should be used only for a specific purpose and be accurate and secure. Many websites have statements to this effect. The following extract from the Melbourne 2006 Workforce Privacy Policy illustrates how this should be done:

> **Disclosure of personal information**
>
> *Melbourne 2006 Commonwealth Games Corporation does not use or disclose personal information about an individual for a purpose other than that for which it was collected, unless such use or disclosure would be reasonably expected or consent from you has been obtained. Please note that if at any time Melbourne 2006 Commonwealth Games Corporation is required by law to release information about you or your organisation, Melbourne 2006 Commonwealth Games Corporation must fully co-operate.*
>
> *Information provided by you is used primarily for the purpose of recruitment. The information is disclosed only to our staff who are on the selection panel and any recruitment agency used in the recruitment process. Melbourne 2006 Commonwealth Games Corporation may keep an electronic copy of your application to be considered for future employment. This information is confidential.*

Human rights

Respect for others is demonstrated in a number of ways, an example being a breach of confidentiality regarding a high-profile sports person or celebrity. Most codes of conduct include a requirement that staff and volunteers do not behave in inappropriate ways such as taking photographs, asking for autographs or generally being a nuisance. Members of the event audience also expect exemplary conduct. Problems can occur when conversations between staff members are overheard (sometimes with bad language) or a volunteer may make a joke embarrassing someone in front of a crowd. In the most serious cases, athletes and celebrities may be the target for stealing souvenirs and this is particularly serious if the item is needed for the performance.

Equity

In the staffing area the focus for this is the planning and organization of the event, resulting in the equitable treatment of everyone on site. Suitable arrangements may need to be made including, for example, access to the venue by wheelchairs and arrangements for people with hearing or sight impairment.

Child protection

Staff training, working practices and codes of conduct need to be put in place to minimize situations where abuse of children may occur. In some countries, such as the United Kingdom and Australia, screening processes are in place to assess an applicant's suitability for working with children. In particular, procedures are needed for employees or volunteers dealing with missing children and general guidance is needed on appropriate behaviour of adults around children.

Drugs and alcohol

For safety reasons, nobody on site should be working under the influence of drugs or alcohol (see Case study 11.1). For some music events, this is somewhat problematic, Woodstock being a good example.

Case study 11.1

Ottawa Folk Festival Volunteer Code of Ethics

- *Always present the festival to the public in a positive way, both in your behaviour and in the way you speak. Nothing shall be said or done to intentionally embarrass the festival.*
- *NO ALCOHOL, NO DRUGS, no audio or video recorders and no pets.*
- *If you will be consuming alcohol after your shift, do not wear your festival shirt.*
- *Refer ALL questions involving policy or sensitive issues to the Festival Director or the Festival Co-ordinator.*
- *Refer members of the media to the Media Relations Check-in, located inside the Ron Kolbus Lakeside Centre.*
- *ALL volunteers shall treat staff, performers and other volunteers with respect.*
- *Volunteers shall make every effort to complete all duties assigned. Failure to contribute a minimum effort will result in dismissal from the festival.*
- *Your Festival Access Pass and crew T-shirt are NOT transferable. They remain the property of the CKCU Ottawa Folk Festival throughout the event.*
- *The space in front of Main Stage is for paying audience only.*

(Reproduced with permission of Ottawa Folk Festival; for further information see www. ottawafolk.org/forms/2005_forms/2005_Volunteer_Form.pdf)

Reflective practice 11.1

1 What is the purpose of developing a code of practice for volunteers?
2 Give an example of unsatisfactory behaviour covered by one of these policies that would be reason for dismissal.

Dealing with the public

Members of the workforce team should understand that they are not spokespeople for the event organization. However, as representatives of the organization, their dealings with the public should be positive and pro-active. Many event organizers go to great pains to ensure that their staff do not admit liability in case of an accident or incident.

Grievance procedures

A grievance policy and related procedures should be developed and explained to all members of the workforce. This topic will be covered in more detail at the end of the chapter.

Sexual harassment and equal opportunity

Harassment should not be tolerated and should be reported in accordance with carefully constructed guidelines. The policy should define harassment, state that it is not tolerated, define the role of managers in preventing and dealing with harassment and set out specific procedures.

Occupational health and safety

Everyone should be aware of their responsibility to report health and safety hazards. Furthermore, they should also report behaviour of others that is risky or dangerous.

Personal advantage

Members of the event workforce should not use their position for personal advantage, including receiving gifts and personal use of equipment.

Confidentiality

All event-related information is confidential. Staff should refer the media to the media centre or event control room. Many large events profiling celebrities require staff to sign confidentiality statements.

Lost and found

Any lost and found items should be reported and submitted for storage.

Use of the Internet

Some organizations develop a policy to explicitly monitor private use of the Internet.
   All employees and volunteers should be given a copy of the policy and procedure guidelines and should sign that they understand that violations may lead to dismissal.

   While many organizations express their policies in a fairly negative 'will not' way, the well-known Burning Man Festival (2005) expresses their ten guiding principles in a more positive, pro-active way:

1 Radical inclusion ('welcome and respect the stranger')
2 Gifting ('unconditional')
3 Decommodification
4 Radical self-reliance
5 Radical self-expression
6 Communal effort

7 Civic responsibility
8 Leaving no trace
9 Participation ('transformative change')
10 Immediacy.

At this values-based event, the workforce are expected to uphold and demonstrate these principles.

Staffing logistics and procedures

Each of the following logistics issues needs to be considered. These are common consequences of not planning these in detail:

- Not having enough staff rostered
- Not having enough small volunteer t-shirts
- Running out of hot meals
- Losing track of where people are (may be watching rather than working!)
- Finding staff in the wrong areas
- Losing valuable equipment to theft
- Receiving reports of staff/volunteers misbehaving (in the bar perhaps).

Rosters

Fortunately, not many events have the numbers of staff illustrated in Table 11.1. However, this table illustrates the level of attention needed for roster planning. The benefits of a contingency group of multiskilled roving workers are also evident from this illustration. For larger events, timetabling online has been a progressive step, enabling staff to access and change their roster themselves, sometimes so that they can work with friends, which is a major benefit.

When planning the staffing schedule, decisions are not just about which days people should work. Micro-level planning is needed to identify the peaks and ebbs of staffing. For example, a large number of staff might be needed in the hour before a performance and again during an interval. This is quite predictable. If, however, the timetable is being done for a multi-venue, multi-session series of events, crowd flow planning forms a key part of planning. Many anxious punters arrive very early, even for ticketed events, and the level of readiness is important. The alternative is that some staff and volunteers are still checking in while the venue fills and this is where things can start to slide. Those key hours before the gates open are critical.

Uniforms

Uniforms are a major expense for a winter event, so care must be taken in the design and sizing. The design of uniforms or t-shirts is often determined with the audience in mind. However, it is also necessary to consider staff's response to uniforms, the size and colour of t-shirts being the most elementary consideration. Many events supply too few very small t-shirts. If a men's small is the smallest size, it will be more like a dress than a t-shirt on a tiny woman. Differentiation of status between paid,

Table 11.1 Peak shift numbers by venue and day, 2002 Manchester Commonwealth Games

Venue	15-Jul-02	16-Jul-02	17-Jul-02	18-Jul-02	19-Jul-02	20-Jul-02	21-Jul-02	22-Jul-02	23-Jul-02	24-Jul-02	25-Jul-02	26-Jul-02	27-Jul-02	28-Jul-02	29-Jul-02	30-Jul-02	31-Jul-02	1-Aug-02	2-Aug-02	3-Aug-02	4-Aug-02	Peak
Sportcity	109	104	97	129	169	95	101	114	477	95	504	611	650	553	540	657	488	306	603	539	862	862
Commonwealth Games Village	34	31	32	34	33	31	31	35	33	32	58	173	200	192	183	202	220	218	205	217	219	220
Bessmer Street (MAUC)	30	27	28	30	29	27	27	33	32	30	57	172	198	191	182	199	219	28	30	31	25	219
Rivington Mountain Biking Crowd Management	–	–	–	–	–	–	–	–	–	48	–	–	125	–	–	–	–	–	–	51	–	125
Salford Quays	–	–	–	–	–	–	–	–	–	–	–	–	2	2	–	21	–	14	14	13	88	88
MEN-Arena	–	–	–	–	–	–	–	–	–	–	–	62	84	70	75	69	74	87	66	60	–	87
International Broadcast Centre	69	43	43	63	52	55	61	51	53	45	50	44	48	60	44	43	60	45	47	53	46	69
National Cycling Centre	9	9	9	9	9	9	9	9	9	9	11	9	9	11	11	31	45	36	43	10	10	45
Bolton Arena	14	11	10	12	10	10	10	9	9	8	11	37	32	35	24	25	26	36	37	27	26	37
G-Mex	12	7	14	15	15	18	24	17	15	22	22	34	34	34	35	32	36	35	33	33	33	36
Flying Squad (attrition – covering all venues)	–	–	–	–	–	–	–	–	–	–	23	17	21	20	22	22	20					23
Heaton Park	–	–	–	–	–	–	–	–	–	–	–	15	14	20	21	22	20	19	16	18	22	22

(Continued)

Table 11.1 (Continued)

Venue	15-Jul-02	16-Jul-02	17-Jul-02	18-Jul-02	19-Jul-02	20-Jul-02	21-Jul-02	22-Jul-02	23-Jul-02	24-Jul-02	25-Jul-02	26-Jul-02	27-Jul-02	28-Jul-02	29-Jul-02	30-Jul-02	31-Jul-02	1-Aug-02	2-Aug-02	3-Aug-02	4-Aug-02	Peak
Hough End Fleet Car Park	16	16	16	16	16	16	16	16	16	16	16	16	16	16	16	16	16	16	16	16	16	16
Aquatics Centre	15	15	15	15	15	15	15	15	15	15	15	15	15	15	15	15	15	15	15	15	15	15
Belle Vue	12	12	12	12	12	12	12	12	12	12	12	12	12	12	12	12	12	12	12	12	12	12
Heron House	8	8	7	7	7	6	7	7	7	9	8	10	6	7	8	10	9	9	8	10	9	10
International Convention Centre	–	–	–	–	–	1	1	1	1	1	1	1	1	1	1	8	8	9	10	5	1	10
Forum Centre, Wythenshawe	–	–	–	–	–	–	–	–	–	–	1	1	1	1	1	1	1	9	7	7	9	9
Fleet Commissioning Depot Redvers Street	7	7	7	7	7	7	7	7	7	7	–	–	.	–	–	–	–	–	–	–	–	7
Technical Officials' Village	2	2	2	2	2	2	2	4	5	4	–	5	4	5	–	5	5	–	5	5	5	5
Bus Operations Depot Sheffield Street	4	4	4	4	4	4	4	4	4	4	4	4	4	4	4	4	4	4	4	4	4	4
Commonwealth House	4	4	4	4	4	4	4	4	4	4	4	4	4	4	4	4	4	4	4	4	4	4
Fleet Operations Depot Bessemer St	4	4	4	4	4	4	4	4	4	4	4	4	4	4	4	4	4	4	4	4	4	4
Main Press Centre	1	1	1	1	1	2	2	1	2	2	2	2	2	2	2	2	2	2	2	2	2	2
Mobile Drivers	–	–	–	2	2	2	2	2	2	2	2	2	2	2	2	2	2	1	2	2	2	2
Broadcast & Rate Card Car Parks	–	1	1	1	1	1	1	1	1	1	1	1	1	1	1	1	1	1	1	1	1	1

(Manchester City Council (2003), Manchester Commonwealth Games Post Games Report; for further information see www.gameslegacy.com)

volunteer and contractor staff may be highlighted in the design of uniforms and this can cause some dissatisfaction if not handled well. At many events these three groups are not easily distinguished as they form one workforce in one uniform. This is an important decision, with implications for motivation.

Accreditation

Workforce members need to be identifiable by security, by one another and by the event audience. A name badge is the simplest method, although for sophisticated events an accreditation badge would be produced, with precinct and access codes, a photograph and provision for electronic access to specific areas.

Sign-on and sign-off

A sign-on and sign-off system is important, both for staff and volunteers. For legal and ethical reasons, the event organizers should be able to account for everyone on duty.

Meal vouchers

The earlier example of staff numbers at different venues in Table 11.1 raises the issue of meal planning. Members of the workforce all need to be fed at least one hot meal per day. Forecasting is thus vitally important to avoid waste or, worse still, run out of food. There are two things that make catering planning a nightmare. First, many of the staff, such as security, have wide-ranging access and might eat at a different venue on each shift depending on where they are at the time. Generally, the news of which menu is best travels on two-way radio pretty quickly. Second, contract staff need to be catered for, requiring some sort of voucher system to allow the event organizer to redeem the cost of contractor meals post-event.

As Figure 11.1 illustrates, detailed planning is needed to estimate and account for the number of meals served at each meal period. Using the system illustrated, each contractor group (e.g. police, transport, security, cleaning) would need to be issued with a different coloured voucher.

Camping

At many music festivals, facilities for camping are provided for people working on site. In some cases they bring their families, friends and pets too. The need for a policy, procedures and control measures for this aspect of the event is immediately evident. At the Falcon Ridge Folk Festival, Hillsdale, New York, volunteers can expect three meals a day as well as camping facilities. The expense of running a three-meals-a-day canteen for staff (and possibly family and friends) is enough to give the event organizer the jitters – catering for the event audience would be a difficult enough task.

Lockers

If lockers are not provided for staff, they need to be aware of this and the fact that they are responsible for their own valuables.

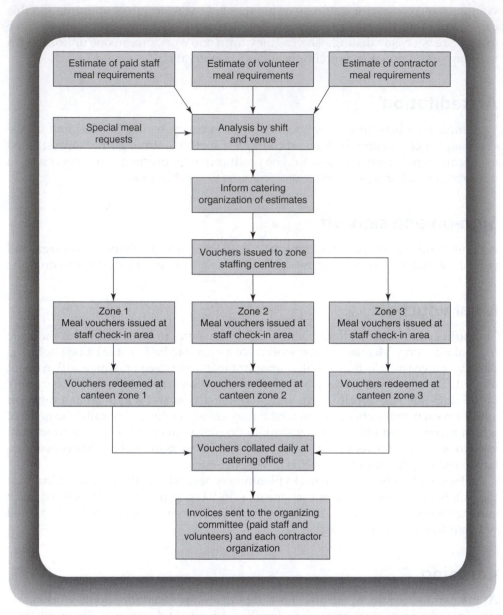

Figure 11.1 Estimating meal requirements and accounting for meals served

Communications equipment (two-way radios)

Management and supervisory staff require communication equipment, usually in the form of two-way radios. These may be issued on arrival at the staff desk or from the adjacent communications command centre.

Briefing and debriefing

It is traditional for staff arriving at an event to be given a briefing, regardless of whether they have already attended a training session. The briefing allows management to

Food safety training and systems are essential for commercial kitchens

Customer demands go from zero to 100 per cent within minutes

communicate important recent changes in operational planning. Likewise, the debriefing enables staff to air their thoughts about operational problems that may be able to be ironed out overnight. For the smaller event, the pre-event briefing could be all the training that is required.

Authority

When arriving for work people need to be told what to do and a checklist is exceptionally useful for this purpose. A common reason for frustration on the part of volunteers is that they are underemployed and therefore don't feel that their support is valuable. Furthermore, all staff, supervisors and volunteers should understand the limits of their authority.

Incident report forms

Employees and volunteers should report all criminal or suspicious behaviour, so on arrival they should be shown where the incident report forms can be found and where to put them when completed. At this time they can also be reminded about potentially more serious emergencies and how to respond to them. Strategically placed posters in staff areas are useful for informing personnel of these important aspects of events.

Dealing with no-shows

It is inevitable that some people will not turn up, and estimates need to be made for how many extra people will be needed to take their place.

Surveillance

Some events have cameras placed in many of the working areas. In Australia, for example, it is necessary to advise staff of their existence as covert surveillance of work areas is not permitted.

Access

Employees and volunteers should not enter areas where they do not have authorized access. A policy is often required on after-hours access to events which, for some, is an anticipated benefit of working at them. At other events, people are asked to leave the precinct on completion of their shift. The author remembers a volunteer, accompanied by two small children, fraternizing with sponsors at the bar. When she became very intoxicated, she and the children were sent home by taxi by a sponsorship manager. Unfortunately this was not reported until the next day.

Performance management

While most long-life organizations have formal performance appraisal systems, this is seldom the case in the project environment of the event business where performance management takes a different format. This is not to say, however, that the absence of a formal programme of annual interviews and appraisal precludes performance management. A simplified system of using the job description as the basis of an interview form was recommended in Chapter 7. Elements of performance management thus appear in the processes of job analysis, selection, induction and training.

Any organization, whether it has a formal or informal system, needs to do the following:

- Set standards of performance
- Set deadlines and outcomes
- Monitor and facilitate performance
- Provide feedback
- Develop and implement remedial action plans if necessary.

Kramer *et al.* (2002) suggest that there are five criteria for evaluation of performance management systems: strategic congruence, validity, reliability, acceptability, and specificity. The first of these, strategic congruence, 'refers to the extent to which performance appraisals encourage job performance that supports the organisation's strategy, goals and culture' (p. 307). Thus, in the event organization, any performance management system, whether project based or formal performance appraisal in the traditional sense, needs to serve the needs of the event. These authors recommend linking strategic objectives to a set of financial and operational measures. This would sit very comfortably with most event organizations.

Grievance procedures and dismissal

The first question it is necessary to ask is whether a grievance procedure is necessary. For small temporary teams operating for short periods of time such a procedure may be unnecessary as most problems will be readily solved. However, for large-scale events, this type of procedure is an invaluable way to deal with grievances, including those put forward by volunteers. The aims of an effective grievance procedure are immediate and confidential attention to conflict issues, consistency and a fair outcome. A grievance procedure should have the following features:

- It should be agreed between all stakeholders.
- It should be explained in plain English to everyone involved.
- The steps to be taken in making a complaint should be clear.
- People should be dealt with consistently and objectively.
- Confidentiality of all concerned should be maintained.
- There should be a means of escalating the issue through several levels of the organization.
- The process should be fully documented.

Essentially, this procedure ensures that people are dealt with fairly and objectively, particularly when there is a performance deficiency. Furthermore, allegations of unfairness can be investigated. There are two significant benefits of such a system: first, conflicts can be resolved and work resumed in a harmonious environment; and second, litigation can be avoided for most cases of alleged discrimination and unfair dismissal once the matter has been given this level of attention.

Dismissal procedures should include counselling and a series of warning letters. At each stage the full facts must be evident, the performance gap clearly identified and the individual given the opportunity to remedy the situation.

Disciplinary procedures

These are the issues that need to be considered in disciplinary procedures:

Specific issue

- What specifically was the offence, the action or inaction, or misconduct?
- Was this clearly a breach of the written code of conduct?
- Was this a minor or major disciplinary issue?
- How does this disciplinary issue relate to the person's job performance?

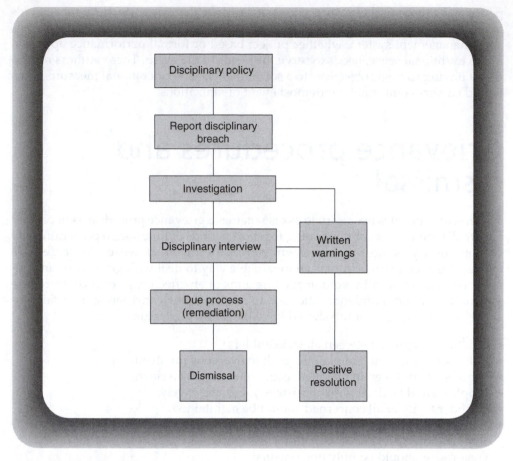

Figure 11.2 Disciplinary process

Awareness and evidence

- Did the person know that they were doing something wrong?
- Was the person warned?
- What are the facts and sources of information?
- Are there witnesses or evidence?

Circumstances

- Were there extenuating circumstances?
- Have these been taken into account?
- Have other people been committing the same offence?

Safety and crisis management

- Does the breach impact on workplace safety?
- What are the risks associated with the misconduct?
- Is this a potential media issue?

In a case of gross misconduct, the employee is asked to leave immediately without following the full process of warnings. This is known as summary dismissal and can apply also to volunteers.

Grounds for summary dismissal include:

- Gross dishonesty
- Willful damage to property
- Endangering the safety of self and others
- Assault and fighting
- Gross insubordination or insolence
- Intoxication on duty.

Procedural fairness in respect of a disciplinary hearing proposed by Labour Protect (2005) in South Africa includes:

- Adequate notice
- The hearing must precede the decision
- The hearing must be timely
- The employee must be informed of the charge/charges
- The employee should be present at the hearing
- The employee must be permitted representation (fellow employee or union member)
- The employee must be allowed to call witnesses
- The presiding officer should keep minutes
- The presiding officer should be impartial.

Case study 11.2

Conditions for volunteers for Melbourne 2006 Commonwealth Games

The following conditions were placed on becoming a volunteer for the Melbourne 2006 Commonwealth Games:

Step 7 – Agree Terms and Conditions

As a pre-condition of you becoming a Volunteer with the Melbourne 2006 Commonwealth Games Corporation ABN 22 088 659 705 ('Melbourne 2006') for the XVIII Commonwealth Games ('the Games'), you agree:

1 To give your voluntary services to Melbourne 2006 for the Games without pay, to the best of your abilities and to comply with all directions given to you by Melbourne 2006
2 That you complete the Volunteer Application Form to the best of your ability and information divulged is entirely true and correct
3 To undertake assessments to ascertain your suitability for a Volunteer role with Melbourne 2006 and to accept the outcome of a fair and merit based assessment

4 To attend required training sessions, work the minimum number of shifts notified by Melbourne 2006 and wear Melbourne 2006's official uniform and accreditation

5 That M2006 reserves the right not to offer you a Volunteer role

6 To keep confidential all information and/or materials concerning Melbourne 2006, the Australian Commonwealth Games Association, the Commonwealth Games Federation ('the CGF'), any national or international sporting organisation and any Commonwealth Games teams (collectively, the 'Commonwealth Games Bodies') which you know or should reasonably know is confidential

7 To notify Melbourne 2006 of any ideas or materials which you may create relating to your provision of voluntary services and, by signing this Application Form, transfer to Melbourne 2006 all rights and interests in these creations (such as copyright) and waive all moral rights in such creations

8 To safeguard your personal property (for example bags and money) located at our premises or Games venues and to understand that Melbourne 2006 will under no circumstances be responsible for any lost, stolen or damaged personal property

9 That you will not do anything to compromise your safety or the safety of others and you understand that there may be risks associated with providing particular Volunteer services

10 Not to make comments to any media organisation, disparaging or otherwise, which relate in any way to the business of Melbourne 2006, the Commonwealth Games Bodies, this agreement, or the Games without Melbourne 2006's express written consent

11 To the conduct of identity verification checks, background security checks, traffic checks and other security checks on you (which may include inspecting your personal property) prior to your entry to and departure from our premises or any Games sites or venues

12 That in conducting background checks, you will be required to consent to a national police record check which will identify whether you have:
   a. any convictions, findings of guilt and/or pending charges against you (non-traffic), in any Australian State or Territory
   b. any adult convictions (including being found guilty of an offence but discharged without conviction) which are less than ten years old (five years for juvenile offences)
   c. any adult convictions over ten years old (five years for juvenile offences) where the sentence imposed was imprisonment for a period greater than thirty months, and
   d. any traffic violations, criminal or traffic charges still pending before an Australian court

13 To participate at your own risk. You undertake to take all reasonable measures to protect yourself from the risks of participating in the Volunteer Programme and you release Melbourne 2006, the State of Victoria and all Commonwealth Games Bodies (and their respective executive members, directors, officers, employees, volunteers, contractors and agents) from any liability of any loss, damage, personal injury, death, economic loss or consequential loss whether in tort, in contract, under statute or otherwise, for any default, failure or negligence (to the extent permitted by law) in relation to your Volunteer role with the Games

14 That you are responsible for all property you bring to the Games and that Melbourne 2006, the State of Victoria and all Commonwealth Games Bodies accept no responsibility for any loss or damage to this property

15 That your name, image and likeness ('the Images') may be photographed, filmed, broadcast or otherwise recorded during competition or any other events incidental to your Volunteer role in the Games

16 To give your unconditional and irrevocable consent to Melbourne 2006, the State of Victoria, the Commonwealth Games Bodies and anyone authorised by them to record the Images during the Games and to copy, publish, broadcast, distribute and communicate the Images to the public by any other means, in any format and on any media without payment to you. You also consent to the use of the Images for all other current or future purposes authorised by Melbourne 2006, the State of Victoria, or the Commonwealth Games Bodies including marketing and promotional activities in connection with the Games. The Images shall be Melbourne 2006's sole and exclusive property for the duration of the Games, and after that, the sole and exclusive property of the CGF. You also release and discharge Melbourne 2006 from all claims whatsoever in connection with the use of the Images and your rights in them

17 That you do not have, and cannot imply that you have, any marketing or promotional rights of association in relation to the Games, Commonwealth Games Bodies, Volunteer Programme or any other event associated with the Games. For the avoidance of doubt, you must not promote or sell any product or service while undertaking your role as a Volunteer

18 To irrevocably waive any and all moral rights in connection with the Images referred to in 15

19 To Melbourne 2006's administration of first aid and/or medical treatment if you are injured or ill while giving voluntary services

20 To perform all duties and requirements in accordance with every policy, procedure and lawful direction provided by Melbourne 2006, as varied from time to time

21 To accept the shifts offered to you in accordance with your specified availability and request changes only where changes are absolutely necessary

22 To reside within a reasonable distance from your rostered venue, representing a travel time of no greater than one hour

23 Not to engage in any form of harassment, bullying or discrimination

24 That Melbourne 2006 may terminate your appointment as a Volunteer if you do not comply with these provisions or engage in misconduct which, in Melbourne 2006's opinion, adversely affects the interests of any Commonwealth Games Body.

(Reproduced with permission of Melbourne 2006 Commonwealth Games Corporation)

Reflective practice 11.2

1 Why is it necessary for an event of this size to develop such a comprehensive code?
2 This list of rules is quite extensive. Assume that you are running a much smaller event and consolidate them to develop your own guidelines in plain English.

Revision questions

1 What is the difference between a policy and a procedure?
2 List and describe some of the logistics challenges of the workforce co-ordinator.
3 Write a short code of conduct for volunteers at a small community festival.
4 How would you go about communicating the above code to staff and volunteers?

References

Burning Man 10 Principles (2005). Viewed 29 December 2005, www.burningman. com/whatisburningman/about_burningman/principles.html.

Kramer, R., O'Connor, M. and Davis, E. (2002). Appraising and managing performance. In *Australian Master Human Resources Guide*. CCH, pp. 301–22.

Labour Protect (2005). Dismissal for misconduct. Viewed 31 January 2005, www.labourprotect.co.za/unfair_dismissals.htm.

Manchester City Council (2003). Manchester Commonwealth Games Post Games Report. Viewed 17 May 2006, www.gameslegacy.com.

Melbourne 2006 Commonwealth Games (2005). Melbourne 2006 workforce privacy policy. Viewed 29 December 2005, www.melbourne2006.com.au/employment/ Melbourne+2006+Workforce+Privacy+Policy.

UK Sports (2005). Major sports events – the guide. Viewed 29 December 2005, www.uksport.gov.uk/generic_template.asp?id=12237.

Chapter 12
Event organizational culture

Learning objectives

After reading through this chapter you will be able to:

- Define the term organizational culture and describe an event organizational culture
- List and describe ways in which organizational culture is established
- Discuss service culture in terms of the event product and its features
- Describe stakeholders and how they impact on event organizational culture.

Introduction

The culture of an organization is reflected in the way things are done within the organization. For example, the level of formality with which senior management are addressed is one feature of an organization's culture. Wimbledon would have a fairly formal culture, with highly developed policies and procedures based on the event's long history. In contrast, relationships between staff planning the Woodstock 1969 Music and Art Festival would undoubtedly have been quite frenetic, given that 50 000 people were expected and 500 000 turned up! In fact, it would have been quite different from any similar event held today, given the values held by those who staged the event and the fact that it was the climax of the hippie era.

Organizations mould a common set of attitudes and values, whether intentionally or not. In most cases it is done intentionally, the culture developing through selection and socialization of members. The language used in the organization is another feature of its unique culture; indeed, the field of event management has a language of its own, summarized in the glossary. Staff at mega events often use more acronyms than words, with the result that outsiders find it hard to understand what they are saying!

Shone and Parry (2004, p. 194) sum up, in general terms, the culture of events: 'events are significant social activities; they are often communal and good natured, and this is reflected in their culture.'

What is organizational culture?

Culture is a system of learned patterns of behaviour, ideas and products characteristic of a group or society. Organizational culture can be described in terms of patterns of cross-individual behavioural consistency within an organization. For example, when people say that culture is 'the way we do things around here', they are defining the consistent way in which people perform tasks, solve problems, resolve conflicts, and treat customers and employees. Culture is also defined by the informal values, norms and beliefs that guide how individuals and groups in an organization interact with each other and with people outside the organization. A strong organizational culture gives people a sense of identity, encourages commitment to the organization's values and mission, and promotes stability.

A culture is conveyed internally through the following means.

Organizational structure

This may be stable or unstable. It is unstable, for example, when there is constant reorganization or when there is a high turnover of staff. It can be tall, with many levels to the hierarchy, or low, where there are few levels to the hierarchy.

Mission and objectives

Many organizations and events have very clear mission statements that encapsulate their culture, as those of the Indigenous Heritage Festival and the Southeastern Surgical Congress indicate:

> The Indigenous Heritage Festival provides crucial opportunities for indigenous peoples of the world to share self-expression and wisdom with communities and initiate inter-tribal relationships that promote cultural exchange and build economic co-operation. Our ultimate vision is to witness the establishment of a united network of flourishing indigenous nations and our global society enriched and strengthened by cultural diversity.
> (www.indigenousfestival.org/MissionStatement.asp)

> The Southeastern Surgical Congress was founded to provide opportunities for surgeons and surgeons in training to come together for educational, scientific and social purposes to promote and advance the study and practice of surgery.
>
> (www.sesc.org/member/information/MissionStatement.htm)

Devolution of decision making

Where there are few levels to the hierarchy, individuals at the lower levels are more likely to be empowered to make decisions without sending them up the line. Thus they have higher levels of responsibility.

Policies and procedures

Approvals for equipment acquisition, petty cash systems, grievance procedures, and reward and recognition programmes are all examples of policies with associated procedures, and their content is indicative of the organization's culture.

Language specific to the workplace

Unfortunately, the specific language of the workplace becomes second nature to those immersed in the culture, making them oblivious to the fact that some of their communication is incomprehensible to others. For example:

> *Our contingency plan must be linked to the risk assessment which is weighted according to probability and consequence. The VCC [venue command centre] will be the base for implementing the VERP [venue emergency response plan].*

(Van der Wagen, 2004)

Distribution of rewards

Remuneration at different levels of the organization is another feature of the culture, with large differences in some organizations and smaller differences in others. This has a major impact on how people work together.

Communication flows

Both vertical and horizontal communication varies from organization to organization. There is also the 'grapevine', the informal communication network, where supposition and rumour prevail, which at times can be damaging.

Resource allocation

The amount of financial and other resources allocated to different departments distinguishes their position in the pecking order. In the event business, if the functional area of waste management is given a very small budget and only one staff member, this is indicative of the value placed on environmental impact by the organization.

How does event organizational culture differ?

Primarily events are service enterprises, not manufacturing enterprises, so it is necessary to look at the event product and service features in order to better grasp the concept of event organizational culture.

Service orientation of events

Here we are looking at the organization's culture as it is expressed in its external relationships. Customers have contact with the event at the following four points and at each point the organization's service culture is communicated (Van der Wagen, 2004):

1. Pre-purchase
   (a) *interactive website*
   (b) *email*
   (c) *telephone enquiry*
2. Purchase/pre-event
   (a) *ticket sale*
   (b) *transportation*

      (c) parking
      (d) queuing
      (e) entry
      (f) security check

3. Event
      (a) seat allocation/usher
      (b) food and beverage
      (c) information
      (d) entertainment
      (e) performance/participation (e.g. in concert/fun run)
      (f) first aid
      (g) merchandise sales
      (h) lost and found

4. Post-event
      (a) exit
      (b) queue
      (c) transport
      (d) online results
      (e) photographs/memorabilia

Furthermore, the event product is characterized by the following services marketing characteristics, which have implications for human resource management.

Intangibility

Services cannot be seen, touched or taken home, and for this reason the customer has difficulty assessing quality and value until after the service experience. A ticket to an event, such as a concert, is often the only tangible reminder of an experience that is judged worthwhile, but it is difficult for the customer to describe, particularly the fleeting points of service contact described earlier. All form part of a cumulative experience which is intangible.

The implication for human resource management is the necessity for a strong culture built on induction and training. Consistent and positive responses by staff and volunteers that reflect the organization's values need to be developed for every service interaction. Some workforce members refer to orientation as 'indoctrination' as this form of training aims to have everyone understand the event's mission and in some cases (particularly fundraising events) to be inspired and motivated by it. This mission and culture could be peace and harmony; novelty and extremism; political posturing; appreciation of a unique artform; or a love of books. For many events, there is an upbeat mood of community celebration.

Perishability

An event organization cannot keep an event experience such as a seat in a stadium for a cricket match and sell it the next day because by then the match is over – the commodity is perishable. In contrast, a hardware store can sell a hammer any time for months and years after it is put on the shelf. The perishability of the event product means that it must sell at the time it is offered and marketing efforts are generally directed at developing demand for tickets. This often means that large crowds attend and there are queues for tickets, entry, cloakrooms and exits. This puts pressure on service personnel to deal with sudden peaks and high-level consumer demands. If there is any prospect of missing the show, tempers flare. Training to deal with these possibilities is essential. The event organization has to capitalize on the moment, and needs staff to help it do so at an optimal level of efficiency.

Inseparability

Services quality and consistency are subject to great variability because they are delivered by people, and human behaviour is difficult to control. The service is inseparable from the service provider. The mood or facial expression of the service provider characterizes the service for that encounter. Judgements are made by both service provider and customer affecting subsequent communication. By paying careful attention to recruitment of staff and volunteers and selecting for sound customer relations skills, it is possible to achieve higher levels of service quality. Training, specifically in service provision, is also recommended. For a service-based enterprise, the investment is in preparing the workforce and not in developing systems of quality control checks as would be done for a production line.

Variability

Following the concept of inseparability, every interaction with the customer is a unique communication. It is thus subject to considerable variation, and in most cases so it should be. The provider customizes their response to meet the customer's needs. However, for this to work successfully, the provider must be empowered to make decisions and solve customer problems. Working closely with management during briefings and debriefings can lead to resolution of many problems, which in turn leads to greater consistency in customer service interactions between staff and clients. Better decision making on the part of frontline personnel is essential for quality service.

Dynamic quality of events

It is difficult to describe the culture of an event organization unless it is an ongoing concern such as a music promoter (multiple shows with a permanent staff) or an exhibition hire company. Even this type of organization would be quite a turbulent environment in which to work. Each new performance, road show or exhibition would provide different challenges. Often the culture of the pre-event period is quite different from the culture of the operational and post-event periods. One thing that is common to all events is that they tend to operate in an environment of relative uncertainty:

> The more complex and the more unique an event is, the more likely it is to be more labour-intensive, both in terms of organization and operation. The organizational issue relates to the need for relatively complicated planning to enable the service delivery to be efficient, or put more simply, for the event to be a good one (this is why some events may be outsourced to event management companies, caterers or other types of suppliers). The uniqueness of this type of service implies a high level of communication between the organizer and the event manager. Such a high level of communication and planning will take time and effort, even where the event may be repeating a well-known formula, or operating within a common framework such as a conference. The operational element may also require high levels of staffing in order to deliver the event properly.
>
> (Shone and Parry, 2004, p. 17)

Much has been made of the idea that the event organization is dynamic and responsive to many situational changes in the life of each event project, and thus theorists are now looking more carefully at the role of human resource managers in non-static organizations. Tyson (1999) suggests that greater weighting needs to be given to process and diagnostic skills on the part of the human resource practitioner than to detailed technical knowledge of human resource management. This is a valuable perspective. From the growth of the event workforce over time, as shown for paid staff

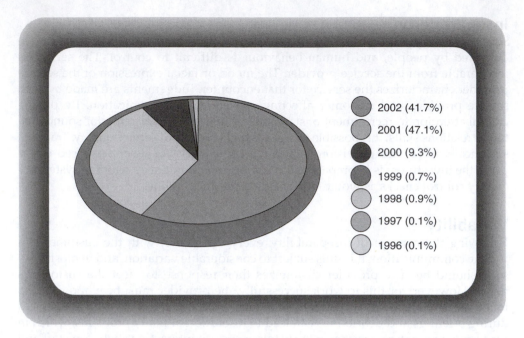

Figure 12.1 Yearly recruitment of full-time employees for the 2002 Manchester Commonwealth Games
(Manchester City Council (2003), Manchester Commonwealth Games Post Games Report; for further information see www.gameslegacy.com)

alone for the Manchester Commonwealth Games in Figure 12.1, it is easy to see that a process and diagnostic focus would better serve the evolutionary character of events.

Relationships with external stakeholders

It would be impossible to discuss event organizational culture without covering the important relationships developed with external organizations. Multiple stakeholders are part of the event communication structure and these external bodies have a profound impact on operational planning and execution. Police and traffic authorities are an example of stakeholders; sponsorship providers are another, having considerable input into ensuring that the event meets their sponsorship and branding expectations.

Eunson (2005) uses the term 'boundary spanner' to describe people working at the interface between the organization and the environment of stakeholders. Boundary spanners have a job role that places them in contact with clients and others, sometimes spending more time with people outside the organization than within it. This role is also played out within the event organization, for example, where the marketing manager has considerable ongoing communication with the naming rights sponsor. Figure 12.2 illustrates the most common stakeholders with which the event organization has relationships, and these are described in more detail below.

Government

Legislative compliance and approval processes are often quite taxing, involving long periods of negotiation by the event organizer with local and regional government bodies, tourism bodies, and authorities such as police, traffic management and environmental protection (see Case study 12.2).

Working with media stakeholders

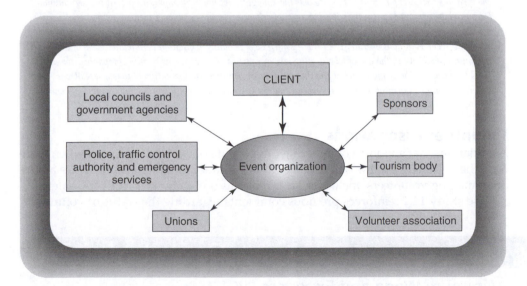

Figure 12.2 Common stakeholder relationships with the event organization

Sponsors

The level of interaction with sponsors varies in accordance with their financial commitment to the event. In some cases sponsors are happy to leave the running of the event to the organizers; in others, sponsors have a great deal at stake and play a significant role in staging the event to suit their aims. This requires endless communication and negotiation, and approval at every step along the way. Sponsors might wish to play a part in designing the event programme, providing goods and services at the event, and managing marketing and publicity, and many sponsors like to run corporate hospitality programmes for their business contacts and staff.

Unions

The role of unions in events was discussed in Chapter 6. For organizations operating in South Africa, United Kingdom and Australia, for example, these relationships are an important consideration for organizational communication. Keeping the unions in the loop can be a pro-active measure with significant and positive outcomes, including simplified planning and improved staff retention (Webb, 2001). Also important are the relationships between contractors and unions, which have been highlighted in Chapter 5. While, theoretically, these contractor organizations operate at arms length from the event organization, the relationship between contractor and union/s is crucial to meeting deadlines. The alternative could be a dispute which could disrupt planning and execution of the event.

In the United Kingdom interest is growing in the role trade unions play in supporting those people employed in freelance or contingent work. Research conducted by Heery *et al.* (2004) has focused on case studies of the media and entertainment unions as well as those representing freelance guides, interpreters and translators. These members of the event workforce have mobile careers and are increasingly concerned with the security, tenure and development potential of their appointments:

> *The focus of our research was on trade unions but also yielded information on the reactions of employers. What emerged most strongly from this evidence was the ambiguity with which employers regard the regulation of freelance labour markets, an ambiguity that arguably characterizes the employer view of institutionalized job regulation per se. They cavil at constraint, and avoidance of union-authored rules is common in the industries in which freelance unions operate. The primary purpose of avoiding regulation is to reduce costs and ensure maximum flexibility in the use of labour although, in some cases, such as major film companies, avoidance takes the form of offering high rates of pay that allow the recruitment and retention of the most skilled labour. Where regulation is institutionalized, however, employers frequently accept it and acknowledge its efficiencies.*
>
> (Heery *et al.*, 2004, p. 32)

Volunteer associations

Associations that support volunteering can provide outstanding support when planning the volunteer programme. For example, Volunteering England provides advice on managing volunteers, including such topics as occupational health and safety.

Case study 12.1 reinforces previous comments regarding the status of volunteers.

Case study 12.1

National Minimum Wage and Expenses UK

The National Minimum Wage Act 1998 *came into force in April 1999. The act gives all workers the right to a set minimum wage. In theory, this should not affect volunteers. However, there have been a small number of cases in which individuals volunteering have been able to prove that they have been working under a contract. This has resulted in their being regarded as employees entitled to full employment rights, or included in a wider definition of employment (usually described as 'worker'), used by the anti-discrimination legislation and the* National Minimum Wage Act. *The legislation behind the*

National Minimum Wage Act *can look complex, and the safeguards that organizations need to impose may seem pernickety, but there are some fairly simple steps that organizations can make to ensure that their volunteers are volunteers, and not employees, in the eyes of the law.*

Employee or volunteer?

To prove that they are employed by an organization rather than volunteering for it, individuals would have to show that they had a contract. This may seem fairly straightforward. Volunteers often sign agreements stating that they understand what the organization expects of them and will do their best to turn up on time and follow policies and procedures etc. etc. However, it is usually made clear to the volunteer that this is a statement of what will happen ideally and that it is not legally binding, which means that it is not a contract. Therefore most organizations working with volunteers would assume that their volunteers have not got a contract with them.

What many people do not know is that a contract does not have to be a written document or even a verbal agreement. A contract is created when an individual agrees to carry out a task in return for something. So, for instance, if you agree to water your neighbour's garden while they are on holiday in return for £10, a contract of employment has been set up. If your neighbour does not agree to pay you but says that if you water their garden then they will bring you back some duty-free cigarettes, a contract is still created because you are doing something in return for something with an economic value (legally referred to as a 'consideration').

(Reproduced with permission of Volunteering England; for more information see: www.volunteering.org.uk/missions.php?id = 432)

Reflective practice 12.1

The website for Volunteering England also contains advice regarding expenses, training and rewards, as well as:

- Planning advice
- Source of experienced volunteer co-ordinators
- Source of experienced volunteers
- Examples of good practice
- Codes of conduct
- Management programmes.

Visit the website and answer the following questions:

1 For an employment contract to be valid, there has to be some form of consideration (usually money). How does an event organization ensure that volunteers are clear about their status and entitlements?
2 Identify five ways in which volunteer best practice can be demonstrated and visit an event (online if necessary) to evaluate volunteer management principles of that event.

Some event organizations have an outstanding relationship with their highly motivated volunteers, so much so that these volunteers meet for years after the event and even continue to wear their colourful uniforms! However, in other cases, this level of camaraderie is not achieved and volunteers leave feeling that they have been exploited or underutilized. Developing relationships with volunteer organizations to support the volunteer programme can lead to more effective management of such programmes.

Clients

Of course, the most significant stakeholder for most events is the client. This could be the person booking the meeting, organizing the company conference, planning the incentive trip or booking the wedding or party. Communication with the client needs to be frequent and clear, so that every expectation is realized. Of course, in some cases, it is impossible to meet every need for the price quoted! Communication with the client needs to be supported by written documentation such as the booking contract. However, from that time on there are likely to be many meetings and conversations that likewise need to be recorded (however briefly), with any changes to service provision and contract price agreed in writing, for which emails will generally suffice.

Reliance on customer satisfaction

In their study, Getz *et al.* (2001) constructed a service map for an event in which they identified the processes – listed earlier in the chapter – through which visitors experienced the event, judged the effectiveness of encounters with staff, viewed tangible evidence of services provided, conducted observations of crowd behaviour, and applied knowledge of management systems and operations. The study was undertaken using trained observers to supplement visitor surveys. The resulting narratives produced by observers led to numerous recommendations for service improvement, including providing more visible and welcoming staff/volunteers.

While it is impossible to cover all aspects of this study and their implications for evaluation, service mapping was one of the main recommendations. This study also provides a baseline for comparative research.

The authors concluded:

> *Events are different from other service encounters, as demonstrated by this research. The event product is unique each time it is offered, and there are no routine service encounters. No matter what management systems are in place, interactions between setting, management and visitors result in unpredictable elements. Indeed, customers help shape the experience through expectations, emotional states and their social interaction.*
>
> (Getz *et al.*, 2001, p. 389)

Case study 12.2

Planning guidelines for events in London's Royal Parks

The following extract is from the planning guidelines for London's Royal Parks:

5.2   Liaison with local authorities

Local authorities can be involved in events through highway management, emergency planning, environmental health (noise, catering, refuse, water and similar) and building control, or as promoters or partners in the event.

Noise. The local authority has the statutory powers to issue noise abatement notices for events in the Royal Parks as elsewhere. Ultimately this could lead to prosecution if statutory notices were ignored.

Food hygiene. The officers responsible for food hygiene must be advised of any temporary arrangements for catering at events. The local authority has the statutory power to inspect caterers in the parks as elsewhere and to take action against them if they consider it necessary.

Toilets and waste disposal. For major events the local authority may also want to comment on your arrangements for toilets, water and refuse collection.

Temporary demountable structures are required to be licensed by some local authorities.

Particularly large events may have an impact on the streets surrounding the park, such as litter, parking, traffic, evacuation or emergency planning. In such cases the local authority should be invited to join event planning meetings.

5.3 Liaison with other public authorities

Transport for London (TfL) are responsible for London's buses, the tube network and some roads. Event planning will need to involve TfL representatives if the event could generate significant additional use of public transport in the area.

The Royal Parks Constabulary will normally make the decision as to when and how to liaise with the *Metropolitan Police.*

London Fire Brigade. The approval of LFB should be sought for the emergency action plans and site plans of all major events. The Fire Brigade should be invited to inspect the event site, particularly if it is an enclosed site.

The *London Ambulance Service* will normally only be consulted for the very largest events. However, first aid requirements should be established for all events and the Event Safety Guide provides useful guidance on this.

(www.royalparks.gov.uk/docs/guidelines_ for_event_organisers.doc)

Reflective practice 12.2

1 Illustrate communication relationships with these bodies by means of a diagram.
2 Explain some of the communication considerations you would have when dealing with these authorities, for example, expectation and points of difference.

Social impacts of events

From a study of the key impacts currently being used for event evaluation, Jago (2005) has proposed the concept of triple bottom line evaluation of events, which covers economic, environmental and social impacts. While it is impossible to do justice to the topic of event evaluation here, suffice it to say that human resource management contributes, at least in part, to the social impact of an event. For example, an estimate of the workforce for the Soccer World Cup 2010 in South Africa is the equivalent of 159 000 annual jobs (Swart and Urmilla, 2005). Large-scale events can contribute to direct short-term employment at the event and, in some cases, to long-term employment if there is significant tourism impact. Depending on the scale and scope of the event, training initiatives can be quite significant in attaining such an outcome, particularly if they cover the full scope of training, from management development through to specific skill acquisition.

There are also more intangible benefits such as increase in community pride, leading to greater self-confidence and a 'can do' attitude on the part of individuals and the community. The culture of the event can thus transmit to the general community, bringing long-term benefits. This is what Shanghai is aiming for with Expo 2010 (see Case study 12.3).

While it is tempting to consider only the positive outcomes of events, we must be mindful that some events are not successful. In his analysis of why some festivals fail, Getz (2002) points to the following reasons:

Human resources
- Incompetent event managers or staff
- Volunteer burnout
- Corruption or theft from within
- High turnover among volunteers

Organizational culture
- Lack of strong leadership
- Internal divisions over goals, programme, strategy, etc.
- The event founders had not permitted needed changes
- The structure of the organization prevented necessary changes

Further, he goes on to point out that an event might fail, not because it has reached the end of the product life cycle or because of market forces, but due to an absence of strategic planning and a sound organizational culture.

Case study 12.3

Shanghai World Expo 2010

11th-Five Year is a key period for the Expo preparations. It is not only a major task for the city of Shanghai but also for the nation as a whole. At the routine news press by Shanghai municipal government yesterday, it was revealed that to host a successful, excellent and unforgettable Expo has become one of the key missions for the Shanghai government. All preparations and efforts will centre around this target to make it materialize in a satisfactory way.

The spokeswoman for Shanghai municipal government Jiao Yang said joint efforts from both home and abroad are needed for an impressive Expo. 'We will try our best to make our target come true, including to invite 200 nations and international organizations to participate and to build the Expo park …'

According to Jiao Yang, the mind and wisdom of Shanghai citizens and the whole nation, as well as the ideas of the world, are a must for such a grand gathering. Successful experience should be learned from. Excellent achievements of human beings should also be made full use of. That's the precondition of hosting a successful, excellent and unforgettable Expo.

Shanghai Expo 2010 is in need of a full understanding and participation of people from all walks of life.

(www.expo2010china.com/expo/english/eu/eh/userobject1ai26930.html)

Reflective practice 12.3
1 Discuss the host city's expectations for this event.
2 If 200 nations and international organizations participate, explain how a 'best fit' between national cultures can be achieved.
3 If you were responsible for training the workforce for this event, what would you list as five priorities?

Chapter summary and key points

This chapter has looked at organizational culture and has highlighted some of the dimensions of an organizational culture, such as policies, practices, communication flows and resource allocation. Looking specifically at the event industry's organizational culture, we saw that the emphasis was on characteristics of the service culture as they apply in this context, that is, intangibility, perishability, inseparability and variability. Providing quality service in this complex environment (with a temporary workforce) is exceptionally challenging and, from a human resource perspective, the importance of careful labour force planning, selection and training cannot be underestimated. Other defining features of the event organizational culture were seen to include the dynamic nature of events, the network of relationships with external stakeholders and the heavy reliance on customer satisfaction for the event's success.

Revision questions

1 Select an event on the Internet that you can investigate or visit one in person. Describe the culture of the event organization through your observations and by using the dimensions suggested in this chapter.
2 Elaborate on the statement, 'Events provide services that are intangible and inseparable, therefore staff communication and customer service training is vitally important.'
3 For a specific local event, describe three of the stakeholders and their communication relationships with the event organizers.
4 Events have social impacts. Compare two events in terms of their human resources impact.

References

Eunson, B. (2005). *Communicating in the 21st Century*. John Wiley and Sons.

Geert Hofstede Cultural Dimensions (2006). *ITIM International*. Viewed 12 February 2006, www.geert-hofstede.com/hofstede_brazil.shtml.

Getz, D. (2002). Why festivals fail. *Event Management*, **7(4)**, 209–19.

Getz, D., O'Neill, M. and Carlsen, J. (2001). Service quality evaluation at events through service mapping. *Journal of Travel Research*, **39**, 380–90.

Heery, E., Conley, J., Delbridge, R. and Stewart, P. (2004). Beyond the enterprise: trade union representation of freelancers in the UK. *Human Resources Management Journal*, **14(2)**, 20–34.

Hofstede, G. (1991). *Cultures and Organizations: Software of the Mind*. McGraw-Hill.

Jago, L. (2005). The impacts of events: triple bottom line event evaluation. In *The Impacts of Events*. University of Technology, Sydney.

Manchester City Council (2003). Manchester Commonwealth Games Post Games Report. Viewed 17 May 2006, www.gameslegacy.com.

Shone, A. and Parry, B. (2004). *Successful Event Management*, 2nd edn. Thomson Learning.

Swart, K. and Urmilla, B. (2005). Leveraging anticipated benefits associated with hosting the 2010 Soccer World Cup in South Africa. In *The Impacts of Events*. University of Technology, Sydney.

Tyson, S. (1999). How HR knowledge contributes to organizational performance. *Human Resource Management Journal*, **9(3)**, 42–53.

Van der Wagen, L. (2004). *Event Management*, 2nd edn. Pearson Education.

Volunteering England (2006). Managing volunteers. Viewed 4 January 2006, www.volunteering.org.uk/missions.php?id=432.

Webb, T. (2001). *The Collaborative Games: The Story behind the Spectacle*. Pluto Press.

Chapter 13
Organizational communication

Learning objectives

After reading through this chapter you will be able to:

■ Describe the communication challenges of the event environment
■ Discuss the issue of knowledge management: transmission of knowledge within and beyond the event
■ Describe the factors that can lead to conflict
■ Evaluate ways in which collaborative work practices can be improved
■ Describe the difference between national and organizational cultures
■ Briefly discuss research into cross-cultural communication.

Introduction

This chapter looks at communication processes. The event environment, due to its turbulent and temporary nature, can provide real challenges for effective communication. Sharing knowledge within and across events can be unreliable, although new technologies are assisting in storing and disseminating a wide range of information. Therefore, the importance of data collection, research and evaluation cannot be stressed enough. For the industry to become more professional, the process of event operational planning needs to be improved and consolidated, particularly where there are serious threats to safety. As O'Toole (2000) has suggested:

> For too long the event industry has ignored the past problems. Ask many event managers about their events and it's as though it went from 'go to o' without a hitch – except for the client changing their mind and the suppliers turning up with the wrong equipment. I suppose they are protecting their good name. The trouble arises when there is a major problem – it seems to come from nowhere and the results are often devastating. One only has to consider the Sydney to Hobart Yacht Race [see Case study 13.1]. If we do look at the past problems then it is often with 20/20 hindsight – of course 'if we had only planned better!' But this does little to help with future events. Each event is a unique combination of suppliers, venues, clients, sponsors, audience. Even if all these event elements are exactly the same, the weather is different, the Australian dollar goes up, a key company collapses or is merged, or there is new legislation pertaining to the event.

If we do not learn from our mistakes, as the saying goes, we are condemned to repeat them. The individual event manager, on their own, can hardly do this. Certainly they can learn from their own mistakes – but this does not make an industry. An association such as ISES can provide a repository of the 'lessons learned' that can be used to strengthen the industry.

Fortunately the event manager has a tool that can be used for their future events. This is the risk management methodology as set out in project management.

Event communication

Goldblatt (2005) points out that event management is a profession where success or failure depends on communication. He also stresses that there are often barriers to communication, such as noise and visual distractions in the event environment. Regardless of the communication channel chosen, and the barriers to communication, it is essential that messages are clear, action oriented and, in most cases, recorded for future reference. This is particularly the case if a contract variation is involved, where customers ask for more, and more, and more! While a good customer service orientation is essential, it is also essential to recognize when additional services have cost implications.

There are numerous ways in which communication can be conveyed in an organization, the most common being:

- memos and emails
- phone calls
- meetings.

The information booth is at the centre of customer service

In the event environment there are two stages where good communication is essential: developing plans and communication on site. For the first of these, the intranet can be a useful tool, facilitating the storage of project plans on the network and updating by anyone on the team. Generally an email is automatically generated to advise team members of changes made. If this is not the case, another procedure needs to be developed to guard against timelines being modified without anyone noticing. As enticing as this technology sounds, it is not user friendly, and many people prefer to have ownership of part of the project rather than have teams contributing to a common plan or budget.

For communication on site two-way radio is the preferred option, although smaller events usually get by using mobile phones. Two-way radio allows multiple people to work together on the same channel. However, this runs the risk of there being too much communication and staff members are often advised to use the radio channel sparingly so that priorities can be managed effectively. And if the radio is used for chitchat others will be excluded, although there are, of course, overrides or alternative channels for emergency reporting.

Case study 13.1

Sydney-to-Hobart disaster: Who's to blame?

Three years after the tragic deaths of six sailors in the 1998 Sydney-to-Hobart race, the Australian coroner in charge of the case has issued his report on the circumstances surrounding the deaths and blasts both race officials and meteorologists alike. Of the 115 boats involved in the 650-nautical-mile race, 5 sank, 66 retired and 55 crew members had to be rescued as a result of the unforecast storm.

State Coroner John Abernethy's 331-page report criticizes the organization of the race management team, and their lack of timely response to a very serious situation. He said the race organizers lacked the necessary knowledge of meteorology and 'failed to appreciate the impending storm'. Also found at fault were Australian meteorologists who were not steadfast enough in assuring that the racing fleet was informed of the danger that was in their path.

Hours after the race began, the Australian Bureau of Meteorology (BOM) issued a storm warning, but upon calling the race director about the gathering storm, they received no answer. Instead of tracking down anyone in the management team and impressing upon them the severity of the storm, the BOM merely faxed a copy of the warning to the sponsoring yacht club. Unfortunately, the race managers were already aboard the committee boat.

Although race officials did finally receive the faxed storm warning, 22 hours before the sailors reached the treacherous waters and gale force winds in Bass Strait, they failed to grasp the severity of it, and did not inform the race boats. As conditions worsened and reports of 75-knot winds were brought to the race committee, they still did not attempt to relay the warning to the race crews. Once the storm hit the boats and they were in imminent danger, the race management team had no crisis plan ready.

(*Boat/US Magazine*, May 2001, www.findarticles.com/p/articles/mi_m0BQK/is_3_6/ai_74699537)

Reflective practice 13.1

This article illustrates the communication issues that emerged between the Australian Bureau of Meteorology and the race management team. Explain how they occurred and how they could have been avoided.

Transmission models of communication emphasize that a 'message' be transmitted from one person to another. This message is converted into a signal, which is transmitted via a channel. If, for example, the channel is the telephone, there are various ways in which the transmission can be disrupted. First, there is mechanical noise, making it hard for the receiver to hear the message. Or there could be poor reception on a mobile phone (another form of mechanical noise), interfering with the transmission of the message. The second type of disruption is semantic noise. If your communication is unclear and the message confusing, through the use of words the receiver does not understand, this too can contribute to poor message transmission. Use of jargon or complex words contributes to semantic noise. Finally, psychological noise causes the receiver to block or object to the message, perhaps due to the tone or language used. If, for example, a supervisor used a swear word on a two-way radio this could interfere with the message content. The receiver might get offended and ignore the instruction. Ultimately, the aim is to ensure that the meaning of the sender is interpreted correctly by the receiver.

Knowledge management

Broadly, knowledge management is the process of systematically managing the stores of knowledge in an organization and transforming these information and intellectual assets into enduring value for the organization. Within the event operation, the focus of knowledge management is on the development and dissemination of information to the workforce and the management of post-event evaluation.

One of the characteristic features of the event environment is the speed at which decisions are made. When talking about the Wave Aid concert put on in quick response to the 2004 tsunami, Matthew Lazarus-Hall said that decisions were made in record time. On one occasion, he left a meeting to find that the decisions made there had changed before he reached the parking lot.

Responsiveness to operational contingencies often requires quick dissemination of information to staff and volunteers who are dealing with the public. Systems need to be in place to ensure that this happens. As seen above, two-way radio is used for this purpose, although today many event staff rely more on their mobile phones for communication. The advent of a new generation of mobile phones, or personal digital devices, will enable central updates of core information, all of which will be available immediately to those on the ground with micro touch screens.

Knowledge management in relation to event evaluation is increasingly viewed as a priority. The Olympic Games Knowledge Management repository is an example of an initiative developed in 1998 so that future events could build upon the planning of past events by accessing and transferring historical information. A similar system was developed by the Manchester Commonwealth Games and built on by the Melbourne Commonwealth Games. All events – whether one-off productions or annual events – can create a useful legacy for those that follow by assembling, storing and evaluating data related to the event.

Unlike the hotel industry in which standard accounting procedures and reporting statistics have been developed, the event industry has had a limited focus on knowledge management and analysis. Communicating knowledge gained from one event context to another occurs mostly informally through transmission of information by individuals who are experienced in the field. For knowledge to be used as the asset that it is, it has to be systematically collected and categorized. While it may appear that technological solutions are the answer, the question of human intent is critical as well. The right organizational climate is needed for people to willingly share information and to learn collaboratively in the interests of the industry.

There are a number of ways in which human resources can contribute to knowledge management:

- Developing a culture of trust and open communication
- Developing systems for capturing tacit knowledge
- Using training and mentoring as a means of disseminating expert knowledge
- Providing rewards for projects which capture expert knowledge
- Writing reports, such as training evaluation reports, to contribute to knowledge management in the area of human resources
- Co-ordinating briefing and debriefing meetings
- Developing and presenting training sessions on project management and evaluation, including post-event reporting for the event as a whole.

Conflict management

What better time to raise the subject of conflict management? Due to the dynamic nature of the event planning environment and the many pressures faced by the organizers, conflict is endemic. It can be resolved positively, leading to creative and innovative event designs and concepts, but equally it can lead to teams becoming dysfunctional. As Eunson (2005) points out, conflict can have positive payoffs, leading to better decision making. Equally, it can block communication.

According to Eunson, any of the following four factors may lead to conflict:

1 *Resource scarcity.* This may include lack of time, money, people and tangible resources such as computer hardware and software.
2 *Workflow interdependence.* Gantt charts, frequently used for event planning, illuminate the dependence of one task on another, thus impacting on the critical path.
3 *Power and/or value asymmetry.* People with high–low power relationships or significantly different values may find it extremely hard to work together. For example, the 'bean counters' are often derided by the creative team for harnessing their ideas.
4 *Goal incompatibility.* Goals of different departments, functional areas and teams can clash. For example, the demands made by the waste management team to ban the use of polystyrene and foil may seem unrealistic to the catering team.

Many studies have been done into the nature of conflict in building projects, which is similar to that occurring during event projects and different from the conflict which occurs in business enterprises (Payne, 1995; Sommerville and Langford, 1994; Vaaland, 2003). Vaaland, in particular, looks at the adversarial attitudes of the client and the contractor in construction projects, which often results in loss of productivity and cost increases. This author suggests that if the perceptions of the two parties are properly managed, insights can be gained which help to restore the ability to manage the relationship under pressure. These different perceptions have been studied in the building industry to show that contractors put more emphasis on minimizing project cost and duration, while clients put more emphasis on satisfying the needs of other stakeholders (Bryde and Robinson, 2005). Research in the event industry along similar lines would be extremely useful (see Case study 13.2 on perception at the end of this chapter).

Working collaboratively

For an event to be successful issues need to be resolved by working collaboratively and productively. Issues may evolve around inequity in distribution of resources; problems with decision making and lines of communication; different values and interpersonal styles; inadequate project planning; or lack of leadership and direction.

So what do we know about collaboration? Here are some assumptions:

• Management involvement in collaborative work planning is essential.
• Teams benefit from regular, professional and neutral facilitation.
• Conflict is inevitable.

Conflict can be reduced by:

• Developing clear roles and responsibilities
• Setting ground rules
• Developing boundaries for acceptable behaviour
• Developing clear goals and targets
• Empowering individuals to negotiate and make binding decisions
• Focusing on super-ordinate goals (the event programme and deadline)
• Establishing conflict resolution processes
• Establishing procedures for conflict escalation
• Meeting regularly and monitoring progress towards agreed goals.

On an individual level, conflict negotiation techniques include:

• Asking questions
• Listening and providing feedback
• Refraining from taking absolute positions
• Repeating key phrases and statements of fact
• Restating the question as a point of focus
• Developing targets and action points
• Focusing on tasks and behaviours
• Avoiding emotional terms and personal blame
• Searching for alternatives
• Reaching agreement on the steps forward.

One of the most interesting features of the event business that has not been widely documented is the 'magic moment' when everyone realizes that only collaboration from this point onwards will enable the event to meet its deadlines. This is the point at which everyone knows that the moment of doors opening to visitors is imminent, and that only positive teamwork will ensure that this will happen. This intense but positive period of co-operation occurs at different times, depending on the size and scope of the event. Complaining, sabotage, arguments and blaming cease and compromise is reached on almost every issue. Super-ordinate goals are those that sit above the nitty gritty conflicts of every day. In the event business the super-ordinate goal is generally the successful production of the event programme on the date and time specified. Since this deadline is invariably inflexible this becomes the super-ordinate goal for negotiation.

Cross-cultural communication

Multinational teams are a feature of events. In addition, many event organizations work in many different cities and countries. For example, specialists working in the fields of pyrotechnic displays and opening ceremonies typically work around the world. Cross-cultural communication is thus a significant issue for such individuals and organizations.

A company called Pyrovision in the United Kingdom produced the Lord Mayor's Show in London in 2005. In addition to numerous shows done in their home country, employees have worked in Monaco, China, Germany, France, USA and Russia, to name just a few places. To work in a global environment cross-cultural communication skills are essential for negotiation and operational implementation.

Writers in the field of communication differentiate between *national* and *organizational* cultures (Arasaratnam and Doerfel, 2005; Eunson, 2005; Griffith, 2002). In this text we have described many of the common features of the event organizational culture, the most dominant being the project management orientation and the dynamic nature of the working environment (Allen *et al.*, 2005; Hanlon and Cuskelly, 2002). When discussing national culture, and the impact this has on organizations, we are looking instead at international business relationships and the impact that national culture has on communication. Communication effectiveness is affected by the 'fit' between one national culture and another. Hofstede (1991) is one of the best known theorists in this field and he describes national cultural dimensions in terms of:

- *Power distance* – focuses on the degree of equality, or inequality, between people in the country's society
- *Individualism* – focuses on the degree to which the society reinforces individual or collective achievement and interpersonal relationships
- *Masculinity* – focuses on the degree to which the society reinforces, or does not reinforce, the traditional masculine work role model of male achievement, control and power
- *Uncertainty avoidance* – focuses on the level of tolerance for uncertainty and ambiguity within the society
- *Long-term orientation* – focuses on the degree to which the society embraces, or does not embrace, long-term devotion to traditional, forward-thinking values.

This last dimension was added after Hofstede completed a study of Chinese managers. As an example, Brazil's highest Hofstede dimension is uncertainty avoidance, suggesting that, as a result, the society does not readily accept change and is very risk adverse (*Geert Hofstede*™ *Cultural Dimensions*, 2006). This would have implications for event planners.

While this research has prompted much debate and discussion (largely over the sample chosen for the research), most writers agree that intercultural communication requires a global outlook. They also concur that knowledge and motivation are the key elements of this outlook (Arasaratnam and Doerfel, 2005; McCabe *et al.*, 2000).

A model for communication effectiveness developed by Griffith (2002) includes three communication competencies. Cognitive competence is the ability of the individual to ascertain meaning from verbal and nonverbal language; affective competence relates to an individual's emotional tendencies (e.g. willingness to accept culturally diverse communications); and behavioural competence. The last of these is indicated by flexibility and adaptability – the ability to respond appropriately in different cultural contexts.

Griffith goes further to suggest the following steps as an action plan to monitor and improve communication effectiveness in international organizations:

- Assess communication competence of internal managers
- Match internal and external manager competencies
- Assess the effectiveness of the communication environment
- Develop an appropriate communication strategy
- Audit performance effectiveness of communication.

Event planning involves extensive negotiation with stakeholders, so event organizations operating offshore need to develop their knowledge of local conditions (including rules, regulations, laws and practices) and fine tune their negotiation skills. An ability to work and communicate effectively in a global environment is a priority for those organizations and individuals working under these circumstances.

Case study 13.2

Different perceptions of crowd control

True picture on the parade 'problems'

I am writing to express my disgust at the one-sided piece of reporting on page three of the journal last week, headlined: 'Animal magic ends in upset.'

Maybe you should make yourself aware of all the acts before publishing such rubbish. Why did you publish only one person's point of view?

I was travelling with my daughter in Black Thunder, we were supposed to be part of the parade through Barnstaple with Father Christmas. Lantern FM were kind enough to take children from the Children's Hospice in their cars to see Father Christmas.

The problems started as we left the service ramp at Green Lanes, the crowd surged forward behind Father Christmas thus making it impossible for the Lantern cars to follow.

There were many children dressed up, I believe they were also supposed to be a part of the parade, but were swamped by the crowd.

As we reached the top of Joy Street a gentleman from the Rotary Club stood in front of the Lantern vehicles and refused to let us pass. Did he not understand that children from the hospice would want to be part of the parade, or did he not appreciate the support and generosity of the Lantern team?

At this stage the police stepped in and diverted us down Joy Street as all three cars quickly became surrounded by people, demonstrating a frightening lack of crowd safety or control.

We sat in the cars at the bottom of Joy Street for about half an hour or so, until Father Christmas came past and we could rejoin the parade to the entrance at Green Lanes, where the children were supposed to follow Father Christmas to the Grotto.

We were advised by the police not to leave the cars as there were too many people, it would not be safe or possible for the children to follow. We sat in the cars until the crowds cleared and the reindeer moved off. We went straight back to the hospice.

The situation could have been a disaster, not only from our point of view in that the children could have become distressed or scared.

It was all thanks to PJ and the Lantern team that the situation was turned into a fun experience. From the crowd point of view, it shows credit to the people of North Devon (most of whom seemed to be in Barnstaple that night!) in that it was their goodwill and humour that kept the atmosphere happy.

Maybe the Rotary Club should think long and hard before marshalling an event of this size, or that has the potential to be this size, as it seems they were ill-equipped to deal with this situation.

But all credit and thanks should go to the police who were brilliant throughout, and to PJ and the Lantern FM team, not only for their support for the children from the Children's Hospice, but for also creating a fun atmosphere to salvage a potentially disastrous evening.

MRS CINDY STONE
Barnstaple

(Reproduced with permission of *North Devon Journal*, 2 December 2004)

Rotarians role was not crowd control

In response to the letter by Mrs Cindy Stone headed 'True picture on the parade problems' in last week's journal may I take the liberty of correcting one of her misconceptions, namely the role played by the Rotary Clubs of Barnstaple.

The Christmas parade was organised by the Town Centre Management who in turn asked for volunteers from the Rotary Clubs, fourteen of us duly gave up our evening at home and turned up.

On arrival at the Green Lanes ramp we were given specific instructions. Two members were sent to Joy Street and told that under no circumstances were they to let any vehicle pass while the remainder were instructed to surround Santa's sled to prevent (for health and safety reasons one assumes) children touching the reindeer.

The assumption by Mrs Stone that we were in some way responsible for crowd control is ludicrous, such tasks are best left to the professionals, the police.

Volunteering for unenviable jobs is what we Rotarians do. We also raise vast sums of money for local, national and international charities one of which is the Children's Hospice to which it would appear Mrs Stone also lends a helping hand.

She is to be congratulated, as is the Town Centre Management, for putting on the parade, and the people of Barnstaple for responding so wholeheartedly.

EDWARD O'NEILL
President, The Rotary Club of Barnstaple Link
Copley Drive, Barnstaple

(Reproduced with permission of *North Devon Journal*, 9 December 2004)

Reflective practice 13.2

1 Explain how these problems occurred.
2 How could clear communication have prevented these problems occurring?
3 Write a letter to the Rotarians, thanking them for their help and clarifying the situation.

Chapter summary and key points

Having a clear purpose regarding communication can go a long way towards improving its effectiveness. Different people can make different meanings of the same message because of their different perceptions, but if communication is purposive and clear, fewer misunderstandings will occur. In this chapter we have also covered cross-cultural communication, explaining briefly how differences in cultural background can impact upon communication. It is dangerous, however, to stereotype cross-cultural communication. Instead, an emphasis on understanding differences in perception (by individuals and groups) and a focus on developing effective listening and clear communication is a more constructive approach.

Inevitably, conflict will arise at times in the pressured event environment, so conflict management skills and conflict negotiation techniques have been outlined in this chapter to help event personnel deal with such situations.

Finally, the field of knowledge management has been introduced briefly and its role in professionalizing event management emphasized. Assembling, storing and evaluating data on events provides a useful legacy for future event planning and implementation.

Revision questions

1 Select one communication channel and describe how it is commonly used in the event environment.
2 Visit two event websites and compare their communication effectiveness with their audiences.
3 Give three reasons why conflict might emerge at an event.
4 Using an example, explain how collaborative processes can assist in developing win–win solutions.
5 Discuss the statement: 'Studies of cultural differences are counterproductive as they lead people to stereotype others.'

References

Allen, J., O'Toole, W., Harris, R. and McDonnell, I. (2005). *Festival and Special Event Management*, 3rd edn. John Wiley & Sons.

Arasaratnam, L. and Doerfel, M. (2005). Intercultural communication competence: identifying key components from multi-cultural perspectives. *International Journal of Intercultural Relations*, **29**, 137–63.

Bryde, J. and Robinson, L. (2005). Client versus contractor perspectives on project success criteria. *Journal of International Project Management*, **2(8)**, 622–9.

Eunson, B. (2005). *Communicating in the 21st Century*. John Wiley and Sons.

Geert Hofstede™ Cultural Dimensions (2006). *ITIM International*. Viewed 12 February 2006, www.geert-hofstede.com/hofstede_brazil.shtml.

Goldblatt, J. J. (2005). *Special Events: Event Leadership for a New World*, 4th edn. Wiley.

Griffith, D. (2002). The role of communication competencies in international business relationship development. *Journal of World Business*, **37**, 256–65.

Hanlon, C. and Cuskelly, G. (2002). Pulsating major sport event organizations: a framework for inducting managerial personnel. *Event Management*, **7**, 231–43.

Hofstede, G. (1991). *Cultures and Organizations: Software of the Mind*. McGraw-Hill.

McCabe, V., Poole, D., Weeks, N. and Leiper, N. (2000). *The Business and Management of Conventions*. John Wiley & Sons.

O'Toole, W. (2000). Towards the integration of event management best practice by the project management process. *Event Management Research Conference*, University of Technology, Sydney.

Payne, J. (1995). Management of multiple simultaneous projects. *International Journal of Project Management*, **13(3)**, 163–8.

Sommerville, J. and Langford, V. (1994). Multivariate influences on the people side of projects: stress and conflict. *International Journal of Project Management*, **12(4)**, 234–43.

Vaaland, T. (2003). Improving project collaboration: start with the conflicts. *International Journal of Project Management*, **22(6)**, 447–54.

Chapter 14
Leadership

Learning objectives

After reading through this chapter you will be able to:

- Differentiate between management and leadership
- Describe stages of project management
- Discuss the appropriateness of project management approaches for providing leadership in the event environment
- Describe context factors for event leaders
- Describe theories of leadership and their relevance to the event industry
- Prepare leadership training.

Introduction

In this chapter we will look at the topic of leadership. In some respects this is quite problematic as so much has been written on the subject, but with the traditional business in mind. In the normal business environment, everything is pretty stable: policies and procedures are in place and there are ready-made systems for dealing with market force changes. Even if staff turnover is high, many organizational characteristics remain unchanged. Systems and procedures in hospitals, banks, supermarkets and fast food outlets come to mind. In these organizations, there is generally a legacy on which to build and move forward, and the organizational culture is well established.

For many events, however, it is a ground-up development, sometimes at an alarming pace. This involves new venues, policies, operational procedures and, most importantly, new temporary people. While some events, such as small meetings held in hotels and exhibitions staged at convention centres, have ready-made formulas, the majority of events, including diverse events in arts and entertainment, are unique in concept and execution, thus requiring flexible leadership.

Management or leadership?

Most people would agree that not every manager is a leader (although he or she should be) and that every leader is not a manager (some workers appoint themselves to this role). Informal leaders often emerge in the event environment: for example, an experienced business person might step in to lead a group of volunteers where there appears to be a leadership vacuum. The problematic informal leader is one who takes the lead, but is essentially clueless!

Management is generally characterized as tactical, i.e. following the processes of planning, organizing, leading and controlling. Planning involves setting the direction and operationalizing organizational strategies; organizing means creating structures and assigning tasks; leading means inspiring effort; and controlling ensures that tasks are completed (see Figure 14.1). From this can be seen that leading is part of a manager's role. Some are better at it than others!

Project management was discussed in Chapter 3 because of its similarity to event management, but here we will outline the five phases of project management to see what they can tell us about leadership:

1 *Initiating*. During this phase the vision for the project is developed and the goals are established. The core planning team is in place and the planning process begins.
2 *Planning*. Work breakdown is analysed, resources are allocated and schedules are developed. During this phase tasks and activities that lead to project goals are defined more clearly. Throughout this phase there is an emphasis on determining the scope of work.
3 *Executing*. Here the work is completed according to the project plan. The focus is on task completion, meeting milestones and managing critical paths. Communication is vitally important during this phase.
4 *Controlling*. Monitoring the outcomes achieved, rescheduling and reallocating resources occurs during the controlling phase, helping to keep the project on track. Where project goals are varied, approval is required from stakeholders. Note that in the event environment a project timeline overrun is seldom possible; the media and the audience are waiting for the performance to begin. Viewers around the world are ready for kickoff!
5 *Closing*. Before the team is disbanded, the project needs to be reviewed, bills paid and people acknowledged. An evaluation of the project is essential, the final report being the legacy of achievement and results.

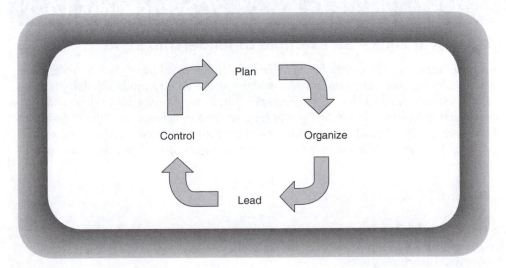

Figure 14.1   Management

Readers will notice that throughout these phases, the issue of leadership does not emerge clearly and the process appears quite clinical. Perhaps this is because projects in information technology or engineering are not as creative, complex, problematic, dynamic or stakeholder reliant as special events. However, this is doubtful, because vision and leadership are required in all workplaces, particularly when working on ground-breaking projects. Thomsett (2002), in his discussion on the project management revolution, talks about the increasing technical complexity of projects making it impossible for project managers to undertake technical reviews. He differentiates between content and context. Content includes the project tasks, the technical deliverables, while context involves the business, social and political environment of the project. He argues that the role of the project manager is shifting to ensuring that the project achieves its business goals: 'Build a relationship with your stakeholders and you will be doing your job. It is all about relationships' (p. 26). In fact, he goes further to suggest that the less the project manager knows about the technical details the better! Thus the project manager's role is all about power and influence, about making things happen. Thomsett concludes by pointing out that leadership is about change whereas management is about order and consistency.

Other authors highlight the association between leadership and vision. Schermerhorn *et al.* (2004) suggest that visionary leadership involves having clear ideas for new directions and being able to commit others to the fulfilment of these ideas. Christenson and Walker (2004, p. 45) emphasize the importance of vision in project success: 'We argue that much of the skill of project management leadership is about ensuring that the project need is adequately articulated into a project vision statement that facilitates enthusiasm and commitment for its successful realization.

In this chapter we will look in more detail at leadership in the event context, sources of power, and old and new theories of leadership, including contemporary ideas about transformational leadership.

Case study 14.1 illustrates contemporary views on visionary leadership.

Case study 14.1

Edinburgh Festival 2005 – an example of leadership style

'Most critics over here are stupid,' Danielsen fumed in the Edinburgh press. 'There's not the widespread culture of cinematic criticism that there is in Europe.' Speaking to The Australian *in Edinburgh on the weekend as the film festival drew to a close, Danielsen said: 'I want the film festival to speak with one voice and that voice has to be mine. I'm not saying that because I'm a megalomaniac. Film festivals are usually bland, they are run by conciliation, compromise and committee. If you are taking a pay cheque as the artistic director, you have to have the balls to stand up and say this is good and this is not, or this is in and this is out.'*

(Emma-Kate Symons, *The Age*, 30 August 2005)

Reflective practice 14.1
1 Summarize the issues emerging from this case study.
2 Explain the festival director's vision.

Definitions of leadership

'Leadership is the ability to inspire confidence and support among the people who are needed to achieve organizational goals' (DuBrun, 2004, p. 12); it is about the capacity of an individual to inspire and motivate. As stated earlier, leadership can be exhibited by non-managerial personnel such as union leaders. In recent years researchers have looked at leadership in terms of 'near' and 'far' leadership (Alimo-Metcalfe and Alban-Metcalf, 2005). They have done this because most previous analysis has been of very senior executives and they believe that the focus for leadership study should be 'near leadership', that is at lower levels of the organizational structure where leaders define organizational reality rather than exert wide-ranging influence over goal achievement.

The concept of 'followership' has also been introduced in more recent times, possibly in response to the diverse nature of the workforce. Leadership and 'followership' are distributed through every level of organizations.

Recent studies are more inclusive of gender and culture (Alimo-Metcalfe and Alban-Metcalf, 2005; White *et al.*, 2001). The women's perspective claims that finding collaborative, interdependent relationships between leader and followers is more common in gender inclusive research. It also suggests that linear models of group development, particularly those that view power struggles as one of these phases, are unsuited to the modern work environment. In start-up organizations, in particular, mutual learning occurs and the interactive leader works on building consensus, inclusion and participation (White *et al.*, 2001).

Leadership is variously defined as:

- Exerting influence
- Having followers
- Lifting people to a new level
- Persuading others to act towards achieving a common goal
- Leading by example so that others follow.

The theme of influence is found in most definitions.

Organizational contexts for leadership

Before looking at leadership theory, past and present, let us revisit the topic of the event context discussed in Chapter 1. Here we will contrast various contexts for leadership: long-life organizations, short-life organizations and organizations manned primarily by volunteers.

Shone and Parry (2004) use the description 'short-life' to describe the special event context. This is a helpful basis on which to review leadership literature since the short-life organization is quite different from the long-life organization, which has been the basis for most leadership research.

Long-life organizations

Strategic planning for a long-life, stable organization requires a vision of the future in which the organization operates: the internal and external forces that might impact on the organization as time progresses; competitive forces; and responses that the organization may need to make to remain ahead of the game. This is generally the role of executives in large corporations, such as media, finance and telecommunications. However, this is also the general direction for many event suppliers, such as hire companies, who plan to run their organizations over a long period and remain profitable in a changing climate.

Short-life organizations (project based)

In contrast to long-life organizations, most events and event organizations do not operate on the scale of major corporations. Rather, their vision is more creative than strategic. As we have seen, many events have project characteristics, such as defined timelines and resources. In this context, leadership is about harnessing energy and commitment to achieve the creative vision of the director (Shone and Parry, 2004). These authors stress the non-routine and unique features of special events, while Watt (1998) stresses the complexity and challenge associated with staging a unique event.

Volunteer-based organizations

When people are not paid they are not easily coerced into doing things. In fact, to keep attrition of the workforce to a minimum, programmes need to be designed to reward and retain volunteers for the period of the event. Leadership is vitally important in the volunteer-based organization in conveying the event's purpose, as volunteers frequently cite their commitment to an ideal as their primary motivation for event volunteering (Bussell and Forbes, 2001; Elstad, 2003).

Leadership is tested in an environment in which many of the event components are outsourced to contractors and subcontractors. As with volunteers, contractors are not paid staff of the organization and therefore highly effective communication, negotiation and conflict management skills are needed to manage them. The earlier definition of leadership is useful in that it referred to 'the people who are needed to achieve organizational goals' and is thus inclusive of contractor employees.

Leadership is also tested when an event organization shifts into emergency mode, for example, in the case of a fire, bomb threat or crowd control issue. When there are sudden and dramatic threats such as these, leadership is sometimes handed over to other authorities such as emergency services, as a military-style command and control mode is generally more useful in response to this type of situation.

Sources of power

A leader has various sources of power. The most common in most organizations is the legitimate power of employer over employee. This power is of course limited in the case of volunteers and contractor representatives.

In the event environment, as in most organizations, influence can be exerted in a number of ways depending on the power source (Mintzberg, 1983):

- Legitimate power comes from the person's place in the managerial hierarchy and is vested in the position. People working as police officers, fire fighters, etc. also carry legitimate power vested in them through legislation.
- Reward power is the realm of leaders who are in a position to provide rewards, both tangible (salary increase, prize, bonus) and intangible (praise, recommendation).
- Coercive power is the ability to use negative means to control behaviour. These can include criticism, demotion, written warnings and ultimately dismissal.
- Expert power is gained by a leader through the admiration by subordinates of his or her expertise and knowledge.
- Information power is achieved through the access to and control of information – those 'in the know' have more data on which to base decisions and to exert their power.
- Referent power comes from loyalty and admiration. This leader is admired and people identify with him or her.

In most situations subordinates will resist coercion (and volunteers will simply walk off the job), while referent and expert power are most likely to lead to commitment.

Theoretical models of leadership

The following theories of leadership are summarized more or less in historical sequence. The evolution of leadership theory has resulted from changes in society, including changes to work practices and increased diversity in the workforce.

Leadership traits

Early theorists were keen to identify the traits of highly effective leaders, as they assumed that people with these traits would become equally effective leaders. Some of the traits identified were confidence, decisiveness and charisma. Edwin Locke (2000) identified the following personality traits among successful leaders: drive, self-confidence, creativity and cognitive ability, among others. More recent work in the United Kingdom has led to the development of leadership scales in which personal qualities include being honest and consistent, acting with integrity, being decisive, inspiring others and resolving complex problems (Alimo-Metcalfe and Alban-Metcalf, 2005).

Emotional intelligence is a construct that has great popular appeal – managing one's emotions and having empathy for others are believed to improve interpersonal effectiveness. Goleman (1995) suggests that there are four dimensions to emotional intelligence: self-awareness, self-management, social awareness and relationship management.

Goldblatt (2005) lists the most important leadership qualities as integrity, confidence, persistence, collaboration, problem solving, communication skills and vision. As he suggests, 'it is important to note that event leadership is neither charisma or control, the ability to command nor the talent to inspire. Rather, it is that rare commodity, like good taste, that one recognizes when one sees it' (p. 153).

Leadership style

Leadership-style theorists looked at the two dimensions of leadership, concern for production (task orientation) and concern for people. The best known of these is the Leadership Grid of Blake and Mouton (1985). Their argument was that the best leader would exhibit concern for both people and production, with a resultant team management style.

Contingency theories

Recognizing that different contexts required different leadership approaches led to the development of contingency theories. Broadly speaking, contingency theories suggest that leaders need to be responsive to a range of situational variables. Many such variables exist. Fiedler (1967) matched style (task orientation and relationship orientation) to situational variables of leader–member relations, task structure and position power. The Hersey-Blanchard (1993) model, on the other hand, looked at the maturity of followers. Here it was suggested that new (low job maturity) employees needed a telling style of leadership, graduating to selling and participative styles. However, once an employee had high job maturity, little guidance was required and a delegating style was appropriate. Looking at the relevance of this approach to the events business, it is clear that most personnel, who see the event infrastructure only just before the event and are briefed only minutes before the gates open, would need a telling style of clear instructions.

In this book there has been much discussion about the event context. There are many situational factors that could be considered in relation to leadership style: primarily the amount of time available to issue instructions and make decisions; and the level of risk associated with, for example, delegating a decision about crowd management.

Transformational leadership

Burns *et al.* (2004) and Avolio and Bass (1994) have worked on the concepts of transactional and transformational leadership. *Transactional leadership* is characterized by rewards contingent upon goal achievement, while *transformational leadership* requires that the leader convince followers of the task importance and value, that everyone is committed to the vision. In most cases this is leadership by inspiration. This can work positively when positive goals and values are espoused by the leader and genuine concern for others' well-being is exhibited. In rare cases, however, there is the visionary-charismatic leader whose power is used for antisocial purposes, leading to corruption or corporate scandal, so it is necessary to remain mindful of the dark side of charisma.

In the event business there is occasionally a scandal or two: in Sydney, Olympic Games tickets were allocated to the rich and famous leaving scarce pickings for the general public (all in the interests of 'revenue maximization'), and the marching band fiasco led to loss of face (and legal costs) when a decision to import bands from the US and Japan was labelled unpatriotic. One person's creative vision can lead to unexpected reactions despite positive intentions.

Avolio and Bass (1994) define transformational leadership in terms of how the leader affects followers, who are intended to trust, admire and respect the transformational leader. They identified three ways in which leaders transform followers:

- increasing their awareness of task importance and value
- getting them to focus on team or organizational goals
- activating their higher order needs and enabling self-actualization.

Avolio and Bass suggest that authentic transformational leadership is grounded in moral foundations, and that transformational leaders are value-driven change agents.

Doyle (2002) has a delightful descriptor of a high change business context as a 'high velocity' environment. This would undoubtedly describe the short period immediately before a major concert, festival, exhibition or conference. In his research, he suggests that the notion of a singular change agent in an organization is inappropriate and should be replaced with a much more diverse range of people, all of whom are change agents in their own right. This he suggests is not commonly considered at the recruitment stage, but recommends that it should be. He describes it as a capability to withstand challenges and stresses, and an ability to manage in ways suited to the contingencies of the environment. He suggests, for example, involving those who are already acknowledged change agents in conducting the screening process.

This argument is useful in that it prioritizes change management attributes as selection criteria for event people in senior roles. While the absence of these attributes might be discovered during a performance appraisal process, this could already be too late for remedial action. In the event business, there are few opportunities to learn and grow and mistakes can have serious repercussions, including delays to the project timeline. If, for example, a poor decision about ticket releases created a storm in the media, the whole organization could be scuttled for a time as plans were changed in response to this pressure. It would also be embarrassing for the organization and could damage morale. This highlights the importance of recognizing the pace of change in the event planning environment and selecting people who can manage well in this context.

Leadership and decision making

Leadership is exhibited in decision making. Each time a manager makes a decision there are a number of factors that come to bear. First, the leader brings his or her attributes, knowledge and experience, and the attributes of followers to the decision. These could be their personal traits, cultural background or their status in the organization (employee, volunteer, contractor). The given task needs careful consideration, perhaps the most important being the level of risk involved. Finally, every decision is situated in the wider context of the event environment or the socio-political environment in which the leader finds him or herself. Given that each time a leader acts, these factors are likely to vary, so each decision is unique. This is shown in Figure 14.2 in which the leadership behaviour/decision is illustrated at the intersection of the four factors. Note that this is not a leadership style, but a fleeting, instantaneous decision or action.

Readers might remember the example from Matthew Lazarus-Hall where the decision made in a meeting had changed by the time he reached the car park. Wave Aid, the concert he was planning, was a relief concert organized in record time (one

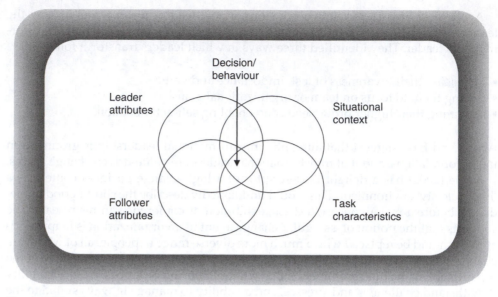

Figure 14.2 Decision-making model

month from start of planning), featuring high-profile performers. The quote that follows is a good description of the situational context. As Lazarus-Hall describes it, the planning was a roller-coaster of decision making and the level of co-operation experienced was unprecedented. However, as soon as all parties returned to their convention business mode, everyone returned to 'normal'.

> To ensure that maximum money is raised, the event organizers are engaging suppliers to either work free of charge or at cost. All those including the bands, management, promoters and publicists, web designers and hosts involved in staging this event are donating their time free of charge.
>
> The income expenditure analysis will be published straight after the concert on this website, and via a press release and in print media. The net proceeds from the event will be distributed to AUSTRALIAN RED CROSS, OXFAM/COMMUNITY AID ABROAD, UNICEF, and CARE AUSTRALIA charity organizations. We urge Sydneysiders to support this event and our fellow citizens of the world (www.waveaid.com.au/about.html).

At the end of this chapter there is a case study (14.2) about the feud between Michael Knight, Olympics Minister for the Sydney 2000 Olympic Games, and Sandy Hollway, head of SOCOG. This story tells of just one decision, Knight's recommendation to the Olympic Committee that Hollway not receive the highest award, an IOC gold medal for services to the Games. It illustrates the dramatic differences between the two men, Hollway adored by his staff and Knight described as being 'mean spirited', with an aggressive style, by Dick Pound (Clune, 2001).

Leadership training

Event leadership training is conducted for most major events, the main purpose being to enable participants to better understand the event environment and the people they will need to supervise. The training must therefore cover the factors in Figure 14.2.

First aid volunteers, also a source of general event information, need briefing

Situational context

Most event training starts with a description of the aims of the event, whether they are to meet a business client's brief, celebrate culture or make a profit. This section answers the broader questions of 'Why are we here?' and 'What are we trying to achieve?' This part of training may involve a presentation by the CEO of the sponsor organization, the event creative director or the fundraising manager.

Task context

The specifics of the tasks to be supervised may or may not be covered in detail depending on the diverse roles of the leaders attending training. Job-specific information is generally covered in other training sessions. However, human resource planning for rosters, uniforms, pay, meals, discipline policy, etc. is important.

Follower attributes

A volunteer speaker often features at training if leadership of volunteers is a key part of the supervisor's role. Understanding workforce composition and expectations is a training objective.

Leader attributes

A degree of self-analysis is useful, many trainers using personality profile tests and games to introduce this session. However, since leader attributes are not easily changed, the focus for this part of training is more likely to be self-acknowledged deficiencies such as inexperience in the event environment and lack of knowledge of event conditions. Developing event leaders' knowledge of the new environment is often done using problem-based scenario exercises.

Leader decision making/behaviours

Tools and tips for leadership can be provided by experienced personnel who may be called upon in this part of the training. Specific ideas for motivating staff, planning rosters, dealing with staff problems and tackling unexpected staffing crises may be provided for discussion. In the ideal situation, leaders in training are provided with a range of problems and issues that require solutions. These can be table-based exercises, games or role plays. The illustrated plan for event leadership training in Figure 14.3 incorporates these elements in various ways.

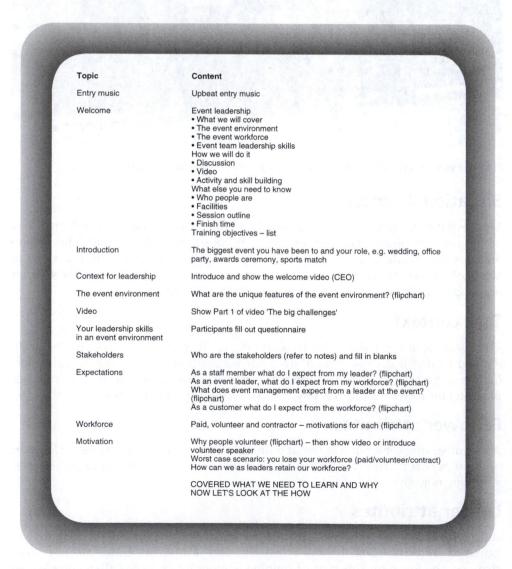

Topic	Content
Entry music	Upbeat entry music
Welcome	Event leadership • What we will cover • The event environment • The event workforce • Event team leadership skills How we will do it • Discussion • Video • Activity and skill building What else you need to know • Who people are • Facilities • Session outline • Finish time Training objectives – list
Introduction	The biggest event you have been to and your role, e.g. wedding, office party, awards ceremony, sports match
Context for leadership	Introduce and show the welcome video (CEO)
The event environment	What are the unique features of the event environment? (flipchart)
Video	Show Part 1 of video 'The big challenges'
Your leadership skills in an event environment	Participants fill out questionnaire
Stakeholders	Who are the stakeholders (refer to notes) and fill in blanks
Expectations	As a staff member what do I expect from my leader? (flipchart) As an event leader, what do I expect from my workforce? (flipchart) What does event management expect from a leader at the event? (flipchart) As a customer what do I expect from the workforce? (flipchart)
Workforce	Paid, volunteer and contractor – motivations for each (flipchart)
Motivation	Why people volunteer (flipchart) – then show video or introduce volunteer speaker Worst case scenario: you lose your workforce (paid/volunteer/contract) How can we as leaders retain our workforce? COVERED WHAT WE NEED TO LEARN AND WHY NOW LET'S LOOK AT THE HOW

Figure 14.3   Event leadership training session plan

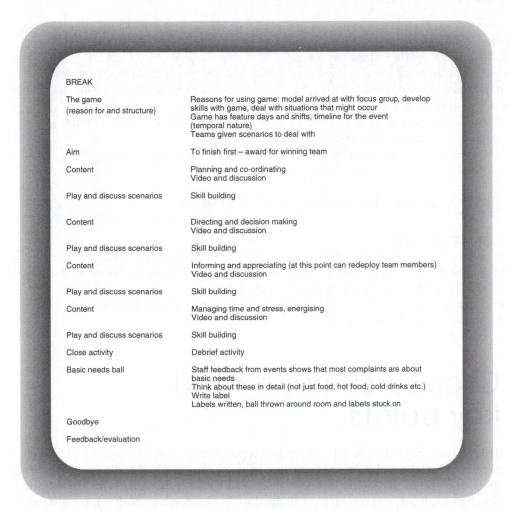

BREAK

The game (reason for and structure)	Reasons for using game: model arrived at with focus group, develop skills with game, deal with situations that might occur Game has feature days and shifts, timeline for the event (temporal nature) Teams given scenarios to deal with
Aim	To finish first – award for winning team
Content	Planning and co-ordinating Video and discussion
Play and discuss scenarios	Skill building
Content	Directing and decision making Video and discussion
Play and discuss scenarios	Skill building
Content	Informing and appreciating (at this point can redeploy team members) Video and discussion
Play and discuss scenarios	Skill building
Content	Managing time and stress, energising Video and discussion
Play and discuss scenarios	Skill building
Close activity	Debrief activity
Basic needs ball	Staff feedback from events shows that most complaints are about basic needs Think about these in detail (not just food, hot food, cold drinks etc.) Write label Labels written, ball thrown around room and labels stuck on
Goodbye	
Feedback/evaluation	

Figure 14.3 *(Continued)*

Case study 14.2

Sydney 2000 Olympic Games – another example of leadership style

Australia's Olympics minister, Michael Knight, resigned from politics on Wednesday following wide-spread personal criticism only three days after what were billed as the most successful Games ever.

Knight, who has become embroiled in a bitter row over his veto of a top IOC award for the chief of the Sydney Olympics organizing body, said he and his family decided last Christmas that he would quit politics after the Games.

'We decided that on the first day after the athletes' parade I would communicate with you the decision we made then – that I would leave parliament at the end of this year,' Knight said.

'I didn't want to do it the day after the closing ceremony, I wanted the athletes to have their day, I wanted the athletes to have their parade,' he said.

It took only a few days for politics to sour Sydney's post-Olympics party.

International Olympic Committee senior vice-president Dick Pound on Wednesday labelled Knight as 'mean-spirited' for blocking a top IOC award to the chief of the Sydney Games organizing body.

Australian media rallied against Knight, calling him a vindictive politician intent on 'payback' who had shattered the afterglow of the Sydney Olympics.

Pound said Knight threatened to publicly reject his IOC gold order only hours before it was bestowed on him by IOC president Juan Antonio Samaranch at the closing ceremony last Sunday, if his colleague Sandy Hollway was also granted the same honour.

Pound said the IOC board was unanimous in its wish to award Hollway its gold Olympic Order because he had 'made an exceptional contribution to the Games'.

'This was not a view apparently shared by Michael Knight and it went so far that he said he would not accept his if Sandy got one,' Pound told Australian radio.

(http://news.bbc.co.uk/sport1/low/olympics2000/955423.stm)

Reflective practice 14.2

1 From reading the above extract, how would you describe Knight's leadership?
2 Discuss the following statement, 'Leadership decisions are historically and socio-politically situated.' You may use your own examples of leader decision making.
3 Leadership training in the event context is typically short, a day or less. How can the trainer best prepare team leaders for their roles?

Chapter summary and key points

This chapter has discussed the important topic of leadership, the ability to influence people in order to achieve organizational objectives. Simply put, this means getting the work done. Leadership has been discussed in the context of short-life and long-life organizations, and research on leadership and leadership models has been evaluated in terms of 'near' and 'far' leadership.

We have returned again to the topic of project management because of its similarity to event management and have stressed the importance of effective leadership in this challenging environment, particularly where the workforce comprises volunteer and contractor employees. And we have seen that effective decision making is a key element of good leadership and that leadership training is a must for managers and supervisors in the event environment.

Revision questions

1 What is leadership?
2 How does leading differ from managing?
3 How is leadership exhibited in the project management model of EMBOK?
4 List and describe a leader's sources of power?
5 Select one theory of leadership, study it in detail by reading more widely, and then evaluate the usefulness of the theory to the event team leader.

References

Alimo-Metcalfe, B. and Alban-Metcalf, J. (2005). Leadership: time for a new direction. *Leadership*, **1(1)**, 51–71.

Avolio, B. J. and Bass, B. M. (1994). *Improving Organizational Effectiveness through Transformational Leadership*. Sage.

Blake, R. R. and Mouton, J. S. (1985). *The Managerial Grid III: A New Look at the Classic that has Boosted Productivity and Profits for Thousands of Corporations World-wide*. Gulf Pub. Co.

Burns, J. M., Goethals, G. R. and Sorenen, G. (2004). *Encyclopedia of Leadership*. Sage.

Bussell, H. and Forbes, D. (2001). Understanding the volunteer market: the what, where, who and why of volunteering. *International Journal of Nonprofit and Voluntary Sector Marketing*, **7(3)**, 244–57.

Christenson, D. and Walker, D. (2004). Understanding the role of 'vision' in project success. *Project Management Journal*, **35(3)**, 39–52.

Clune, D. (2001). Political chronicles. *Australian Journal of Politics and History*, **47(2)**, 243–309.

Doyle, M. (2002). Selecting managers for transformational change. *Human Resource Management Journal*, **12(1)**, 3–17.

DuBrun, A. (2004). *Leadership*, 4th edn. Houghton Mifflin Company.

Elstad, B. (2003). Continuance commitment and reasons to quit: a study of volunteers at a jazz festival. *Event Management*, **8**, 99–108.

Fiedler, F. E. (1967). *A Theory of Leadership Effectiveness*. McGraw-Hill.

Goldblatt, J. J. (2005). *Special Events: Event Leadership for a New World*, 4th edn. Wiley.

Goleman, D. (1995). *Emotional Intelligence*. Bantam Books.

Hersey, P. and Blanchard, K. H. (1993). *Management of Organizational Behavior: Utilizing Human Resources*, 6th edn. Prentice-Hall.

Locke, E. A. (2000). *The Blackwell Handbook of Principles of Organizational Behaviour*. Blackwell.

Mintzberg, H. (1983). *Power in and around Organizations*. Prentice-Hall.

Schermerhorn, J. R., Poole, D. A., Wiesner, R. and Campling, J. (2004). *Management: An Asia-Pacific Perspective*. John Wiley & Sons.

Shone, A. and Parry, B. (2004). *Successful Event Management*, 2nd edn. Thomson Learning.

Thomsett, R. (2002). *Radical Project Management*. Prentice-Hall.

Watt, D. (1998). *Event Management in Leisure and Tourism*. Addison Wesley Longman.

White, J., McMillen, C. and Baker, A. C. (2001). Challenging traditional models: towards an inclusive model of group development. *Journal of Management Inquiry*, **10(1)**, 40–57.

Chapter 15
Motivation and retention

Learning objectives

After reading through this chapter you will be able to:

- Discuss the topic of workforce retention
- Describe the differences between content and process theories of motivation
- Use the concept of psychological contract to analyse volunteer expectations
- Describe some approaches to reward and recognition
- Develop strategies for workforce retention
- Discuss issues relating to motivation of management personnel.

Introduction

When an event is staffed primarily by volunteers, motivation is a significant concern for the organizing committee who are sometimes themselves volunteers. In the business world, staff turnover is measured by the human resource department as the number of staff leaving as a percentage of the workforce. In the event business the terms most often used are retention and attrition – attrition more commonly because many volunteers quit before they have started. For example, prior to the 2006 Commonwealth Games, there were reports that more than 1200 Commonwealth Games volunteers had resigned their posts in the ten weeks prior to the event (Phillips, 2006). These volunteers did not take up positions offered to them to participate in the 15 000 strong volunteer programme.

There have been numerous studies on volunteer motivation, some of which were mentioned in Chapter 4. These studies have mostly investigated the antecedent motives for volunteering (Coyne and Coyne, 2001; Strigas and Newton Jackson 2003). Essentially, the diversity of event type and scale is reflected in the diversity of motivations that volunteers put forward for volunteering. Other studies have looked at reasons why volunteers quit, Elstad (2003) finding that the top three reasons were workload, lack of appreciation, and poor event organization. Cuskelly *et al.* (2004) did an extensive study on the behavioural dependability of volunteers, arguing that a study of behaviour is more meaningful than a study of attitudes. One of the points they make is that many event organizers deal with retention problems by overrecruiting volunteers, but are then faced with increases in the cost of selection and training, as well as the cost of uniforms, accreditation, etc. An oversupply of volunteers has the potential also to cause dissatisfaction when underutilization occurs. This is problematic as one of the highest level satisfiers is feeling skilled, useful and productive. Using the theory of planned behaviour, Cuskelly *et al.* (2004) found that the most consistent predictor variable was perceived behavioural control, measured as having the confidence and skills to be a volunteer.

Motivation and retention of volunteers is not however the only concern. From a risk management perspective, a much more significant concern is retention of event planning staff, those involved in the lead-up period to an event. When a key person quits at a crucial time, this can have a major effect on other members of the team, increasing their workload and impacting on goal achievement. For this reason, retention of management and other paid personnel is a significant consideration. One suggestion for retention of staff is to provide employment contracts with loyalty bonuses.

Hanlon and Jago (2004) have drawn up a schema for retention of both paid and seasonal event staff working for major sporting events, which will be discussed later in the chapter.

Theories of motivation

There are two main groups of theories of motivation: *content* theories assume that all individuals possess the same set of needs and therefore prescribe the characteristics that ought to be present in jobs; *process* theories, in contrast, stress the differences in people's needs and focus on the cognitive processes that create these differences.

One example of a content theory is that of Frederick Hertzberg (1987) who proposes that job satisfaction and dissatisfaction appear to be caused by different factors (see Figure 15.1).

According to this theory, the factors listed as hygiene factors would lead to dissatisfaction if they were not up to standard. To support this concept, Elstad (2003) found that food had a significant effect on the volunteers' continuance commitment at a jazz festival. However, food is not a satisfier; if adequate, it is taken for granted and does not contribute to feelings of job satisfaction. The factors that do motivate

Hygiene factors (dissatisfiers)	Motivators (satisfiers)
Supervision	Goal achievement
Policy	Recognition
Work environment	Intrinsic nature of the work itself
Relationships with colleagues	Responsibility
Pay/reward	Advancement

Figure 15.1 Hertzberg's two factor theory

are goal achievement and recognition. For management personnel, the intrinsic nature of the work itself, particularly the creative development of the event concept and plans, is also highly satisfying. To sum up and simplify, motivators provide reasons to stay, while unsatisfactory hygiene factors can provide reasons to leave.

What all process theories have in common is an emphasis on cognitive processes in determining a person's level of motivation. For example, equity theory assumes that one important cognitive process involves people looking around and observing what effort other people are putting into their work and what rewards follow. This social comparison process is driven by a concern for fairness and equity.

Expectancy theory resulted from Vroom's (1973) work into motivation. His argument is that crucial to motivation at work is the perception of a link between effort and reward. Perceiving this link can be thought of as a process in which individuals calculate, first, whether there is a connection between effort and reward and, second, the probability that rewards (valences, as Vroom called them) will follow from high performance (instrumentality). The motivational force of a job can therefore be calculated if the expectancy, instrumentality and valence values are known (see Figure 15.2).

If the individual perceives that no matter how much they try they will never reach the work performance level indicated, they will not make an effort. For example, a goal may be to serve 300 banquet guests within 15 minutes. This may be regarded as unachievable due to the number of floor staff available and delays in kitchen production. However, the floor staff may also be thinking about the promise of a reward. Perhaps they were promised an early finish once and instead had to stay back to set up for breakfast the next day. The promised reward has to have a high valence, or value, and there needs to be a level of trust that rewards will be delivered.

The main contribution of process theory has been to highlight the effects of cognitive and perceptual processes on objective work conditions.

A different theory of motivation involving goal setting has been proposed by Locke and Latham (1984). This theory states that goals direct effort and provide guidelines for deciding how much effort to put into each activity when multiple goals exist, and that participation in goal setting increases the individual's sense of control.

This theory is well suited to the project management environment of event planning where goals such as audience size, throughput at turnstiles, food service during intermission, delivery times and scoring accuracy can be measured and communicated to event personnel. At a more personal level, control systems such as safety checklists, cash balancing and voucher reconciliation can provide a level of satisfaction when such goals are achieved.

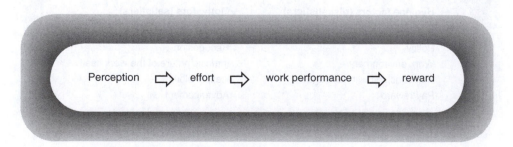

Perception ⇨ effort ⇨ work performance ⇨ reward

Figure 15.2   Expectancy theory of motivation

Workforce expectations

Guest and Conway (2002) talk about the psychological contract in terms of perceived promises and commitments in the employment relationship, which is usually discussed in the literature in terms of *employee* expectations. These authors look instead at *employer* views on this topic. Ultimately, of course, the psychological contract works both ways, each party making promises and commitments and having certain expectations. Indeed, managing expectations is also crucial to the management of volunteers, so this concept of the psychological contract is a very useful one to use in the event context. The following quote talks about psychological contracts in the context of event volunteering:

> First, it seems that regardless of previous experience, volunteer background and reason for participating, volunteers are seeking fulfillment of a psychological contract from the outset and not simply during the period of volunteer engagement during the event. As the early stages of the psychological contract are based largely on trust, then any early contact or activities are essential in validating this trust that expectations will be fulfilled. In this case, the welcome afforded to all volunteers had an impact on expectations.
>
> Secondly, there appears to be an ideal set of expected outcomes regarding planning, recruitment, training and communications but also a realism that expectations are not always met. Thus, there appears to be a degree of compensation afforded in circumstances where expectations are met but barely. However, it is clear that if expectations are not met with a degree of adequacy then the level of concern and in some cases withdrawal from the process can be expected. This happened for many volunteers in relation to the lack of communication between management and volunteers and in relation to transport. There is a fine line between perceptions of breach of the psychological contract and violation. Although some volunteers have more tolerance of uncertainty and unmet expectations, it would be unwise for management to become complacent. The desire to be part of a special or unique event may attract volunteers in the first place, but it may not be strong enough to influence their attitudinal or behavioural responses to management reneging on expectations and perceived promises.
>
> The third key issue the research raises is that such events seem to arouse optimism and positive word-of-mouth marketing not at a level expected given the perceived lack of planning. This optimism extended into expectations regarding long-term outcomes. Thus, if effectively managed, volunteers can generate a positive wave of expectation and citizenship in the period leading up to the Games. The challenge is for managers to plan these outcomes well in advance of such an event to reap the benefits of a highly charged, if temporal, volunteer workforce.
>
> (Ralston *et al.*, 2004)

Guest and Conway (2002) also look at the psychological contract in three phases, at initial entry, in day-to-day work and in more future-oriented, top-down communication. These three phases will be discussed here, where we look further at workforce expectations.

Initial entry – planning phase

The hype that is often a feature of the lead-up period of an event is likely to develop a strong sense of ownership on the part of employees and volunteers (Hanlon and Jago, 2004). However, as Ralston *et al.* (2004) point out in their study of volunteers for the 2002 Commonwealth Games, early communication with volunteers is vital. These authors also found that volunteers were motivated primarily by altruism, involvement and the uniqueness of the special event. Events of this scale have the added advantage of positive publicity contributing to building relationship between volunteer and event organization. Negative press can result in reduced enthusiasm and lower than expected numbers of volunteers committing to work from the recruitment pool. In fact, prior to the 2006 Commonwealth Games the organizers were forced to contact volunteers who had been rejected to compensate for the 1200 who had pulled out two months before the Games.

Positive publicity is even more important for organizers who carry responsibility for the infrastructure and the programme. These external forces (often uncontrollable) have considerable impact on those in the hot seat at the time. It takes a seasoned operator to withstand this type of pressure. Thus motivation of paid staff is something that needs considerable attention. Stress and burn-out are common, some people 'falling over' just before the event and others totally exhausted before the execution phase when the highest levels of energy are needed. It is also possible that some members of the team are looking for alternative post-event employment during the final phases of planning. This, too, has implications for the organization, some of which have post-event placement programmes to assist the transition.

Retention strategies for this phase should focus on internal communication, regular and efficient meeting updates, and celebration of targets and achievements. Well-facilitated training and change management can also contribute to perceptions that the train is on track and there is light at the end of the tunnel.

Daily event operations

Motivation and retention of staff and volunteers day to day during the event operational period are essential components of the human resources plan. Such strategies can take the following forms.

Tickets

Many event volunteers expect to watch part of the performance and are provided with tickets for periods when they are not working. For many mega events this is a ticket to the rehearsal of the opening or closing ceremony. However, according to one study, volunteers' satisfaction with the opportunity to use free tickets had no impact on volunteers' continuance commitment (Elstad, 2003, p. 107).

Sponsor products

Quite often sponsors are prepared to provide their products as rewards for volunteers. However, good intentions can have serious repercussions if it is perceived that these rewards are distributed inequitably. As an example, Swatch provided Sydney Olympic Games volunteers with commemorative watches. However, the logistics of distribution were less than adequate and some volunteers missed out, including ceremonies volunteers who were not included in the headcount (Webb, 2001).

Loyalty schemes

Loyalty schemes have been used to assist retention of employees and volunteers. This may be a passport which is stamped for each shift and qualifies the volunteer or worker for entry in a draw for a major prize, such as a motor car. These have been used in hotels and by Games organizing committees (Byrne *et al.*, 2002). However, the odds of winning seem slim to most and it is doubtful that the link between shift attendance and the prize is strong.

Loyalty bonuses

A loyalty bonus, as an addition to an hourly rate, may be paid on completion of all allocated shifts. This requires careful planning to ensure that work times are recorded and payroll systems modified accordingly.

Celebrity meetings

Inviting high-profile people from the events committee, charity, sponsor organization or government to address the workforce can raise morale. Everyone wants to meet celebrities and this brush with fame can be accompanied by permission for large group photos with athletes and/or entertainers.

Photo boards

While many codes of conduct preclude the use of cameras at events, volunteers in particular love to have their photographs taken on site, and these can be displayed on notice boards (with permission, of course).

Briefings and debriefings

A pre-shift briefing is one of the most important communication strategies for the event workforce, enabling everyone to have the latest information. Likewise, debriefings allow people to contribute their concerns and suggestions. No amount of extrinsic rewards such as pins and caps can solve the frustrations of a member of a team who is bombarded with questions from the event audience and cannot answer them.

Daily newsletters

Staff newsletters, highlighting milestones and achievements, can be distributed at the start of shifts or be kept in the staff canteen area. Notice boards can be used for the same purpose. Production of the newsletter requires a budget and plan and distribution needs to cover all venues.

Posters

Posters highlighting goal achievement, such as the size of the crowd, media stories or television coverage all contribute to a sense of satisfaction that the event concept is being realized.

Food and beverage surprises

Ladies carrying bags of boiled sweets appear to be appreciated, particularly if they have a sunny personality and can visit staff members at remote sites. More exciting are donut days, cappuccino days and ice-cream treats. When these come as a surprise they are much appreciated. Once again a budget and planning are required.

Parade of volunteers

While some mega events have a parade of volunteers after the event, there is nothing to prevent this happening at some stage during the event so that the audience can express their appreciation.

Media support for volunteers

To obtain media support, the public relations department needs to find stories and write press releases. As with previous recognition strategies, this needs pre-planning.

Games

Games are used as ice-breakers and for stress relief. The choice of games and timing are crucial. They can be simple things like competitions to guess the outcomes of matches or spectator numbers. The higher the relevance, the greater the value the game is perceived to have.

Entertainment

Entertainment in the staff area is much appreciated, although for a sporting event the link to work performance is tenuous. However, at a folk festival, volunteers would love to watch musicians jamming.

Concluding party for staff

Little needs to be said about the traditional post-event party. However, decisions do need to be made about when to hold the party – even pre-event is a possibility – and whether to make it a family or adult affair.

Certificates of appreciation

References and certificates of appreciation are highly valued, particularly if they are specific to the individual and to the role they played in making the event a success. A computer printout with a floral border and no individualization has little value.

Careful consideration must be given to the cost of all recognition and reward programmes. These strategies need to be planned on a day-to-day schedule for the event as it progresses with, for example, templates in readiness for staff newsletters and people allocated to writing and printing them. A budget is needed for all such activities. The budget for the Melbourne Commonwealth Games volunteer programme was A$3 million for 5000 volunteers. This included the cost of meals and uniforms, which are significant.

All smiles and hugs when it's over

Case study 15.1

Annual Summer Solstice Folk Music, Dance and Storytelling Festival

Volunteering to work at the Annual Summer Solstice Folk Music, Dance and Storytelling Festival is a **GREAT** *way to experience a wide range of folk art styles and modes. One of the BEST parts about volunteering is that YOU GET INTO THE FESTIVAL FOR FREE! In addition, you get to be part of the 'back-stage scene' of the festival, including having the chance to listen to and even jam with the festival artists in the evenings at the festival hotel.*

(Reproduced with permission of Annual Summer Solstice Folk Music, Dance and Storytelling Festival, www.ctmsfolkmusic.org/volunteer/festival/default.asp)

Reflective practice 15.1

1 Many music festivals offer their volunteers free tickets to performances. How would you ensure that they do not take advantage of this offer and abandon their posts?
2 Why might some volunteers not value free tickets but look for other rewards?

Future-oriented expectations

At management level, the event personnel are ever mindful of their future careers. Being associated with a successful event will enhance their reputation, while an event that fails to reach expectations or is exposed to media criticism can be irredeemably harmful to their career prospects. In traditional business environments, lack of job satisfaction is the primary antecedent to resignation. Holtom *et al.* (2005) show from their research that precipitating events, or shocks, are more often the immediate cause of turnover. This is a most interesting perspective and, as the authors suggest, the organization should look at strategies to manage shocks and thus improve retention. Many mega events are subjected to intense criticism in the lead-up to the event: for example, for the ticketing fiasco in Sydney and in Athens for the incompletion of the infrastructure for the Games not long before the opening ceremony.

Tactics are needed to help staff weather such storms, which affect morale across the board. An understanding of the patterns of a mega event – the positive honeymoon period following the successful bid, then the ever-growing concern about the budget and negative reports – should be linked to the employee communications strategy. Negative press, even when 'par for the course', can be demoralizing. Some individuals don't have the stamina to deal with the lows and thus miss out on the buzz of the final, dramatic success that ensues.

To further illustrate the variables impacting on retention of staff in event management, Hanlon and Jago (2004) show from research into two major annual events that the period immediately following the event is typically flat in contrast to the adrenalin rush of the previous weeks. It is during this period that a number of retention strategies should be considered for permanent staff. Additionally, for organizations running annual events such as the Australian Open, efforts need to be made to maintain contact with seasonal workers who return annually to the event.

Table 15.1 is a guide to retaining both full-time and seasonal staff at two major annual events.

Table 15.1 A recommended guide for retaining full-time and seasonal personnel at the Australian Open Tennis Championship and the Australian Formula One Grand Prix

	Retention strategies for personnel categories	
Event cycle	Full-time	Seasonal
Lead-up	Event's status Recognition Ownership	Event's status Recognition Ownership Timing of the event
During an event	Team debrief Team activities	Team debrief Team activities
After an event	Team debrief Thank-you function Performance appraisal Remuneration Career management programmes Updated job descriptions Re-establishing teams Positive direction from management Exit interviews Loyalty payments	Team debrief Thank-you function
During the year	Team meetings	Continuous contact (i.e. Christmas cards, birthday cards, organization's newsletter, team meetings)
	Remuneration	Career opportunities Survey needs Employed for additional events

(From Hanlon, C. and Jago, L. (2004). The challenge of retaining personnel in major sport event organizations. *Event Management*, **9**, 47. Reproduced with permission.)

This area is undoubtedly ripe for investigation. Research into changing expectations and workforce motivation would be most valuable for human resource practitioners in this field given the rapidly changing scale of the workforce and the diversity of employment and volunteer options. No doubt as technology progresses and people working at events are able to check in and out electronically, more reliable data will be available on the level of retention of both full-time employees and volunteers.

Performance appraisal

Large event organizations that employ a permanent workforce usually have a performance appraisal programme, although for many others performance management is largely informal. A formal performance review session is an opportunity to discuss present performance and future aspirations with an employee. The elements of this programme include:

- Assessing performance against goals, objectives, target and outcomes
- Providing feedback on performance, particularly positive feedback and constructive advice
- Providing an opportunity for the employee to provide feedback on their level of motivation and satisfaction
- Reaching agreement regarding action plans or learning programmes.

Ongoing performance feedback, both formal and informal, contributes significantly to clear expectations for all concerned. Long-term volunteers also require performance feedback. Performance management contributes in constructive ways to a positive organizational culture, which was discussed in Chapter 12, and in turn the event organizational culture affects volunteer retention and motivation. Some of the elements of this culture include:

- *Feedback* – encouragement and a sense of direction
- *Cohesion* – everyone wants to feel part of a team that has a positive dynamic, as dysfunctional teams fall apart very quickly. Shared goals contribute to a sense of cohesion
- *Resources* – lack of resources to do the job efficiently or correctly frustrates volunteers, while being well equipped assists productivity
- *Support* – being neglected by team members or supervisors makes volunteers most unhappy, particularly those left isolated at remote spots without relief or encouragement
- *Fairness* – like permanent employees, volunteers get extremely upset by inequitable treatment
- *Improvement* – in the ongoing event operational environment, suggestions for improvements need to be taken seriously and acted upon
- *Information provision* – to provide good service, volunteers need to be in the information loop. This also contributes to a sense of collaborative teamwork.

Performance management is a vital component of the human resource strategy. Whether the event organization is a long-life or short-life concern, everyone needs to be working at an optimal level. This involves meeting expectations, providing motivational opportunities and managing performance that is below par. For the most part, there are many intrinsic elements in the event environment that can be relied upon to maintain motivational momentum.

Case study 15.2

Staging a Shakespeare Festival

You are the organizer of a Shakespeare Festival. There will be four week-long plays performed over the summer holidays with matinee and evening performances. The event will be preceded by a main street procession. The production of the plays will be professionally managed by a theatre team using amateur performers. A number of volunteers will be assigned to minor roles in costumes, set and lighting. The administrative team will be a core of event management paid staff with support from volunteers in the ticket office, at information and on merchandising. Volunteers will also assist with ushering. You will need to suggest a naming rights sponsor and some minor sponsors. Marketing and promotions volunteers will need to be appointed early. Overall, your paid staff to volunteer ratio will be 1:4.

Reflective practice 15.2

1 Identify the phases of this project, and allocate timings to the workforce appointments (paid and volunteer).
2 Develop a simple organization chart for the planning of the event and another for the production period.
3 Describe ideas for motivating the core team of senior staff during the pre-event phase.
4 Develop strategies for motivating the workforce during the event production phase.

Chapter summary and key points

This chapter has covered some of the research pertaining to motivation, looking mainly at longer term paid staff and volunteers. Theories of motivation fit mainly into two categories: content theories prescribe a series of characteristics that should be present in jobs, while process theories stress differences in people's needs and their perceptions of the circumstances in which they find themselves. Motivation and retention strategies were considered at different points in the event cycle, from initial entry to final celebration. The concept of the psychological contract was used to analyse the relationship between the event organization and the volunteer.

Revision questions

1 What are the implications if there is poor retention of management/planning staff?
2 What are the implications of overrecruitment of volunteers?
3 Explain the idea of the psychological contract.
4 Discuss the following statement, 'to understand motivation you need to understand the planning cycle for the event'.

References

Byrne, C., Houen, J. and Seaberg, M. (2002). One team. *Communication World*, 28–32.
Coyne, B. and Coyne, E. (2001). Getting, keeping and caring for unpaid volunteers for professional golf tournament events. *Human Resource Development International*, **4(2)**, 199–216.

Cuskelly, G., Auld, C., Harrington, M. and Coleman, D. (2004). Predicting the behavioural dependability of sport event volunteers. *Event Management*, **9**, 73–89.

Elstad, B. (2003). Continuance commitment and reasons to quit: a study of volunteers at a jazz festival. *Event Management*, **8**, 99–108.

Guest, D. and Conway, N. (2002). Communicating the psychological contract: an employer perspective. *Human Resource Management Journal*, **12(2)**, 22–39.

Hanlon, C. and Jago, L. (2004). The challenge of retaining personnel in major sport event organizations. *Event Management*, **9**, 39–49.

Hertzberg, F. (1987). One more time: how do you motivate employees?. *Harvard Business Review*, **65**, 109–20.

Holtom, B., Mitchell, R., Lee, T. and Inderrieden, E. (2005). Shocks as causes of turnover: what are they and how organizations can manage them. *Human Resource Management*, **44(3)**, 337–52.

Locke, E. A. and Latham, G. P. (1984) *Goal Setting: A Motivational Technique That Works!*. Prentice-Hall.

Phillips, S. (2006). Volunteer dropouts soar. *Herald Sun*, 7 January.

Ralston, R., Downward, P. and Lumsdon, L. (2004). The expectations of volunteers prior to the XVII Commonwealth Games 2002. *Event Management*, **9**, 13–26.

Strigas, A. and Newton Jackson, E. (2003). Motivation: volunteers to serve and succeed. *International Sports Journal*, **7(1)**, 111–23.

Vroom, V. (1973). *Work and Motivation*. John Wiley and Sons.

Webb, T. (2001). *The Collaborative Games: The Story behind the Spectacle*. Pluto Press.

Suggested reading

Aiken, L. R. (2000). *Psychological Testing and Assessment*, 10th edn. Allyn and Bacon.

Alimo-Metcalfe, B. and Alban-Metcalf, J. (2005). Leadership: time for a new direction. *Leadership*, **1(1)**, 51–71.

Allen, E. (2005). Creativity on demand. *Harvard Business Review*, **83(7/8)**, 46–8.

Allen, J., O'Toole, W., Harris, R. and McDonnell, I. (2005). *Festival and Special Event Management*, 3rd edn. John Wiley & Sons.

Arasaratnam, L. and Doerfel, M. (2005). Intercultural communication competence: identifying key components from multicultural perspectives. *International Journal of Intercultural Relations*, **29**, 137–63.

Arcodia, C. and Axelson, M. (2005). A review of event management job advertisements in Australian newspapers. In *The Impacts of Events*. University of Technology, Sydney.

Armstrong, M. (2001). *Human Resource Management*, 8th edn. Kogan Page Ltd.

Avolio, B. J. and Bass, B. M. (1994). *Improving Organizational Effectiveness through Transformational Leadership*. Sage.

Baker, A. C., Kolb, D. A. and Jensen, P. J. (2002). *Conversational Learning: An Experiential Approach to Knowledge Creation*. Quorum Books.

Baldwin, C. (2004). Planning and operations for special events in Washington, D.C. – WWII memorial dedication and the funeral of President Ronald Reagan. In *Managing Travel for Planned Special Events*. New Orleans.

Beckett, D. and Hager, P. J. (2002). Life, work and learning: practice in postmodernity. *Routledge International Studies in the Philosophy of Education*, **14**. Routledge.

Blake, R. R. and Mouton, J. S. (1985). *The Managerial Grid III: A New Look at the Classic that has Boosted Productivity and Profits for Thousands of Corporations World-wide*. Gulf Pub. Co.

Blake, R. R., Mouton, J. S. and Allen, R. L. (1987). *Spectacular Teamwork: How to Develop the Leadership Skills for Team Success*. John Wiley & Sons.

Bowdin, G. A. J., O'Toole, W., McDonnell, I. and Allen, J. (2001). *Events Management*. Butterworth-Heinemann.

Brannick, M. and Levine, E. (2002). *Job Analysis*. Sage Publications.

Breaugh, J. and Starke, M. (2000). Research on employee recruitment: so many studies, so many remaining questions. *Journal of Management*, **26(3)**, 405–34.

Brown, S. and James, J. (2004). Event design and management: ritual sacrifice? In I. Yeoman, M. Robertson, J. Ali-Knight *et al.* (eds), *Festival and Events Management: An International Arts and Culture Perspective*. Elsevier Butterworth-Heinemann.

Bryde, J. and Robinson, L. (2005). Client versus contractor perspectives on project success criteria. *Journal of International Project Management*, **2(8)**, 622–9.

Burns, J. M. (1978). *Leadership*. Harper & Row.

Burns, J. M., Goethals, G. R. and Sorenen, G. (2004). *Encyclopedia of Leadership*. Sage.

Burns, S. (2000). *Artistry in Training*. Woodslane Press.

Bussell, H. and Forbes, D. (2001). Understanding the volunteer market: the what, where, who and why of volunteering. *International Journal of Nonprofit and Voluntary Sector Marketing*, **7(3)**, 244–57.

Byrne, C., Houen, J. and Seaberg, M. (2002). One team. *Communication World*, 28–32.

Callow, M. (2004). Indentifying promotional appeals for targeting potential volunteers: an exploratory study on volunteering motives among retirees. *International Journal of Nonprofit and Voluntary Sector Marketing*, **9(3)**, 261–74.

Christenson, D. and Walker, D. (2004). Understanding the role of 'vision' in project success. *Project Management Journal*, **35(3)**, 39–52.

Clune, D. (2001). Political chronicles. *Australian Journal of Politics and History*, **47(2)**, 243–309.

Cook, M. and Cripps, B. (2005). *Psychological Assessment in the Workplace: A Manager's Guide*. Wiley.

Coyne, B. and Coyne, E. (2001). Getting, keeping and caring for unpaid volunteers for professional golf tournament events. *Human Resource Development International*, **4(2)**, 199–216.

Cuskelly, G. and Auld, C. (2000). *Volunteer Management: A Guide to Good Practice*. Australian Sports Commission: Active Australia.

Cuskelly, G., Auld, C., Harrington, M. and Coleman, D. (2004). Predicting the behavioural dependability of sport event volunteers. *Event Management*, **9**, 73–89.

De Cieri, H. (2003). *Human Resource Management in Australia: Strategy, People, Performance*. McGraw-Hill.

Doyle, M. (2002). Selecting managers for transformational change. *Human Resource Management Journal*, **12(1)**, 3–17.

Drummond, S. and Anderson, H. (2004). Service quality and managing your people. In I. Yeoman, J. Rogge, J. Ali-Knight and U. McMahon-Beattie (eds), *Festival and Events Management*. Elsevier Butterworth-Heinemann.

DuBrun, A. (2004). *Leadership*, 4th edn. Houghton Mifflin Company.

Dunning, D. (2004). *TLC at Work*. Davies-Black Publishing.

Elstad, B. (2003). Continuance commitment and reasons to quit: a study of volunteers at a jazz festival. *Event Management*, **8**, 99–108.

Eunson, B. (2005). *Communicating in the 21st Century*. John Wiley & Sons.

Fiedler, F. E. (1967). *A Theory of Leadership Effectiveness*. McGraw-Hill.

Fish, D. and Coles, C. (1998). *Developing Professional Judgement in Health Care: Learning through the Critical Appreciation of Practice*. Butterworth-Heinemann.

Foster, M. (2003). *Recruiting on the Web*. McGraw-Hill.

Garrick, J. and Rhodes, C. (2000). *Research and Knowledge at Work: Perspectives, Case Studies and Innovative Strategies*. Routledge.

Getz, D. (2002). Why festivals fail. *Event Management*, **7(4)**, 209–19.

Getz, D., O'Neill, M. and Carlsen, J. (2001). Service quality evaluation at events through service mapping. *Journal of Travel Research*, **39**, 380–90.

Goldblatt, J. (1997). *Special Events*, 2nd edn. John Wiley & Sons.

Goldblatt, J. (2005). An exploratory study of demand levels for EMBOK. In *The Impacts of Events*. University of Technology, Sydney.

Goldblatt, J. J. (2005). *Special Events: Event Leadership for a New World*, 4th edn. John Wiley & Sons.

Goleman, D. (1995). *Emotional Intelligence*. Bantam Books.

Griffith, D. (2002). The role of communication competencies in international business relationship development. *Journal of World Business*, **37**, 256–65.

Guest, D. and Conway, N. (2002). Communicating the psychological contract: an employer perspective. *Human Resource Management Journal*, **12(2)**, 22–39.

Hall, B. (1997). *Web-based Training Cookbook*. John Wiley & Sons.

Hall, M. *et al.* (2005). *The Canadian Nonprofit and Voluntary Sector in Comparative Perspective*. Imagine Canada.

Hanlon, C. and Cuskelly, G. (2002). Pulsating major sport event organizations: a framework for inducting managerial personnel. *Event Management*, **7**, 231–43.

Hanlon, C. and Jago, L. (2004). The challenge of retaining personnel in major sport event organizations. *Event Management*, **9**, 39–49.

Harris, V. (2004). Event management: a new profession. *Event Management*, **9**, 103–9.

Heery, E., Conley, J., Delbridge, R. and Stewart, P. (2004). Beyond the enterprise: trade union representation of freelancers in the UK. *Human Resources Management Journal*, **14(2)**, 20–34.

Hersey, P. and Blanchard, K. H. (1993). *Management of Organizational Behavior: Utilizing Human Resources*, 6th edn. Prentice-Hall.

Hertzberg, F. (1987). One more time: how do you motivate employees?. *Harvard Business Review*, **65**, 109–20.

Hofstede, G. (1991). *Cultures and Organizations: Software of the Mind*. McGraw-Hill.

Holtom, B., Mitchell, R., Lee, T. and Inderrieden, E. (2005). Shocks as causes of turnover: what are they and how organizations can manage them. *Human Resource Management*, **44(3)**, 337–52.

Hood, C. and Rothstein, H. (2000). *Business Risk Management in Government: Pitfalls and Possibilities*, National Audit Office, London.

Jago, L. (2005). The impacts of events: triple bottom line event evaluation. In *The Impacts of Events*. University of Technology, Sydney.

Jarvis, M. (2005). *The Psychology of Effective Learning and Teaching*. Nelson Thornes.

Kraiger, K., McLinden, D. and Casper, W. (2004). Collaborative planning for training impact. *Human Resource Management*, **43(4)**, 337–51.

Kramer, R., O'Connor, M. and Davis, E. (2002). Appraising and managing performance. In *Australian Master Human Resources Guide*. CCH, pp. 301–22.

Locke, E. A. (2000). *The Blackwell Handbook of Principles of Organizational Behaviour*. Blackwell.

Locke, E. A. and Latham, G. P. (1984) *Goal Setting: A Motivational Technique That Works!*. Prentice-Hall.

Malouf, L. (1999). *Behind the Scenes at Special Events: Flowers, Props and Design*. John Wiley & Sons.

Manchester City Council (2003). Manchester Commonwealth Games Post Games Report.

Maund, L. (2001). *An Introduction to Human Resource Management*. Palgrave.

McCabe, V., Poole, D., Weeks, N. and Leiper, N. (2000). *The Business and Management of Conventions*. John Wiley & Sons.

McCray, G., Purvis, R. and McCray, C. (2002). Project management under uncertainty: the impact of heuristics and biases. *Project Management Journal*, **33(1)**, 49–57.

McDonnell, I., Allen, J. and O'Toole, W. (1999). *Festival and Special Event Management*. John Wiley & Sons.

Mead, R. (2005). *International Management: Cross-cultural Dimensions*, 3rd edn. Blackwell.

Mintzberg, H. (1983). *Power in and around Organizations*. Prentice-Hall.

O'Toole, W. (2000). Towards the integration of event management best practice by the project management process. *Event Management Research Conference*, University of Technology, Sydney.

O'Toole, W. and Mikolaitis, P. (2002). *Corporate Event Project Management*. John Wiley & Sons.

Payne, J. (1995). Management of multiple simultaneous projects. *International Journal of Project Management*, **13(3)**, 163–8.

Plekhanova, V. (1998). On project management scheduling where human resource is a critical variable. In *6th European Workshop on Software Process Technology*. Springer-Verlag.

Project Management Institute (2004). *A Guide to the Project Management Body of Knowledge: PMBOK Guide*, 3rd edn. Project Management Institute Inc.

Ralston, R., Downward, P. and Lumsdon, L. (2004). The expectations of volunteers prior to the XVII Commonwealth Games 2002. *Event Management*, **9**, 13–26.

Rogge, J. (2004), Global viewing of Athens 2004 Olympic Games breaks records. Presented at the 15th edition of Sportel, October 2004.

Rothwell, W., Prescott, R. and Taylor, M. (1998). *Strategic Human Resource Leader*. Davies-Black Publishing.

Rutherford Silvers, J. (2005). *Standards: Fear or the Future?*. Mark Sonder Productions. Viewed 12 December 2005, (http://marksonderproductions.com/about/News/Feb05Standards.html).

Rynes, S., Bretz, R. and Gerhart, B. (1991). The importance of recruitment in job choice: a different way of looking. *Personnel Psychology*, **44**, 487–521.

Salem, G., Jones, E. and Morgan, N. (2004). An overview of events management. In I. Yeoman, M. Robertson, J. Ali-Knight and U. McMahon-Beattie (eds). *Festival and Events Management*. Elsevier Butterworth-Heinemann.

Sanchez, J. and Levine, E. (2000). Accuracy or consequential validity: which is the better standard for job analysis data?. *Journal of Organizational Behaviour*, **21**, 809–18.

Schermerhorn, J. R., Poole, D. A., Wiesner, R. and Campling, J. (2004). *Management: An Asia-Pacific Perspective*. John Wiley & Sons.

Schondel, C. and Boehm, K. (2000). Motivational needs of adolescent volunteers. *Adolescence*, **25(138)**, 335–44.

Shone, A. and Parry, B. (2004). *Successful Event Management*, 2nd edn. Thomson Learning.

Sommerville, J. and Langford, V. (1994). Multivariate influences on the people side of projects: stress and conflict. *International Journal of Project Management*, **12(4)**, 234–43.

Strigas, A. and Newton Jackson, E. (2003). Motivation: volunteers to serve and succeed. *International Sports Journal*, **7(1)**, 111–23.

Swart, K. and Urmilla, B. (2005). Leveraging anticipated benefits associated with hosting the 2010 Soccer World Cup in South Africa. In *The Impacts of Events*. University of Technology, Sydney.

Taylor, P. (2005). Do public sector contract catering tender procedures result in an auction for 'lemons'?. *International Journal of Public Sector Management*, **18(6)**, 484–97.

Thomsett, R. (2002). *Radical Project Management*. Prentice-Hall.

Toffler, A. (1990). *Future Shock*. Bantam Books.

Tomey, A. (2003). Learning with cases. *Journal of Continuing Education in Nursing*, **34(1)**, 34–8.

Tourism Training Victoria (2002). Strategic training issues for the 2006 Commonwealth Games.

TUC (2004). Unions have a vital role in making London 2012 the best Olympic Games the world has ever seen. Viewed 12 October 2005, www.tuc.org.uk/economy/tuc-9023-f0.cfm>.

Tum, J., Norton, P. and Wright, J. (2006). *Management of Event Operations*. Elsevier Butterworth-Heinemann.

Tyson, S. (1999). How HR knowledge contributes to organizational performance. *Human Resource Management Journal*, **9(3)**, 42–53.

Vaaland, T. (2003). Improving project collaboration: start with the conflicts. *International Journal of Project Management*, **22**, 447–54.

Van der Wagen, L. (2004). *Event Management*, 2nd edn. Pearson Education.

Van der Wagen, L. (2005). Olympic Games event leadership course design. In *The Impacts of Events*. University of Technology, Sydney.

Van der Wagen, L. Contexts for Customer Service. Unpublished thesis. University of Technology, Sydney.

Vroom, V. (1973). *Work and Motivation*. John Wiley & Sons.

Walker, M. (2002). Going for gold. *TD*, May, 63–9.

Watt, D. (1998). *Event Management in Leisure and Tourism*. Addison Wesley Longman.

Webb, T. (2001). *The Collaborative Games: The Story behind the Spectacle*. Pluto Press.

White, J., McMillen, C. and Baker, A. C. (2001). Challenging traditional models: towards an inclusive model of group development. *Journal of Management Inquiry*, **10(1)**, 40–57.

Williamson, P. (2005). Event management students' reflections on their placement year: an examination of their critical experiences. In J. Allen (ed.), *International Event Research Conference 2005*. University of Technology, Sydney.

Glossary

accreditation	process of granting approval for entry into a particular event area or zone, usually with badge or swipe card
action plan	a plan that shows what needs to be done and when it needs to be done; projects comprise multiple action plans
activity	a specific project task
audience	people attending an event, also described as spectators or visitors
bidding	competitive process of submitting proposals
breakdown	process of dismantling event infrastructure; also called bump-out
budget	estimate of revenue and expenditure
bump-in	assembling event infrastructure on site, e.g. building exhibition stands or stages; also called load-in or set-up
bump-out	process of dismantling event infrastructure; also called load-out or breakdown
business events	meetings, incentives, conferences, exhibitions
contingency plan	alternative course of action if things don't go according to plan
contractor	an organization that works independently to provide goods and services
control	ensuring that performance meets plans by monitoring and checking
cost centre	business unit, department or functional area to which costs can be attributed
critical path	timeline for project completion based on dependent tasks
crowd management	techniques used to manage crowd flow through an event site
customer	person who purchases goods and services; in the event environment, the audience or spectators
debrief	a short meeting after a shift or an event to discuss the success or problems experienced

deliverables	results required; often physical objects, but also reports, plans and written documents
duty of care	legal responsibility for the safety of every person on site, including visiting workers and the general public
equal employment opportunity (EEO)	providing the same opportunities for all, based on merit
event product	range of goods and services captured as the purchased event product; may include performance, catering, ambience, entertainment, first aid and other services
extrinsic reward	reward from external sources, e.g. praise from supervisors, certificates
functional area	departments of a business that represent individual disciplines, e.g. marketing, purchasing, human resources
Gantt chart	a timeline chart linking tasks with deadlines; a horizontal time scale
gap analysis	an analysis of current skills against requirements; identifies skills and knowledge gaps as a result of a training needs analysis
human resource management	effective use of human resources (people) to achieve organizational outcomes
human resource operational plan	plan to ensure that the right people are in the right place at the right time doing the right thing
human resource strategic plan	long-range plan to identify labour needs and implement workforce strategic plans and policies
induction	introduction to an organization, may be formal or informal
intrinsic reward	a reward that comes from an internal realization that personal goals have been achieved
job analysis	systematic process of describing jobs within an organization
job description	a document that describes the position and the tasks and responsibilities associated with it
job-specific training	work-related training for specific job-related skills
job specification	a document that describes job requirements in terms of the ideal candidate, including his/her knowledge, skill and other attributes; also called person specification

leadership	directing and inspiring commitment to the organization's goals
logistics	the procurement, distribution, maintenance and replacement of materials and staff
matrix organization	organizational structure that uses both functional and project teams – leads to dual reporting relationships and cross-functional teams
merchandising	items for retail sale consistent with the event theme
MICE	meetings, incentives, conferences and exhibitions (now known as business events)
motivation	an individual's interest and effort in achieving a goal
occupational health and safety (OHS)	systems for worksite health and safety for all workers on site
orientation	session at which the individual is introduced to the organization and its various facets (same as induction)
paid staff	employees working in a paid capacity, full-time, part-time or seasonal
performance appraisal	process used to give individuals performance feedback
person specification	see job specification
policy	intended course of action; guiding principle
precinct	zone or area of an event venue, e.g. catering precinct
procedure	specific series of tasks or actions for goal achievement, generally linked to policy
procurement	assembling resources, mainly purchasing goods and services, needed for a project
project management	planning, organizing directing and controlling a system with specific deadlines and resources
recognition	acknowledging work performance in a formal way
recruitment	process of attracting applicants to an organization
risk management	process of identifying, evaluating and dealing with risks in relation to probability and consequence
scope of work	identified parameters of a work project or action plan
selection	process of selecting the best candidates for the position (with EEO in mind)

site	place, usually an outdoor venue
situational management	matching management style to work context variables
staffing	process of recruiting, selecting, inducting and training new personnel
stakeholder	organization associated with an event with significant interest in related goal achievement, e.g. police, sponsor
supplier	an organization that works independently to provide goods and services
training	providing the workforce with the skills and knowledge they need for successful performance
vendor	an organization that works independently to provide goods and services
venue	place at which an event is held, such as convention centre, athletics track
venue area	part of the site which is designated for a special purpose, such as venue catering area
venue training	training relating to the venue or zone, such as the chain of command and evacuation planning
venuization	term used during mega events where the venue is 'taken over' by the organizing committee and the overlay for the sports, for example, is installed
volunteer	unpaid worker
work breakdown structure (WBS)	describes all work that needs to be done to achieve project outcomes; used as the basis for costing, scheduling, organizational design and work allocation
workforce	everyone working, including paid staff, contractors and volunteers
zone	specific area of an event venue or site

Appendix: Assessment project

You are required to develop the human resources strategy for a multi-venue, multi-session event. This can be for any one of the following: international conference, exhibition, music festival, sporting event, street festival, awards ceremony, community celebration or an event of your own conception.

For this project you need to be mindful of the scope that this event provides for human resource planning so at least some of the following challenges need to be addressed:

- Scope of the event – a multi-venue event provides logistics challenges
- Size of the event – the total workforce should number at least 200
- Unique nature of the event – if the concept is untried the challenges will be greater
- Volunteer management – consider the use of volunteers if you choose a community or noncommercial event
- Themed event – service, ambience and congruence with the theme will influence planning
- Stakeholder involvement – a range of contractors, government agencies and emergency services may be part of the planning
- Outdoor or unique venue – infrastructure has to be built from the ground up
- Risk – the level of risk associated with staffing, such as involvement of high-profile VIPs, celebrities or royalty.

Clearly, not all of the above would be part of the concept; however, if the event is too simple, it will not allow you to adequately demonstrate your planning skills.

Your Human Resources Plan should include the following headings and sections:

1 Executive summary
2 Event overview (with an emphasis on the concept and the staffing considerations presented by the concept)
3 Human resources strategic plan (including a labour force analysis; a rationale for the workforce composition; a human resources risk prevention and contingency plan)
4 Human resources operational timelines (including tasks and timelines for significant elements such as recruitment, selection and training)
5 Compliance review (a review of HR legal obligations and insurances)
6 Job analysis (rationale, organization chart and sample job descriptions/job specifications for key positions as appendices)
7 Recruitment and selection plan (identify source of labour, tasks and timelines)
8 Training plan (include orientation, venue and job-specific training)
9 Policies and procedures (identify which policies and procedures are necessary)
10 Organizational culture and communication (review communication plans)

11 Leadership, motivation and retention (provide strategies for human resource management)
12 Human resources evaluation plan (outline ways in which the quality of service and management of personnel can be evaluated during and post event)
13 References
14 Appendices

When presenting this report you may wish to include some components as appendices at the end of the report, for example, a copy of a policy and procedures for accreditation or a training guide. In each case you need to refer to the appendix in your main document.

Index